Pro SharePoint 2010 Disaster Recovery and High Availability

Stephen Cummins

Pro SharePoint 2010 Disaster Recovery and High Availability

Copyright © 2011 by Stephen Cummins

ISBN-13 (pbk): 978-1-4302-3951-2

ISBN-13 (electronic): 978-1-4302-3952-9

Trademarked names, logos, and images may appear in this book. Rather than use a trademark symbol with every occurrence of a trademarked name, logo, or image we use the names, logos, and images only in an editorial fashion and to the benefit of the trademark owner, with no intention of infringement of the trademark.

The use in this publication of trade names, trademarks, service marks, and similar terms, even if they are not identified as such, is not to be taken as an expression of opinion as to whether or not they are subject to proprietary rights.

President and Publisher: Paul Manning
Lead Editor: Jonathan Hassell
Development Editor: Chris Nelson
Technical Reviewer: Jeff Sanders
Editorial Board: Steve Anglin, Mark Beckner, Ewan Buckingham, Gary Cornell, Morgan Ertel,
    Jonathan Gennick, Jonathan Hassell, Robert Hutchinson, Michelle Lowman, James Markham,
    Matthew Moodie, Jeff Olson, Jeffrey Pepper, Douglas Pundick, Ben Renow-Clarke, Dominic
    Shakeshaft, Gwenan Spearing, Matt Wade, Tom Welsh
Coordinating Editor: Jennifer L. Blackwell
Copy Editor: Mary Behr
Compositor: Bytheway Publishing Services
Indexer: BIM Indexing & Proofreading Services
Artist: SPI Global
Cover Designer: Anna Ishchenko

Distributed to the book trade worldwide by Springer Science+Business Media, LLC., 233 Spring Street, 6th Floor, New York, NY 10013. Phone 1-800-SPRINGER, fax (201) 348-4505, e-mail orders-ny@springer-sbm.com, or visit www.springeronline.com.

For information on translations, please e-mail rights@apress.com, or visit www.apress.com.

Apress and friends of ED books may be purchased in bulk for academic, corporate, or promotional use. eBook versions and licenses are also available for most titles. For more information, reference our Special Bulk Sales–eBook Licensing web page at www.apress.com/bulk-sales.

The information in this book is distributed on an "as is" basis, without warranty. Although every precaution has been taken in the preparation of this work, neither the author(s) nor Apress shall have any liability to any person or entity with respect to any loss or damage caused or alleged to be caused directly or indirectly by the information contained in this work.

Any source code or other supplementary materials referenced by the author in this text is available to readers at www.apress.com. For detailed information about how to locate your book's source code, go to http://www.apress.com/source-code.

To Jane and Lia
—Stephen

Contents at a Glance

Contents

About the Author

 **Stephen Cummins** was one of the earliest established experts on SharePoint. He set up the first blog about the platform (www.spsfaq.com) in 2001 and has continued to share what he's learned since then in many forms of media. Since 2001, he has worked with more than 50 clients on three continents and learned a great deal about a great many businesses and people along the way. He has also learned many lessons about what makes the SharePoint platform adopted, valuable, and resilient. He has eight SharePoint Most Valuable Professional (MVP) awards as well as four Microsoft Certified Technical Specialist (MCTS), two Microsoft Certified Professional (MCP) and two Microsoft Certified IT Professional (MCITP) certificates. He is currently preparing to become a Microsoft Certified Master (MCM).

He lives in Ireland with his wife, daughter, three dogs, and an ever-changing number of goldfish. Hobbies-wise he writes science fiction, surfs and plays the ukulele. He likes to write about himself in the third person, too.

About the Technical Reviewer

 **Jeff Sanders** is a published author, technical editor, and accomplished technologist. He is currently employed with Avanade in the capacity of a Group Manager/Senior Architect. He is very happy to have been involved in this project and feels it's a long overdue subject for addressing.

Jeff has years of professional experience in the field of IT and strategic business consulting, leading both sales and delivery efforts. He regularly contributes to certification and product roadmap development with Microsoft and speaks publicly on Microsoft enterprise technologies. With his roots in software development, Jeff's areas of expertise include collaboration and content management solutions, operational intelligence, digital marketing, distributed component-based application architectures, object-oriented analysis and design, and enterprise integration patterns and designs.

Jeff is also the CTO of DynamicShift, a client-focused organization specializing in Microsoft technologies, specifically Office365/BPOS, SharePoint Server, StreamInsight, Windows Azure, AppFabric, Business Activity Monitoring, BizTalk Server, and .NET. He is a Microsoft Certified Trainer and leads DynamicShift in both training and consulting efforts.

He enjoys non-work-related travel as well as spending time with his wife and daughter, and wishes he had more time for both. He may be reached at jeff.sanders@dynamicshift.com.

Acknowledgments

Acknowledgement must first go to my wife Jane and daughter Lia who stayed with me patiently through the process of writing this book.

I would also like to acknowledge Jonathan, Jennifer, and especially Chris and Jeff for guiding me through the writing maze. I learned a lot and your enthusiasm kept me going at times.

Introduction

I wrote this book to share what I have learned about high availability and disaster recovery for SharePoint at this point in time. It is certainly an interesting time. In the past 10 years, SharePoint has gone from a compiled application that just looked superficially like a web application into a more fully fledged cloud platform. The process is far from over, however, and SharePoint will likely look very different in 10 years time. But there is no doubt in my mind that it will still be in use in some form. It will be interesting for me look back on this book and see what's the same and what's different. I tried to focus on general principles in this book so that even as the technology changes, the principles still apply.

The main risk with any information recording system is that once you use it, you become dependent on it. If that information becomes unavailable for any number of reasons, it has a detrimental effect on your organization. We are just as subject to whims of Mother Nature as we ever were, and now technology has become complex enough that it is difficult for anyone but the most specialized to know enough about it to know how to make it resilient, redundant, and recoverable. In relation to SharePoint, this book will give you the knowledge and guidance to mitigate this risk.

Who This Book Is For

If you worry about what would happen to your organization if the data in your SharePoint farm was lost, this book is for you! It is a technical book in parts, but most of it is about the principles of good planning and stories of how things have gone right and wrong in the field. My intention is that it should be instructive and entertaining for anyone whose organization has begun to rely on SharePoint to function.

How This Book Is Structured

Each chapter describes practical steps that can be taken to make your system more resilient and give you the best range of options when a disaster hits your SharePoint farm. Reading, however, is not enough. I offer pointers to inspire you to take what you have learned here and apply it in the real world. After you read each chapter, put into practice what you have learned! At the very least, take notes of your thoughts on what to do so you can do it later.

Chapter 1: Steering Away from Disaster

To protect your content, you must know your technology and realize its importance to your organization. Roles must be assigned and responsibility taken. Moreover, there should be a way to record near-misses so they can be captured and addressed. SharePoint is not just a technology platform; it's partly owned by the users, too. They and management must play a part in its governance.

Chapter 2: Planning Your Plan

Before you can write a plan you will need to lay a foundation. You will first need stakeholder and management buy-in. You will also need to do a business impact assessment. You may need to plan different SharePoint architectures that have different RTO/RPOs and different cost levels relative to the importance of the data within them. You will also need to create a good SLA and plan how to coordinate a disaster.

Chapter 3: Activating Your Plan

Many processes and procedures have to be in place before you can put your SharePoint disaster recovery plan into action. These are not abstract things on paper; they are actual tasks that defined roles have to perform. This chapter details who is going to do what and when, knowing the interdependencies, accessing the plan, and making sure in advance the plan contains what it should.

Chapter 4: High Availability

High availability is something achieved not just through meeting a percentage of uptime in a year. It is a proactive process of monitoring and change management to ensure the system does not go down. It is also about having high quality hardware. Finally, it is about having redundancy at every level of your architecture from the data center down to the components of the individual service applications.

Chapter 5: Quality of Service

The main ways to improve your quality of service are WAN optimization, designing your farm so that content is near the people who need to see it, and caching infrequently changed pages. WAN acceleration can only help so far with the limitations of latency, but there are options in SharePoint 2010 to get a cost-effective compromise between user satisfaction and a not overly complex architecture.

Chapter 6: Back Up a Step

Your farm is a unique and constantly changing complex system. When focusing on how to back up and restore it successfully, you will need clearly documented and tested steps. You can't fully rely on automated tools, partly because they can't capture everything and partly because they can only capture what you tell them to and when.

Chapter 7: Monitoring

SharePoint must be monitored at the Windows and application levels. The SharePoint application is so dependent on the network infrastructure that anything wrong with SQL Server, Windows, or the network will affect SharePoint. The information in this chapter gives you the guidance and direction you need to watch what needs watching.

Chapter 8: DIY DR

This chapter shows that the task of maintaining backups of valuable content need not be the exclusive domain of the IT staff. Giving users the responsibility for and means to back up their own content is an excellent idea from an organizational point of view as it is likely to save resources in both backup space and IT man-hours.

Chapter 9: Change Management and DR

Change management is a collaborative process where the impact of change has to be assessed from a business and a technical perspective. Change is the life-blood of SharePoint; without it the system succumbs to entropy, becomes less and less relevant to user needs, and becomes a burden rather than a boon to the business.

Chapter 10: DR and the Cloud

Analyze the additional problems and opportunities presented by off-premises hosting. There is still a great deal of planning involved in moving to the cloud. This chapter looks at the process by which SharePoint developed into its current form, how cloud architecture options come down to cost and control, and how multi-tenancy and planning federation are key aspects of SharePoint in the cloud.

Chapter 11: Best Practices and Worst Practices

When it comes to best and worst practices in SharePoint, there is no such thing as perfection and no implementation is all bad. But it is possible to improve and to avoid obvious pitfalls. Primarily, you have to avoid the easy path of short term results, the quagmires of weak assumptions, a reactionary approach to change, and an irresponsible approach to governance. Those four principles will get your SharePoint platform off to a good start and keep it on course.

Chapter 12: Final Conclusions

This chapter brings together the key principles contained in this book. The approach has been to create a guide that can be used in any circumstance rather than to define only one approach. Principles are more universal and can be applied to any version of SharePoint irrespective of changes in the underlying technology. Even as SharePoint transitions to the cloud, there are still lessons than can be applied from the four previous versions of SharePoint, and high availability and disaster recovery in general.

CHAPTER 1

Steering Away from Disaster

On my very first SharePoint job back in 2001, I spent hours backing up, copying and restoring the SharePoint installation from an internal domain to the one accessible to users from the Internet. This was not a backup strategy; it was a crude way to get content to the Internet while keeping the intranet secure. But it made the system very vulnerable to failure. Every time content was updated, I had to manually overwrite the production SPS 2001 with the updated staging SPS 2001 out of hours so users could see the changes the next day. This started to become a nightly occurrence. I still remember the feeling of fear every time I had to run the commands to overwrite the production farm and bring it up to date. I would stare at that cursor while it made up its mind (far too casually, I thought) to bring everything in line. I would sigh with relief when it worked and I was able to see the changes there. I still feel the sense of mild panic when it didn't work and I had to troubleshoot what went wrong. It was usually an easy fix—some step I missed—but sometimes it was a change to the network or the Exchange server where the data was stored or a Windows security issue.

Disaster was always only a click away and even back then I knew this way was not the best way to do what I was doing. It made no sense, but I did it every day anyway. The process had been signed off by management, who thought it looked secure and prudent on paper, but in reality it was inefficient and a disaster waiting to happen. Eventually, I left for a better job. Perhaps that's how they still do content deployment there.

Maybe you are in a similar situation now: you know that the processes and procedures your organization is using to protect itself are just not realistic or sustainable. They may, in fact, be about to cause the very thing they are supposed to protect against. Or perhaps the disaster has already occurred and you are now analyzing how to do things better. Either way, this book is designed to focus your thinking on what needs to be done to make your SharePoint farm as resistant to failure as possible and to help you plan what to do in the event of a failure to minimize the cost and even win praise for how well you recovered. The ideal scenario is when a disaster becomes an opportunity to succeed rather than just a domino effect of successive failures. Can you harness the dragon rather than be destroyed by it?

This chapter addresses the following topics:

- The hidden costs of IT disasters.

- Why they happen.

- Key disaster recovery concepts: recovery time objective and recovery point objective.

- Key platform concepts: networks, the cloud, IaaS, and SaaS.

- Roles and responsibilities.

- Measures of success.

- Some applied scenarios, options, and potential solutions.

The Real Cost of Failure

This book focuses on two different but related concepts: high availability (HA) and disaster recovery (DR). Together they are sometimes referred to as Service Continuity Management (SCM). While SCM focuses on the recovery of primarily IT services after a disaster, as IT systems become more crucial to the functioning of the business as a whole, many businesses also assess the impact of the system failing on the organization itself.

No matter what your core business, it is dependent on technology in some form. It may be mechanical machinery or IT systems. IT systems have become central to many kinds of businesses but the business managers and owners have not kept up with the pace of change. Here's an example of how core technology has become important for many types of companies.

Starbucks recently closed all its U.S. stores for three hours to retrain baristas in making espresso. It cost them $65 million in lost revenue. Was that crazy? They did it on purpose; they realized the company was sacrificing quality in the name of (store) quantity. They had expanded so fast that they were losing what made the Starbucks brand famous: nice coffee in a nice coffee shop. They anticipated their seeming success in the short term would kill them in the long term. They had more stores, but less people were coming in. The short term cost of closing for three hours was far less than what they would lose if they did not improve a core process in their business. Making espresso seems a small task, but it's one performed often by their most numerous staff members. If those people couldn't make a quality espresso every time, the company was doomed in the longer term. Focusing on this one process first was a step in improving business practices overall. It was a sign that Starbucks knew they need to improve, not just proliferate, in order to survive.

In this case, falling standards of skill was a seen as reason to stop production. It was planned but it underlines the cost when a business can't deliver that they produce. Your SharePoint farm produces productivity. It does this by making the user activity of sharing information more efficient. SharePoint is worthless if the information in it is lost or the sharing process is stopped. Worse than that, it could seriously damage your business's ability to function.

Perception is reality, they say. Even if only a little data or a small amount of productive time is lost, some of an organization's credibility can be lost as well. A reputation takes years to build but it can be lost in days. If increasingly valuable information of yours or your customers is lost or stolen from your SharePoint infrastructure, the cost can be very high indeed. Your reputation might never recover.

Poor perception leads to brand erosion. IT systems are now an essential part of many businesses' brand, not just hidden in a back room somewhere. For many companies, that brand depends on consumer confidence in their technology. Erosion can mean lost revenues or even legal exposure. The attack on Sony's PlayStation Network where 100 million accounts were hacked (the fourth biggest in history) will cost Sony a lot of real money. One Canadian class action suit on behalf of 1 million users is for $1 billion. What might the perceived antenna problems with iOS4 have cost Apple if they had not reacted (after some initial denial) swiftly to compensate customers?

Large companies like Starbucks, Sony, and Apple know technology is not just part of what they sell, it is core to who they are. If you neglect the core of your business, it will fail. The cost of total failure is much higher than the cost of understanding and investing in the technology that your staff relies on every day. SharePoint has become more than a useful place to put documents in order to share them with other users. It is now the repository for the daily tasks of many users. It has become the core technology platform in many businesses and it should be treated as such.

Why Disasters Happen and How to Prevent Them

In IT there is a belief that more documentation, processes, and procedures means better documentation, processes, and procedures—like the idea that more Starbucks meant Starbucks was doing better. In fact, the opposite is true. Processes around HA and DR (indeed all governance) should follow the principle that perfection is reached not when there is nothing left to add, but when there is nothing left to take away. Good practice requires constant revision and adjustment. Finally, the people who do the work should own the processes and maintain them. In too many businesses the people who define the policies and procedures are remote from the work being done and so the documents are unrealistic and prone to being ignored or causing failures.

Success/Failure

SharePoint farms are like any complex system: we can't afford to rely on the hope that haphazard actions will somehow reward us with a stable, secure collaboration platform. But the reality is most of our processes and procedures are reactive, temporary stop-gap solutions that end up being perpetuated because there's no time or resources to come up with something better. We would, in fact, be better off with "Intelligent Design" than with Evolution in this case because we are in a position to interpret small events in a way that lets us anticipate the future further ahead than nature. At the same time, near misses dangerously teach us something similar but opposite: if you keep succeeding, it will cause you to fail. So who is right and how can we apply this to the governance of our SharePoint architectures?

There is some research from Gartner that has been around for a few years that says that we put too much emphasis on making our platforms highly available only through hardware and software, when 80% of system failures are caused by human error or lack of proper change management procedures. So, what are the thought processes that lead us to ignore near-misses and think that the more success we have, the less likely we are to fail?

If we're not careful, success can lead to failure. We think that because we were lucky not to fail before, we will always be lucky. Our guard goes down and we ignore the tell-tale signs that things will eventually go wrong in a big way, given enough time.

Research shows that for every 30 near misses, there will be a minor accident, and for every 30 of those, one will be serious. SharePoint farms have monitoring software capturing logs, but they only capture what we tell them to; we have to read and interpret them. The problem is that not enough time is allocated to looking for small cracks in the system or looking into the causes of the near-misses.

But a more pernicious cause of failure is the fact that when processes are weak, the people who monitor the system are continuously bailing out the poor processes. Those who have responsibility for the processes are not reviewing the processes continually to keep them up to date. The people who don't own the process are not escalating the problems; instead they are coming up with quick fixes to keep things going in the short term. Sooner or later, they will get tired or frustrated or bored or they'll leave before things really go wrong. Then it is too late to prevent the real big FUBAR.

Thus, management must not ignore the fact that staff on the ground are working at capacity and keeping things going but it will not last. Likewise, staff on the ground must step up and report situations that will lead to system failure and data loss.

Is failure necessary for success? I think that every process has to be the best it can be with the realization that it must be tested and improved continuously. This is the essence of governance: people taking ownership of change and reacting to it constructively. The constant evolution of policies is needed.

Your SharePoint Project: Will It Sink or Float?

Let's use an analogy—and it's one I will revisit throughout this book. Your SharePoint project is like the voyage of a cruise liner. Will it be that of a safe, modern vessel or the ill-fated Titanic? Your cruise ship company has invested a lot of money into building a big chunk of metal that can cross the Atlantic. Your SharePoint farm is like that ship. The farm can be on-premise, in the cloud, or a hybrid of both. You have a destination and high ambitions as to what it will achieve. You know for it to succeed you will need an able crew to administer it plus many happy paying passengers.

This analogy is assuming something inevitable. The ship will sink. Is it fair to say your SharePoint implementation will fail? Of course not, but you should still plan realistically that it could happen. Not being able to conceive of failure is bound to make you more vulnerable than if you had looked at everything that could go wrong and what should be done if it happened. This is why ships have lifeboat drills—because they help prevent disaster. Acknowledging the fact that disasters do happen is not inviting them. In fact, it does the opposite; it makes them less likely to happen as it helps reveal weaknesses in the infrastructure and leads to realistic plans to recover more quickly when disasters do happen.

Figure 1-1 is of a typical SharePoint 2010 farm. Note that more than half of the servers are redundant. The farm could still function if one web front end, one application server, and one SQL server stayed functioning. Let's return to the Titanic metaphor. It was engineered with a hull with multiple compartments; the builders said that the ship could still float if many of these were breached. In fact, ships had hit icebergs head on and survived because of this forethought in the design.

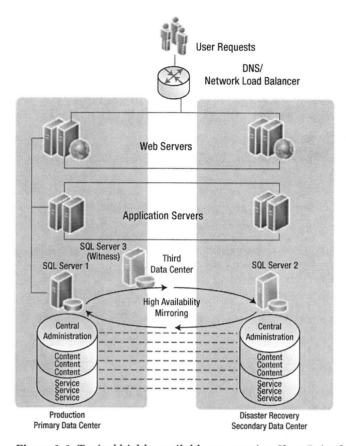

User Requests

DNS/
Network Load Balancer

Web Servers

Application Servers

SQL Server 3
(Witness)   Third
SQL Server 1   Data Center   SQL Server 2

High Availability
Mirroring

Central
Administration   Central
                                              Administration
Content
Content   Content
Content   Content
                                              Content
Service
Service   Service
Service   Service
                                              Service

Production   Disaster Recovery
Primary Data Center   Secondary Data Center

Figure 1-1. Typical highly available on-premises SharePoint farm

So technology convinced experts that very large ships were beyond the laws of physics. It somehow became widely believed that not only was this the biggest, most luxurious liner on the sea, but it was also virtually unsinkable. And we all know how that turned out. The story was very sensational news at the time and still is. The press today is no different from the press 100 years ago; they love big stories. The Titanic was such a compelling story because it was the world's biggest passenger ship on its maiden voyage full of the rich and the poor—a metaphor for modernity and society.

Perhaps your SharePoint deployment will be watched by the press, too, and you will want it to go well for the same reasons. Perhaps it will only be watched by internal audiences, but its success or failure will still be very visible as it involves all kinds of users in your organization. This is certainly a good argument for piloting and prototyping, but the real full-scale system still has to go live and set sail someday.

High Availability: The Watertight Compartments

High availability is the IT terminology for the efforts made to ensure your SharePoint Farm will not sink, no matter what happens to it—its resilience and quality can handle the damage and still keep afloat. Automatic systems that kick in when things go wrong are referred to as *failover systems*. In the case of my analogy, they would be like the bulkhead doors that close to make the compartments watertight (see Figure 1-2). These could be triggered manually but would also kick in automatically if water rose to a certain level in the compartments. In SharePoint, on-premises, clustering, load balancing, and mirroring provide this failover and resilience. But they can be overwhelmed.

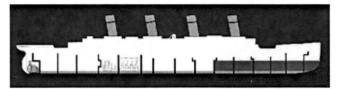

Figure 1-2. High availability on R.M.S Titanic

In most IT systems, it's too easy to provide the minimum or even recommended level of resilience without much active thought. In the Titanic, the 16 compartments exceeded the Board of Trade's requirements; the problem was that 16 watertight cubes in a ship are inconvenient for the crew (administrators) and passengers (business users). There were many doors between the compartments so that people could move freely through these barriers. As a result, safety was trumped by convenience. This is a common reason for the failure of high availability systems in SharePoint, too. The failure is usually in the rush to apply updates and routine improvements to the system. The more complex the high availability systems, the more moving parts there are that can fail.

In a SharePoint on-premise farm, you can achieve high availability through a number of options. A combination of the following is common:

- *SQL mirroring:* Synchronously maintaining a copy of your databases. *Synchronously* means the data is always the same at the same time.

- *SQL clustering:* Spreading a SQL instance over multiple machines. An *instance* is a group of servers that appears as one SQL server.

- *SQL log shipping:* Backing up to file the data and restoring to another SQL instance asynchronously. *Asynchronously* means the data is not exactly the same at the same time. There is a delay of hours in moving the logs from one instance to the other.

- *Multiple data centers (DCs):* This means locating your server farms in independent premises in different geographical locations. For example, Office 365 for EMEA is in Dublin, but there is also another DC in Amsterdam.

- *Load balancing:* Software or hardware, more than one server seems to have the same IP address as they have virtual IP addresses.

- *Stretched farm:* Hosting some servers in your farm in different data centers.

- *SAN replication:* Synchronously maintaining a copy of your data.

- *Redundant disaster recovery farm:* A second farm in another location ready to take the place of the production farm.

- *Availability zones and regions:* Used in Amazon Web Services, these are analogous to servers and data centers.

Disaster Recovery

Disaster recovery is what to do when something has already gone wrong. With a SharePoint Farm, it's the point when users start to lose access, performance, or data. It can also be when security is compromised. Basically, it's when the integrity of the system is compromised. You've hit the iceberg. With the Titanic, the disaster recovery process was the lifeboat drill and the lifeboats themselves. With a SharePoint farm, it's the processes, policies, and procedures related to preparing for and undergoing a recovery from a disaster. Thus, it is the planning that goes into what to do from the point the problem is detected. Note that it may not be the exact time the problem started to occur—only when it is detected. Error detection and reporting will examined in further detail in a later chapter.

On the Titanic there were not enough lifeboats because it was believed that the ship was unsinkable due to its watertight compartments. Also, it was believed that it would take the crew too long to load all the lifeboats in the event of a sinking (the Titanic had a capacity of over 3,500 souls, although there were only about 2,500 on board when it sunk). Finally, the regulations were out of date at the time; the ship was legally compliant, but in actuality had less than half the capacity needed, even if the lifeboats had been full. Relying too much on documentation and the recommended approach is not always enough.

Recovery Time Objective and Recovery Point Objective

Two metrics commonly used in SCM to evaluate disaster recovery solutions are recovery time objective (RTO), which measures the time between a system disaster and the time when the system is again operational, and recovery point objective (RPO), which measures the time between the latest backup and the system disaster, representing the nearest historical point in time to which a system can recover. These will be set in the Service Level Agreement (SLA), which is the legal document the provider has to follow. For example, SharePoint Online as part of Office 365 has set an RPO and RTO in the event of a disaster as the following:

> *"12-hour RPO: Microsoft protects an organization's SharePoint Online data and has a copy of that data that is equal to or less than 12 hours old.*
>
> *24-hour RTO: Organizations will be able to resume service within 24 hours after service disruption if a disaster incapacitates the primary data center."*

Networks and the Cloud

Think of your network or the cloud as the ocean. It's big, unpredictable, and full of dangerous things, most of which the administrator can't control. There are denial-of-service attacks, human error, hardware failures, acts of God, and all manner of things that can happen to compromise your system. Later I will describe the kinds of events that can compromise the integrity of your system and how to mitigate them.

IaaS vs. SaaS

Infrastructure as a Service (IaaS) and Software as a Service (SaaS) emphasize high availability over disaster recovery. Naturally, it makes more sense to keep the system working rather than recover from it failing. With IaaS, high availability is more in the hands of the tenant. With SaaS, like SharePoint Online in Office 365, you are more reliant on the provider to keep the system working. My analogy is that IaaS is like being a crew member; you have training and responsibility to keep the passengers safe. With SaaS, you are more like a passenger, reliant on the provider to keep you safe.

For example, in the case of an IaaS provider like Amazon Web Services (AWS), there is the ability of the tenant to place instances in multiple locations. These locations are composed of regions and availability zones. Availability zones are distinct locations that are engineered to be insulated from failures in other availability zones and provide inexpensive, low latency network connectivity to other availability zones in the same region. Think of these as your watertight compartments.

By launching instances (in your case, your SharePoint servers) in separate availability zones, you can protect your applications from the failure of one single location. There are also regions. These consist of one or more availability zones, are geographically dispersed, and are in separate geographic areas or countries. By spreading your instances across these, you have greater resilience.

With SaaS examples like Office 365, if there is a problem with the platform, you have less control over reacting to that problem. Think of this as a passenger bringing his or her own lifejacket. I will go into more detail later on how to have more control.

SharePoint in the Cloud

The IT world is shifting to where computing, networking, and storage resources are migrating onto the Internet from local networks. SharePoint is a good candidate for cloud computing because it is already web-based. From a setup and administration point of view, it has a growing complex service architecture. Also, many companies would gladly do without the cost of having the skills in house to administer it, not to mention the opportunity to move Exchange to the cloud. This will not happen all at once, but it does mean that hosting your SharePoint farms on-premises is no longer the only option. For that reason I will outline the new cloud options for those unfamiliar with them.

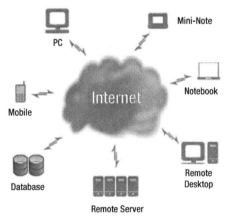

Figure 1-3. The cloud was a metaphor for the Internet.

Once upon a time a picture of a cloud was used on network diagrams to denote the Internet (see Figure 1-3). This is why we use the term *the cloud* now. It had a "here be dragons" feel about it. (Prior to the Europeans discovering big chunks of the world, large areas on maps were labeled "here be dragons," as shown in Figure 1-4. It was a way to fill an empty space that could not be understood. With this lack of knowledge comes fear; hence pictures of dragons.) In the context of this metaphor, the dragon is complacency—a false bravado born of fear. The cloud is full of positive benefits for businesses. It will soon be seen as a New World to be discovered and explored, not an unknown danger.

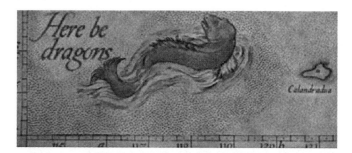

Figure 1-4. Dragons were a metaphor for the uncharted parts of the map.

By moving your SharePoint infrastructure or software into the cloud, there is a danger that too much trust is placed in the platform provider to automatically take care of all the high availability and disaster recovery options. They do, in most cases, provide excellent tools to manage your infrastructure, but you must still know how to use them. The truth is the final responsibility still rests with the owner of the data to understand the options and choose the best ones for their needs and budget.

Instead of some nice, healthy fear, there is dangerous complacency that comes from a reluctance to take control of the infrastructure. It is easier just to assume someone else it taking care of it. I take it, dear reader, that you bought this book because you don't want to get swallowed up by the great chewing complacency.

Why Is Infrastructure Moving to the Cloud?

We live in a more connected world. Wi-Fi, Smartphones, tablets, notebooks, and laptops allow workers to be more mobile and connection options more plentiful. People can access so much and communicate so easily through the Internet they now expect to be able to access their work data from any location with any device with the same ease.

Another major factor in the arrival of the cloud for businesses is technologies like virtualization and cheap hardware that allow for the commoditization of resources to the point that they are like any other utility, such as power, water, or gas. SharePoint 2010 needs a lot of hardware and capacity. The standard build is three farms: Development, Testing, and Production. SharePoint also requires a lot of software and licenses if you want in each farm, for example, three web front-end servers, two application servers, and a SQL cluster.

SharePoint Online (SPO) makes paying for access much simpler. There is no need for a large upfront investment in hardware, software, and licenses. Organizations can just sign on and pay monthly per user. They can even invite users from outside their network; this just requires a LiveID account like Hotmail or an existing Office365 account. This makes collaborating beyond your network with partners or customers so much simpler. This also makes starting small and adding users gradually much easier— and the costs of user licenses up front much lower. It is much easier to remove user licenses, too, because each user has to re-authenticate once every 30 days; thus, once the 30-day license has expired, you no longer have to pay if you don't want to. There's no requirement to buy and configure a number of servers and work out what server and software licenses you will need. This has always been an overly complex and arcane art and any simplification here is very welcome. It is true there are still a range of user licenses to choose from, but the options are clearer and it's easier to identify what you want.

Licenses are also priced differently. They are now per user and not per device with SharePoint Online. The Client Access Licenses (CALs) for SharePoint 2010 are per device, so if you access from home, office, and mobile, you need three licenses, in theory, which is not something most organizations plan for. With SPO, a user can connect with up to five devices but it counts as only one device—a more realistic approach in this connected age and something Microsoft is counting on by building integration with Lync, SharePoint, and Exchange into its Windows Mobile platform.

In theory, administrators will no longer need to install patches. Of course, Microsoft will still be patching the platform, but this is no longer an administrative burden in the hands of the client to test and update servers on-premises. Single sign-on does require ADFS and Directory Synchronization on premises as well as Office Professional Plus and Office 365 Desktop, and these will likely still require patching. This is still less than maintaining a stack of SharePoint and SQL servers.

Another important change is that the concept of versions becomes less significant. Online applications are gradually improving. People don't run different versions of Gmail, for example. So there's no longer a need to upgrade to the latest version of SharePoint every two or three years to get the latest features, maintain compatibility with other software, and keep the product supported.

Will SharePoint Administrators Become Extinct?

No, but they will have to evolve. SharePoint was once more like the manufacturing industry. It was about making and managing real things: servers and software. Now it is more like a service industry. The emphasis is delivering user satisfaction. Meeting the businesses requirements was always the purpose of technology, but now the emphasis is doing it more quickly and directly by listening to user requirements and helping then use SharePoint to meet them. SharePoint is more like Word than Exchange. Its value comes from the users and administrators knowing how to use it. There is also still resource management, user management, and quota management, as well as meeting branding requirements and declarative workflows through SharePoint Designer. Finally, through sandboxed solutions, there is still the ability to develop compiled code solutions through Visual Studio.

SharePoint 2010 Is a Complicated Beast

Moving to the cloud makes the technical aspects of setting up SharePoint much simpler. SharePoint 2010 is more complex than Microsoft Office SharePoint Server (MOSS) 2007 was—and SPS 2003 and SPS 2001. This is mainly because the services now run as applications in their own right. As a result, setting up a SharePoint 2010 farm can mean planning for more than 15 databases and learning how to configure at least as many services. SharePoint Online takes away some of that complexity, since there are only a limited number of services you can access. This is because the SharePoint Online infrastructure is standardized for all tenants; see Figure 1-5. It is the "Any customer can have a car painted any color that he wants so long as it is black" approach employed by Henry Ford.

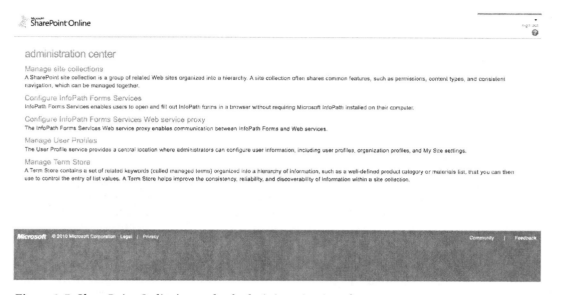

Figure 1-5. SharePoint Online's standard administration interface

The onus is still on you to understand the options that are available and the pros and cons of the different decisions you can make. These decisions will affect the integrity of your system. This book is about helping you understand all the options so you can make an informed choice.

Practical Steps to Avoid Disaster

The art of losing isn't hard to master;
so many things seem filled with the intent
to be lost that their loss is no disaster,

"One Art" by Elizabeth Bishop

Do you think your SharePoint implementation is filled with the intent to become a disaster? This is a message you need to communicate to the people who can take the steps to avert it. Real action and real responsibility must be taken. There has to be consensus, too; it might be tempting to see this as a lone hero's struggle for recognition, but the way to avert disaster will require team co-operation. The art of losing is not hard to master. The art of success is much more difficult, but here are some practical steps.

What Role Will You Play?

It's important to consider what your role will be, both in the setup and later, if there is a disaster, in the cleanup. There are a number of different roles and responsibilities assigned to different people during the creating of a SharePoint deployment, and there are a number of roles and responsibilities that must be assigned in the event of a disaster. Make sure this does not happen in an ad hoc way.

If disaster happens, everyone is initially implicated and there will be an investigation to find out the causes and who, if anyone, has a part in the blame. Which role will you take if your ship flounders?

- An engineer/administrator working to mitigate the disaster?

- A passenger/user, panicking and not helping?

- Someone who saw that the ship was sinking and only worked to save themselves?

- Or a hero who labored selflessly to save what they could?

Stakeholders and Strategy

Ownership of SharePoint is complex. Content is owned by users in the business. Sites and site collections are managed by site owners. Farms or tenancies are owned by IT staff. Branding and the look and feel are owned by the Marketing department. People invariably want ownership but not the responsibility that comes with it. They especially don't want accountability when things go wrong. So the first step in having good high availability and disaster recovery practices is establishing who is accountable for what.

SharePoint ownership is fundamentally a collaborative process. Creating good high availability and disaster recovery practices requires planning and commitment up front. This will also lead to a shared solution that will help the organization meet their top-level goals. Someone must lead this process and lead by example: take responsibility and be accountable, not just own the process long enough to take credit for it before moving on to something else that allows them to advance their career. That, dear reader, is you. If not, why not? If no one is taking responsibility for good high availability and disaster recovery practices in your organization, you should do it. Not just for fame or glory, but because you are a professional and a grown-up.

The next step is to create a cross-functional group that meets every month or six weeks to initially reach a consensus of what the organization is trying to accomplish. Without a shared understanding, you will not gain a shared commitment to the solution. Without a shared commitment, the good high availability and disaster recovery practices will eventually fail. This group must meet every two to three months to revisit the good high availability and disaster recovery practices to ensure they are still current to requirements.

Dependencies

This group must focus on the following key dependencies:

- Reliability will be a key indicator of success for the new SharePoint solution. It drives user adoption and maintains the valuable data already compiled by users.

- It will require a commitment from the owners of the infrastructure, the information architecture, and the content to ensure practices stay current. Keep responsibility with the owners, not one level above, as this disconnection leads to mistakes.

- Content will require the application of metadata and content types, which are part of the information architecture, to leverage the benefits within SharePoint to identify content that may be so valuable it needs its own high availability and disaster recovery policy apart from the rest of the content.

- Good high availability and disaster recovery practices cost time and money, but they cost a lot less than zero availability and zero disaster recovery. Without these, there can't be good practices.

Clear Measurements of Success: Reporting, Analysis, and Prevention

Simply measuring success by the fact that there has not been a disaster yet is not enough. My contention is that reporting of near misses by observers is an established error-reduction technique in many industries and organizations and should be applied to the management of SharePoint systems. Error logs only tell us so much. The majority of problems are those that people are aware of every day. There must be a place to record these observations. This must be a log that tracks these near misses in a transparent way: everyone should be able to read the log. It shouldn't be required to say who recorded the observation but it's better if people do so. This should begin to foster an environment of trust. It must be clear to everyone that the purpose of the log is not to apportion blame but to prevent security breaches or system outages. Table 1-1 shows a simple example form that could be maintained as a SharePoint list.

Table 1-1. A Near Miss Log Form for Your SharePoint Farm

Date/Time	Part of SharePoint	Type	Description	Contributing factors	Learning point	Action taken	People involved

The following are some questions that need to be discussed and reviewed with the cross-functional group. These are the kinds of questions that, when applied in real world situations, can help spot and address any problems sooner.

- Are there any patterns and trends?

- Is everyone competent to carry out the role they are assigned to do?

- Could this near miss combine with other near misses to create a chain of problems that could create an actual system failure?

- What resources are needed to address this problem?

Applied Scenario: The System Is Slowing Down

Ingenious Solutions Ireland has a problem with SharePoint. Users are reporting performance is slower than usual. They have called Support but Support hasn't been able to help. Likewise, the Infrastructure team says they will look into it but nothing further happens.

Members of Management notice, too, and eventually one of them asks the head of Infrastructure about the problem. At this point, the SQL server guy says the SQL servers are at capacity and he's been complaining about this for months but no one has done anything.

Infrastructure tells Management that users are putting too much into SharePoint and it's the user's responsibility to remove unneeded content. There are no policies around what has to be archived or deleted or even what should be put into SharePoint in the first place. The shared drive is full, too, so people have been putting everything and anything into SharePoint.

Content owners respond by saying all the content is necessary and it's the Infrastructure team's job to provide more space. Management realizes they need to buy more capacity but they didn't plan for this; when they see the rising cost, they do nothing in order to avoid having to tell Upper Management that they made a mistake and more money is needed to keep SharePoint going.

Eventually, the morale of the company is affected. Then one day the whole farm stops working. The redundant front end, application, and SQL servers are irrelevant because the problem was not caused by software or hardware. It was caused by people not taking responsibility for their part of the solution. After the disaster, SharePoint is offline for almost a week as some emergency freeing up of space is done to get things going again.

Upper Management hires a consultancy company to fix the problem. They quickly work out the real problem, which is no sense of responsibility or ownership. However, they convince Management that the solution is to buy a new, expensive, trendy content management solution and pay them to support it. They only take responsibility for setting up the new system and some basic training. Thus the process starts all over again.

The Solution

Invariably, there is a cycle of failure and spotting it is the first step. In this example, the shared drives filled up, so SharePoint was used as a solution. Then it filled up and the latest trendy solution was brought in instead.

Upper Management should get the cross-functional group together with a representative from the following groups:

- Content owners

- Site administrators

- Management

- Support

- Infrastructure

They need to work together to reach a consensus on what went wrong. They should communicate without apportioning blame to each other. Upper Management should provide a person to guide and own this process, keep it on track, and keep everyone involved until a course of action is set.

This should be a constructive process where the conclusion is that each member takes responsibility for their contribution to the problem.

- Content owners take responsibility for not uploading content to SharePoint unless it is there for the distinct business processes agreed upon. If these are not known, they must be defined. They also take responsibility for regularly deleting content that is no longer needed. This has the benefit of keeping search results relevant, makes navigation faster, and makes the system less cluttered.

- Site administrators take responsibility for maintaining quotas on sites plus archiving and deleting sites that are no longer needed.

- Management takes responsibility for providing enough money to prevent the system from running out of resources. They also take responsibility for providing resources for training for users, site administrators, and support staff.

- Support takes responsibility for making users and site administrators vigilant in deleting unneeded content. If content needs to be removed but archived, they report this to Infrastructure.

- Infrastructure takes responsibility for having a system in place to archive content and for using that system. They also regularly monitor capacity; if they reach a specific target, say 25% of storage capacity, they report this to Management.

What Is Upper Management's Responsibility?

The role of Upper Management is to maintain ownership of this whole process. They can't simply subcontract it to an external consultancy. If they find they don't understand the technology involved, they need to get themselves the necessary training to understand the issues involved. Technology is now vital to the brand, morale, and financial health of every organization. It is too important to be just ignored in the hope that things will just continue on as they were. The problem is they will—and this will cost money and even good staff, who may leave.

After these steps have been completed, the near-miss log should be implemented. Anyone in the organization can contribute to it, but it should be reviewed weekly by management and all points should be discussed at the monthly SharePoint cross-functional group meeting. It is Upper Management's job to make sure these meetings take place and that the near misses are addressed. In this example, the symptom was slow performance, and the causes were multiple: poor content retention policies, lack of training, and lack of capacity or budget. The cause was actually lack of attention to the importance of IT processes in the business. The cure was Upper Management taking ownership of creating the processes need to prevent problems like this from happening again.

Technology Is Just a Tool

Did you notice I mentioned almost nothing technical in this example? I didn't go into detail about the structure of the SharePoint farm, how many front-end servers, application servers, or even SQL servers in the cluster. I didn't talk about the advantages of mirroring versus clustering or combining the two. I didn't mention stretched farms, DR farms, SQL backups, or tape backup. This is because none of that would have made any difference. It is assumed that whoever created the SharePoint farm initially followed Microsoft's well-documented processes on creating highly available SharePoint farms, or hired someone who knew how to specify the hardware and software and then install and configure a SharePoint farm. The problem was something harder to measure—and what can't be measured can't be managed. In the example, the farm did not fail because of technology; it failed because of people.

There is a tendency to see high availability and disaster recovery as purely technical areas. In my opinion, the technology is the simplest part to manage (even though it still takes a great deal of work to master it—and I don't think anyone ever fully can). Many companies sell the idea that you can buy a magic solution to the problems of high availability and disaster recovery, that their skills or tools to monitor or backup the farm will mean you will never lose access or data.

At the root of the problem is the fact that SharePoint itself is just a tool, like a hammer, a car, or a telephone. Microsoft sells it, but it's up to you to work out what to use it for and, more importantly, how to manage it so that it keeps working and meeting your needs.

Microsoft designs, manufactures, and distributes SharePoint. Partners sell it. Third parties provide add-ons to it. Consultancies install, configure, and support it. They also develop and design custom functionality. Training companies show you how the default functionality works. But in the end, it's up the owners of the tool to use it to its full potential and maintain it in a way that it remains useful.

Applied Scenario: It's Never Simple

Examples tend to be simple and clear. But the real world they try to illustrate is complex and unclear. Complexity and a lack of clarity is the main problem we all face in attempting to solve the high availability and disaster recovery problems of most companies. If a problem is simple to frame, it's usually simple to solve. Here is a scenario involving the kind of messy situation that leads to poor high availability and disaster recovery decisions.

Super Structure is an Infrastructure as a Service (IaaS) company. Their customer, Fancy Flowers, contracts them to design a highly available and recoverable SharePoint 2007 farm. Then they change their mind and ask for a SharePoint 2010 farm. Super Structure doesn't have SharePoint 2010 experience, so they subcontract an external consultancy, Clever Consultants, to provide the expertise. They also subcontract Dashing Development to provide custom coding.

After a long and exhaustive process, the solution architecture is agreed upon. This takes time because 15-20 people (representatives from the four companies) are directly involved. There are multiple meetings and documents. A detailed design is drawn up and the servers are all installed and configured.

Two months later a project manager from Fancy Flowers notices that her idea for high availability and disaster recovery—a stretched farm—is not in the solution architecture. In the minutes of meeting, she sees that everyone agreed that this was the way to go. Actually, the Solution Architect from Clever Consultants argued that a stretched farm across two data centers would only provide high availability up to a point because the SAN was still in the first data center. If that data center went down, the farm would go down too. Super Structure argued that the SLA that Fancy Flowers paid for was their highest level and this would take too long to recover from. The actual solution in the solution architecture was for a disaster recovery farm in the second data center. But Fancy Flowers insisted that this be marked as "part of phase 2" and so it was described in the solution architecture but not actually implemented in the detailed design.

At this late stage, the Fancy Flowers project manager balks and says that is not what they agreed. She doesn't think the cost of the disaster recovery farm is necessary, despite her lack of knowledge of SharePoint, and she insists things must be done her way.

Dashing Development stays out of this because Fancy Flowers is their customer and they don't want to lose the business of designing custom branding and web parts for them.

The discussion now whirls between 15-20 people as to what the SLA means and how this should be delivered. Super Structure offers a third option: log shipping and moving the staging farm to the second data center to double as a DR farm. This will mean uninstalling and reinstalling this farm from scratch as all the accounts and machine names include the name of the data center. Also, log shipping will mean further capacity in the network to store the logs.

Someone brings up mirroring and there is much debate about what databases can, should, and shouldn't mirror in SharePoint 2010. The discussions reach a stalemate as no one seems to be willing or able to make the final decision. In the end, they do nothing. Eventually, the data center is destroyed when a local river bursts its banks. Without a proper disaster recovery plan, everyone sues everyone else and it cost them all a lot of money while they all continue to believe they were right all along.

Some Terminology

Before I go on, I'll explain some of the terms that are useful to know in the context of HA and DR.

- *SAN*: Storage that can be used by SQL or Windows.

- *Latency*: How long it takes data to travel from one server to another. Low latency (1 millisecond latency) is ideal.

- *Data center:* A building with lots of servers in it. Primary and secondary data centers are normally less than 100kms apart because fiber optic cable starts to degrade in efficiency at lengths longer than that, thereby increasing the latency.

- *Replication:* Copying data between farms.

- *Mirroring:* Making a copy of data almost instantly, like a mirror. Referred to as synchronous, which means "at the same time." Because it has to be done constantly, it requires lots of system resources.

- *Log shipping:* This means backing up the SQL data to a file server and then restoring it to another SQL server. Referred to asynchronous because the copying is not done instantly. Typically the log backup might be done at 6 p.m., but the restore done six hours later. This is because it takes perhaps two hours to back up the SQL databases to a file server, two hours to copy them to a file server on in the other data center, and two hours to restore the data to the farm.

- *Hot, warm, and cold standby:* If a standby system can be operational in minutes or less, it's referred to as hot. If it takes several minutes or hours, it's referred to as warm. If it takes many hours or days, it's referred to as cold. These are not exact terms.

Summary of the Options

Later in this book, I will go into the relative merits of these choices in more detail; I will also explain how to implement them. For now, here is a summary of the options in this scenario.

Option 1: Log Shipping/Mirroring

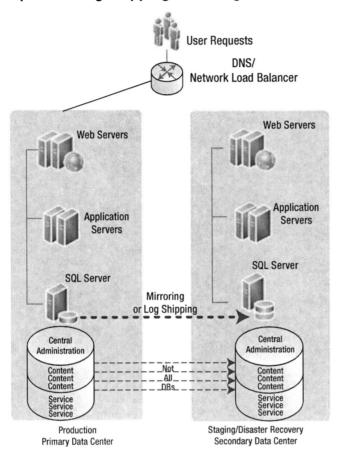

Figure 1-6. *A SharePoint farm with mirroring or log shipping*

This was the option presented by Super Structure. As an IaaS company, they have experience with Windows and SQL Server but not with SharePoint, so they proposed that some of the databases could be mirrored or log shipped to the secondary data center and that the farm intended for the staging of new code could double as the disaster recovery farm. This plan includes separate web servers, application servers, and SQL servers in the two data centers. Only some of the databases can be log shipped with SharePoint 2010, and since they are different farms, the configuration databases are not replicated (I will go into more detail on this later in the book). In Figure 1-6, you can see that some content and service databases are being replicated and that the servers in the same farm are in different data centers. Table 1-2 covers the pros and cons of this approach.

Table 1-2. *The Pros and Cons of a SharePoint Farm with Mirroring or Log Shipping*

Pros	Cons
Standard way to provide HA and DR for SQL Server	SAN not replicated to secondary date center. SAN mirroring/replication costs millions of dollars.
Asynchronous: providing cold standby availability in hours or days.	Logs are not copied in real time between the principal and the mirror servers, so no negative effects on performance.
A compromise of cost versus benefits.	File server space required to hold logs during copy to DR farm.

Option 2: Stretched Farm

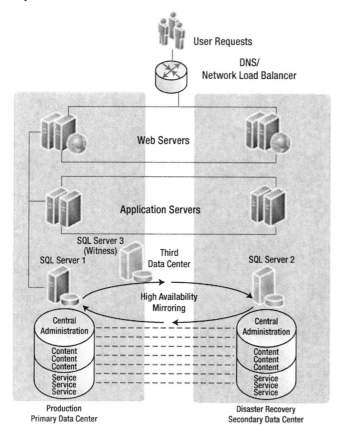

Figure 1-7. *A SharePoint stretched farm with mirroring*

Figure 1-7 shows the architecture Fancy Flowers wanted. They did not specify mirroring specifically as they didn't know the difference between log shipping and mirroring, but to give highest availability of the SQL layer, it would be a good idea. There are web front-end servers, application servers, and SQL servers in the primary and secondary data centers. All are in the same farm. However, there is an important detail not represented in this diagram that Super Structure didn't explain to Fancy Flowers: the SAN. The storage for the whole farm is still in the primary data center. So if that data center became unavailable, it would mean a lot of stretching was done for no real benefit. Replicate the SAN is possible, but it's also a very expensive option—much more expensive than having a separate disaster recovery farm in the secondary data center. But Fancy Flowers is set on this idea and isn't budging. Table 1-3 represents the pros and cons of this approach.

Table 1-3. The Pros and Cons of a SharePoint Stretched Farm

Pros	Cons
In SLA, it corresponds to highest level of availability.	SAN replicated to secondary date center. SAN mirroring/replication costs millions of dollars.
Provides high availability and disaster recovery.	Mirroring is expensive in terms of system resources.
Synchronous, thus providing hot standby availability in seconds or minutes.	

Option 3: Disaster Recovery Farm

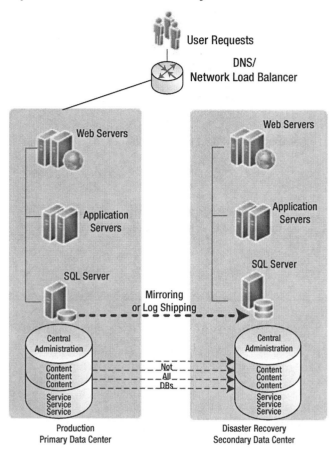

Figure 1-8. *A disaster recovery farm*

This option, shown in Figure 1-8, is almost exactly the same as option 1 except here the disaster recovery farm is only used for that purpose. It is not used for the staging of custom development. This is what was proposed by Clever Consultants but rejected by Fancy Flowers because of the additional cost. However, it is less expensive than SAN replication and certainly better than no disaster recovery at all. Table 1-4 shows the pros and cons of this option.

Table 1-4. The Pros and Cons of a SharePoint Combined Staging/Disaster Recovery Farm

Pros	Cons
In SLA, it corresponds to high level of availability.	SAN replicated to secondary date center. SAN mirroring/replication costs millions of dollars.
Provides high availability and disaster recovery.	Mirroring is expensive in terms of system resources.
Asynchronous, thus providing warm standby availability in minutes or hours.	More costly than no DR farm. Second farm and capacity paid for even when not used.
Same level of performance after failover.	File server space required to hold logs during copy to DR farm.
Database layer is asynchronously log shipped.	Logs are not copied in real time between the principal and the mirror servers, so no negative effects on performance.
No dependency on constant connectivity between data centers.	Requires secondary farm to be maintained/patched to keep same as primary.

The Solution

This is a typical scenario because of the multiple people involved and the multiple technical options. Here the failure came about because there were too many people involved and no one person with enough knowledge or authority to make the decision. There were four parties with different motivations and no cooperation between them. It would be easy to blame the disaster on the river, but in fact it was poor project management that really caused the disaster.

It's not uncommon for organizations to subcontract to other companies because they lack the expertise to make the technical decisions. Here are some details on the four players involved:

- Fancy Flowers: They wanted the most secure solution but also the cheapest. They didn't accept that disaster recovery is expensive and that designing your own solution if you don't understand the technology is a recipe for disaster. Being the client, they had veto power on all decisions; also they reversed the decision on the solution architecture after it was agreed, which caused chaos.

- Super Structure: They had the infrastructure expertise, but SharePoint requires specialist knowledge, which they lacked. When they had to deliver an SLA to Fancy Flowers, they fell back on what they knew: SQL server log shipping as the solution.

- Clever Consultants: They were stuck in the middle. They had responsibility for the solution architecture, but they lacked authority to push their solution through. In the end, they compromised on their initial recommendation of a disaster recovery farm to get the solution signed off.

- Dashing Development: They stayed neutral through all this and managed not to get any of the blame. Their goal was to stay in good graces with Fancy Flowers, so they decided to neither help nor hinder.

Someone needed to have authority over the whole process to make the final decision. This should have been a higher level manager in Super Structure. They should have decided exactly what was required in the SLA and clearly laid out the options for Fancy Flowers in terms of costs and the advantages and disadvantages of each. They could have gathered this information from Clever Consultants. The options were the following:

- Log shipping/mirroring
- Stretched farm
- Disaster recovery farm

With a clear set of choices and the costs of each, Fancy Flowers could have made a decision and the disaster could have been averted.

Summary

To protect your content, you must know your technology and realize its importance to your organization. Roles must be assigned and responsibility taken. Moreover, there should be a way to record near-misses so they can be captured and addressed. SharePoint is not just a technology platform; it's partly owned by the users, too. They and management must play a part in its governance.

CHAPTER 2

Planning Your Plan

This chapter describes the dependencies you will have to address before you can begin to create a disaster recovery plan. The plan itself with consist of what to do when disaster happens, but there are a number of important steps before it can even be created. Firstly, there has to be a will to create it and the funding to do so, plus the input of stakeholder in the business itself and not just IT. There will be barriers to your desire to create a plan and you will have to approach removing them in different ways. I will describe each one and give an example of how you can remove it.

The object at the end of this chapter is to be in a position to create a plan and put it into action. Before you have a plan, though, you have to plan what is required for that plan to exist. You will need to do the following:

- Gain approval from management.

- Build consensus among stakeholders.

- Create a business impact assessment.

- Address the physical and logistical realities of your place and people.

The focus here is "first things first." These are the dependencies that, if not addressed, will either prevent you from creating a plan or mean it can't or won't work when it is really tested.

Getting the Green Light from Management

Since I am assuming your disaster recovery plan does not already exist, step one is to get approval for your plan. In order to initiate a DR planning project, top level management would normally be presented with a proposal. A project as important as this should be approved at the highest level. This is to ensure that the required level of commitment, resources, and management attention are applied to the process.

The proposal should present the reasons for undertaking the project and could include some or all of the following arguments:

- There is an increased dependency by the business over recent years on SharePoint, thereby creating increased risk of loss of normal services if SharePoint is not available.

- Among stakeholders, there is increased recognition of the impact that a serious incident could have on the business.

- Disaster recovery is not something that can be improvised. Therefore, there is a need to establish a formal process to be followed when a disaster occurs.

- There is an opportunity to lower costs or losses arising from serious incidents. This is the material benefit to the plan.

- There is a need to develop effective backup and recovery strategies to mitigate the impact of disruptive events.

The first step to understanding what the disaster recovery plan should consist of will be a business impact assessment (BIA). However, before discussing the BIA, let's consider some of the barriers to organizational consensus and the metaphors that often underlie these barriers.

Barriers to Consensus

There can be many barriers to creating a DR plan. Some will be practical, such as the fact that every business has finite resources. These have to be addressed with facts and figures to back up your arguments.

One paradoxical objection is the existence of a plan already! This plan may be large and complex to such an extent that no one actually understands it or has ever tested it. It may not include SharePoint explicitly. There can also be political reasons to oppose the development of a plan. For example, there may be people who favor the support of a platform they perceive as in competition with SharePoint and so they oppose anything that relates to it. Counteracting political maneuvering like this is beyond the scope of this book.

Another barrier to approval of a DR plan is a lack of awareness by upper management of the potential impact of a failure of SharePoint. This is why, as I will outline in this chapter, having a BIA is the essential first component of the DR plan. It gives management real numbers around why the DR plan is necessary. Creating a DR plan will cost resources (time and money), so the BIA is essential to show you are trying to avoid cost and reduce losses, not increase them.

Some barriers to creating a DR plan will be more nebulous. This is because they have to do with the way people's minds work, especially when it comes to complex systems like technology. There is a mistake we are all prone to making in relation to anything we don't understand: we substitute a simple metaphor for the thing itself. As a result, we make naïve assumptions about what is required to tackle the inherent risks in managing them.

Disaster recovery planning is usually not done very well. This is because the business doesn't understand the technology. At best, it still thinks it should be simple and cheap because copying a file or backing up a database to disk seems like it should be simple and cheap. But the reality is that SharePoint is a big, complex system of interdependent technologies, and maintaining a recoverable version of the system is not simple. While this book will give you the knowledge and facts to back up your system, you will need to construct some better metaphors for your business to help you convince them to let you create a disaster recovery plan that actually fulfils its purpose. But first, you have to understand where these metaphors come from and the purpose they serve.

Weak Metaphors

Metaphors have been used in computing for many years to ease adoption and help people understand the function of certain items. This is why we have "documents" in "folders" on our computer "desktop." These metaphors were just to represent data on the hard disk. John Siracusa of Ars Technica talks about what happened next:

Back in 1984, explanations of the original Mac interface to users who had never seen a GUI before inevitably included an explanation of icons that went something like this:

"This icon represents your file on disk." But to the surprise of many, users very quickly discarded any semblance of indirection. This icon is my file. My file is this icon. One is not a "representation of" or an "interface to" the other. Such relationships were foreign to most people, and constituted unnecessary mental baggage when there was a much more simple and direct connection to what they knew of reality.

(Source: http://arstechnica.com/apple/reviews/2003/04/finder.ars/3)

Zen Buddhists have an appropriate Kōan, although I don't think they had WIMP (window, icon, menu, pointing device) in mind:

Do not confuse the pointing finger with the moon.

The problem is the convenient, simplistic metaphor used to represent the object becomes the object in itself if you don't understand fully the thing being pointed at. When this kind of thinking gets applied to planning the recovery of business information, it creates a dangerous complacency that leaves a lot of valuable data in jeopardy.

Long, Long Ago...

It may seem obvious to some readers, but almost all business information is now in the form of electronic data. We don't think of the fragility of the storage medium. We think of business information as being as solid as the servers that contain it. They say to err is human, but to really mess things up takes a computer. This is especially true when years of data from thousands of people can be lost or corrupted in less than a second and is completely unrecoverable. We find it hard to grasp that the file hasn't just fallen behind the filing cabinet and we can just fish it out somehow.

In many ways, the store of knowledge, experience, and processes is the sum of what your business is—beyond the buildings and the people. Rebuilding a premises or rehiring staff can be done more quickly than rebuilding years of information.

The fragility and importance of electronic information is mainly underestimated because of our outmoded metaphors. We confuse the metaphor with the thing it represents. Those are not really documents; they are just lots of magnetized materials arranged one direction or another on aluminum or glass in a hard drive (see Figure 2-1).

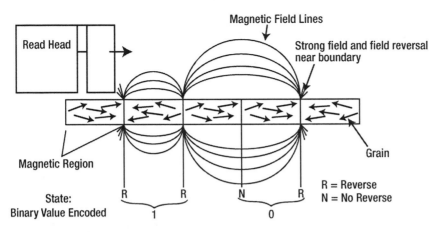

Figure 2-1. *Your documents are actually just little bits of iron.*

A relative of mine had an original way to get around this fragility. When he visited a web page he liked, he would print it out and file it alphabetically in a file cabinet right beside the computer. He complained this was a frustrating process because the web sites kept changing. Once I introduced him to the concept of a bookmark (another metaphor) in the browser, his life got a lot simpler. But I think that from a data retention point of view, perhaps he had the right idea!

Long Ago…

Even if some people have moved on from the perception of files in filing cabinets, they still think that data protection can be addressed exclusively through some form of tape-based backup. A few years ago, copies of backup tapes were retained locally to meet daily recovery requirements for lost files, database tables, etc. Copies of some of those tapes were periodically shipped to remote locations where they were often stored for years to ensure data recovery in the event of a catastrophic disaster that shut down the organization's primary site.

Long term, off-site storage of tapes was the conventional way to "do" disaster recovery. If operation of the business needed to be restarted in some location other than the primary one, these tapes could be shipped to the new location; application environments would be manually rebuilt; the data would be loaded onto the new servers; and business operations would be transacted from this new location until such time as the primary location could be brought back online.

This model is still seen as valid in some organizations and it is insufficient to capture the complexity and scale of a SharePoint farm. As you will see in later chapters, a SharePoint farm has many interdependent and ever changing components. Rebuilding a SharePoint farm with only tape backups and no DR plan would be a challenge for anyone no matter what their technical skill. Combine that with the cost of every second the system is down and it's not a good scenario.

Another Weak Metaphor: Snapshots

Virtualization uses another metaphor that is taken wrongly to promise something it can't deliver in relation to a SharePoint farm. Some people still think they can simply take a "snapshot" of a running SharePoint farm's virtual web, application, and SQL servers. They think this magic camera captures all the information in SharePoint farm at a moment in time and this allows them to restore it at any point in the future back to that point. This is overly simplistic.

Just one example of a part of a SharePoint farm that shows their complexity is timer jobs. SharePoint farms have over 125 default timer jobs (http://technet.microsoft.com/en-us/library/cc678870.aspx). They can run anywhere from every 15 seconds (in the case of Config Refresh, which checks the configuration database for configuration changes to the User Profile Service) to monthly runs of My Site Suggestions Email Job, which sends e-mails that contain colleague and keyword suggestions to people who don't update their user profile often, prompting them to update their profiles.

Timer jobs look up what time it is now to know when next to run. This is because they don't run on one universal time line but follow a simple rule like "after being run, set the timer to run again in 90 minutes." If you take a snapshot of these services and then try to restore them to a previous point in time, they think it's the time of the snapshot, not the current time. Obviously, this can create major problems.

Stronger Metaphors

"Reality is merely an illusion, albeit a very persistent one"

Albert Einstein (attributed)

The point I am making is that these overly simplistic views of the information stored on computers are what leads to poor disaster recovery plans because there is an assumption that it should be cheap and simple to make backups, like taking a photo or making a tape recording. But times have changed, and it is no longer that simple or cheap. Your aim at this point is to get buy-in for your project to create a DR plan. You don't have time to make people experts on SharePoint, but you have to change their weak metaphors to stronger ones.

Weak metaphors operate like superstitions; they can't be counteracted with knowledge and facts. Facts simply make the person's viewpoint more entrenched because there is no 100% true view of anything. To persuade people to open their minds, the more successful indirect approach is to improve their metaphors; you're going to have to substitute better metaphors they can use instead.

Here are some stronger metaphors that may help you convince people SharePoint is a complex system:

- *SharePoint is like a public park*: It needs constant pruning and planning to manage its growth. Now imagine that park has been destroyed and you have to re-create it. You would need a lot of different information to recreate it. A simple snapshot would not be enough, and you can't simply maintain a copy of a constantly changing organic thing.

- *SharePoint is like an office building*: If, due to a natural disaster, you had to relocate everyone and everything in this building elsewhere, how would you do it? This metaphor is useful because no matter what business you are in, you will likely rely on some physical location. SharePoint is a virtual version of that. A home is another variation of this metaphor.

- *SharePoint is like the human body.* It has many interconnected and interdependent parts. Like a body, if one organ fails, it impacts the whole organism. If you had to rebuild a person from scratch using cloned organs, you would need not only the physical aspects but also the years of information stored in the brain. With SharePoint, you can clone virtual servers, but only empty ones. The data is constantly changing and complex.

If you can get across to your stakeholders some idea of the complex and evolving nature of SharePoint, you can win them over to the more concrete step of working out what the impact of a SharePoint system failure would be. This is the next step.

Business Impact Assessment

Business data is an asset and has tangible value. But some data has more value than others. Most organizations don't actually calculate the value of information or the cost to the business of losing some or all of it. Before you can do a disaster recovery plan you have to plan why you need it. And what you need to have to fully appreciate why you need a disaster recovery plan is a business impact assessment (BIA). This will result in knowing the cost of not having a disaster recovery plan in real money. The conclusion most organizations will come to is that the cost of producing and maintaining a BIA is proportionally very little compared to what it will have saved them in the event of a disaster.

A business impact assessment (BIA) should be a detailed document that has involved all the key stakeholders of the business. They are the people key to making the BIA and, by extension the DR plan, a success. It is not something that can only be drawn up by the IT department. This is another fundamental outmoded mind set. It is the responsibility of the content owners to own the business continuity planning for their teams. While that is done in conjunction with the IT department, they are simply there to fulfill the requirements. It is the job of the business to define them.

A BIA should identify the financial and operational impacts that may result from a disruption of operations. Some negative impacts could be

- The cost of downtime

- Loss of revenue

- Inability to continue operations

- Loss of automated processes

- Brand erosion: loss of a sense of the company's quality, like the Starbucks example in Chapter 1

- Loss of trustworthiness and reputation: the hacking of Sony demonstrated this impact

Who Sets the RTO and RPO?

I have offered my theory as to why disaster recovery planning is so underfunded and also why traditionally IT has been the owner of it: the stakeholders don't realize the complexity. In most cases, it is the IT department that determines the recovery time and recovery point objectives. But how are they supposed to determine them accurately without empirical input from the business?

As a consequence, the objectives are typically set based on generic Microsoft guidelines or some arbitrary decision like which managers complain the most about how particularly important their data is. Without a BIA, IT has no empirical way to determine how to measure these objectives (RTO and RPO).

The business users are owners of their content, so by extension they are responsible for business continuity/disaster recovery planning. They should dictate the RTOs and RPOs for their business processes within SharePoint.

The Goldilocks Principle

RTOs and RPOs are either based on simple tape backups or snapshots—or due to overzealousness they go to the opposite extreme of something approaching zero downtime. SharePoint farms sometimes end up with overly aggressive RTO and RPOs because business users believe they can't tolerate any downtime. That is certainly true in some organizations, such as Amazon.com, which relies on uptime to exist as a business. Another example would be air traffic control where every second counts if planes are circling your airport and running low on fuel. These are the exception, not the rule. The more aggressive the RTO/RPO, the more expensive the technology needed to achieve that objective. As you saw in "Applied Scenario: It's Never Simple," in the previous chapter an RTO/RPO in minutes or hours necessitates the use of SAN replication technology which is very expensive to replicate the data at the SAN level to another data center. Log shipping is slower but also much cheaper.

    The objective in disaster recovery planning is to find the perfect equilibrium between what you want to pay for your RPO/RTO and what you can afford to lose. Call it the Goldilocks principle: Not too much or too little. The graph in Figure 2-2 illustrates this principle.

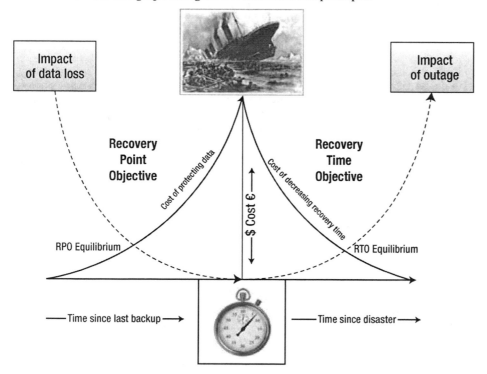

Figure 2-2. Time is money when it comes to RPO and RTO.

    In Figure 2-2, the central axis is cost. It also marks the point in time when the disaster happens. On top, you have your ship hitting the iceberg. From that point what you do is your disaster recovery. The clock is literally ticking and time is money. Beside the stopwatch and to the right is time moving forward. The arrow coming from the Titanic indicates that the cost goes down as you move away from the point of impact. In other words, the longer you can wait to restore the data, the cheaper your recovery will be. However, this descending curve is crossed by an ascending dotted curve pointing up to the Impact of Outage. That is the rising cost to your organization of SharePoint being offline. The further you go from the stopwatch, the higher it will climb.

To illustrate this dynamic, consider the Titanic. Lifeboats took up space on the deck, and space on a ship is very valuable to the passengers and by extension the company because the more comfortable the voyage, the more passengers they will have and the higher their profits. It was also the common wisdom of the time that if a ship that large did sink, there wouldn't be enough time to get all the thousands of passengers onto the lifeboats, so they were useless anyway. Also, it was believed that in such a busy shipping lane, there would be plenty of ships to come to their aid and fish people out of the water in the event of a sinking. Thus, a focus on profits and a dependency on luck were placed over the value of human lives. It is important to point out that White Star Line (who owned Titanic) eventually ceased to exist and was taken over by its competitor Cunard. It is fair to say they did not consider seriously the Impact Of Outage or achieve a reasonable RTO equilibrium.

On the other side of the stopwatch is the time since your last backup. The cost of being able to recover to a point in time seconds or minutes before the disaster is at the highest point on the curve to the left of the cost axis. In other words, if you can only afford to lose seconds or minutes of data, it's very expensive to implement this. But if you can afford to lose hours or days, it is much cheaper.

To give a non-SharePoint example, to keep backups of this book as I wrote it I used Jungle Disk. It is based on Amazon Web Storage. I schedule a timer job to back up the folder with all my chapters and figures to the cloud every night at 1a.m. If it fails at that time because my Internet access is down, it tries again until it gets a connection. I am comfortable with a Recovery Point Objective of at most 24 hours because if I lost a day's work, it would only be 1,200 or so words on average and I could make that up in four days at a rate of 1,500 words a day. Jungle Disk is low cost because you only pay for the storage you use after your initial upload. It is not too expensive for me, so I feel I have achieved my RPO Equilibrium. My RTO is also low because all I need to do is go to another PC, install Jungle Disk, and restore my backup—in less than an hour, I'm back writing. You can read more about Jungle Disk here if you are interested: http://aws.amazon.com/solutions/case-studies/jungledisk/.

The single most important point in this book is that if you are going to implement a disaster recovery plan, you need to start by understanding your requirements and the implications of those requirements. It is a mistake to focus first on the many technologies that are often associated with SharePoint. I knew I needed to protect myself from a potential hard drive crash. I didn't want to rewrite this book from the beginning if I lost it. I knew I wouldn't mind spending a few dollars a month on backup, as long as I'd not lose more than a day's work and I could be back writing within an hour or so. That was my BIA. Once I'd figured out my parameters, I searched until I found the technical solution that met my requirements.

Consensus

A good BIA will result in consensus on RTO/RPOs for critical business processes within SharePoint. To achieve this you will have to involve a representative from all of your organization's business units. Their job is to identify the critical business processes their units perform and how long those processes can be down before there is a critical impact to the organization. Notice the standard is *critical impact*. Critical means if they don't function, the organization can't function and comes to an immediate stop. It's not just the point where SharePoint being down would cause them some inconvenience. It is the point where there is a real, measurable cost. The reality is that there is invariably a manual procedure that can be followed until SharePoint is brought back up. Admittedly, it will be a bit annoying to catch up with re-entering the data, but the cost savings could be very large.

Once you have tangible figures, these business process RTO/RPOs will translate into application and system RTO/RPOs for SharePoint, and IT can support these processes. From IT's point of view, it will give them real requirements to meet. As a bonus, this will also likely help identify dependent systems such as Active Directory or external data sources linked to the prioritized business processes within SharePoint.

You'll never know whether you're really maintaining the "just right" point in your DR spending without producing a thorough BIA with all the necessary inputs. Secondly, if you don't review and revisit it every 6-12 months it will become out of date and irrelevant. Remember the lesson of the lifeboats and the Titanic.

Like the ship, you have to make sure all the stakeholders are on board and understand the risks so they are committed fully to knowing what they will need to do in the event of a disaster. Think of this as making sure your passengers know the lifeboat drill. To understand the importance of the drill, they need to know the impact, literally, of an impact.

People

To prepare a disaster recovery plan the main dependency you will need to make it happen is people. I have already discussed completing a BIA, RTO/RPO, the Goldilocks principle, and finally, consensus. In the event of a disaster, what other people will you need involved in the planning? The answer is, of course, the people to execute the plan. This is another point where planning your plan can fall down before it even begins. What if the person or people who know your SharePoint farm best are not available themselves because of the disaster? Perhaps the disaster is an epidemic and all your SharePoint administrators are ill in hospital or worse. Your plan has to take into account that the people who created it may not be the ones implementing it. The only way to prepare for this and to test your plan properly is to have an independent third party test your recovery plan.

Another issue to consider when testing your plan is that the people who created the plan have a vested interest in it being successfully run. As a result, they will make sure the test of the plan is successful. This is another reason why a third party should do a dry-run implementation of the plan. So now you have everyone in agreement about needing a plan, you have a way to measure what it needs to achieve, and you've avoided the pitfall of relying on one person/group of people as a single point of failure to test and execute the plan. What other dependencies are there?

Physical Dependencies

The physical dependencies in the event of a disaster are the SharePoint farm itself and the data. Many enterprises implement a DR plan for just data, assuming that the servers and application environment will be manually rebuilt. Manually rebuilding SharePoint is not a simple task. Think again of the complex system metaphors. The answer is to use automated application recovery. DR plans that provide for automated SharePoint application recovery will be able to meet much shorter RTOs than those that just recover data and then depend on administrators to manually rebuild SharePoint. Those plans will also be more reliable and perform more predictably because they will not be as dependent upon the skill of the SharePoint farm administrators that are actually performing the recovery, some of whom may not be available when a real disaster hits.

Architectural Impact

Remember that the primary goal of the BIA is to find an equilibrium point for the RTO and RPO objectives where the impact to the organization can be tolerated and the organization can afford the cost of the solution. If you've not built it already, it may result in changing how you plan your SharePoint architecture. You may have separate farms with different RTO/RPOs because you have a prioritized recovery order of the business processes within the business units.

From IT's point of view, it will help identify dependent systems such as Active Directory or external data sources linked to the prioritized business processes within SharePoint. So when planning your plan, realize it will have a comprehensive impact on your architecture. Don't build until you have a BIA. It's tempting to do things the other way around, but the result will be an architecture where, like the Titanic, you have to hope nothing will go wrong because you know it will be a disaster.

Risk Assessment

Outside of your SharePoint farm and its data is a bigger world that is beyond your control. But as part of your pre-DR plan planning you can assess what could happen that might affect your not being able to put your plan into action. This means you will have to evaluate the types of disasters that you are most likely to encounter given where your data centers are located. If you are in an area prone to natural disasters, such as tsunamis, floods, earthquakes, or widespread power outages, you may want to follow the DR best practice guideline of locating your remote recovery site at least 200 miles away from your primary site. If this is your requirement, this will affect any decision you make to implement replication technologies to help address your DR requirements. For example, Microsoft recommends a stretched farm have at worst 1ms of latency between the data centers and fiber optic cable contains imperfections that starts to degrade the light being passed along after about 60 miles. There may be other specific risks associated with your type of organization that should be taken into account when planning what should be in your DR plan.

To assess risk, you'll need to do some research. There will be many sources of information, including the following:

- System interfaces, hardware and software

- Data in logs

- People: Ask! There will be lots of valuable information here.

- History of hacks/attacks on the system from the following sources: internal, police, news media.

- History of natural disasters from the following sources: internal, police, news media.

- External/internal audits

- Security requirements

- Security test results

There are many types of risk that should be considered. The following list is by no means exhaustive but it at least demonstrates the range of possibilities:

- Natural Disasters

  - Tornado

  - Hurricane

  - Flood

  - Snow

- Drought
- Earthquake
- Tsunami
- Electrical storms
- Fire
- Subsidence and landslides
- Freezing Conditions
- Contamination and environmental hazards
- Health Epidemic
- Deliberate Disruption
  - Terrorism
  - Sabotage
  - War
  - Coups
  - Theft
  - Arson
  - Labor disputes/industrial action
- Loss of Utilities and Services
  - Electrical power failure
  - Loss of gas supply
  - Loss of water supply
  - Petroleum and oil shortage
  - Loss of telephone services
  - Loss of Internet services
  - Loss of drainage/waste removal
- Equipment or System Failure
  - Internal power failure
  - Air conditioning failure
  - Cooling systems failure
  - Equipment failure (excluding IT hardware)

- Serious Information Security Incidents
  - Hacking
  - Accidental loss of records or data
  - Disclosure of sensitive information
- Other Emergency Situations
  - Workplace violence
  - Public transportation disruption
  - Riots
  - Health and safety regulations
  - Employee morale
  - Mergers and acquisitions
  - Negative publicity
- Legal problems

The outcome of this will be to identify preventive controls. These are measures that reduce the effects of system disruptions, increase system availability, and potentially reduce your disaster recovery costs.

Synchronicity

Time and distance are big factors in planning your plan. Synchronous means "at the same time." Replication means "make a copy of data." Keeping current is something people have always done. Before we even technology, we used verbal communication to keep in sync. If I haven't seen a friend for a while, we will share news until we "catch up." We exchange the new information of interest since the last time we met. So the key concepts here are time and data. When you connect your Smartphone to your PC, they also catch up and exchange information that may be new on the other until they are in sync again; this includes new downloads, software updates, contacts, e-mails, calendar entries, etc. In both cases, it takes a bit of time to catch up. The longer since you last talked/connected to the PC, the longer it takes to get in sync.

Social networking technologies like Facebook, Twitter etc. mean we tend to know a lot of current information about a lot of people very quickly, almost the instant it happens. Some updates are even from people we don't know; we are just interested in a topic they are sharing their knowledge about. If we constantly check these applications, we can stay constantly in sync. The drawback is you have to spend every waking minute with your eyes glued to a screen reading to ensure you are up to date. The real world is passing you by while you stay in sync with the virtual one.

You can think of talking/Smartphone sync as not happening all the time, only when we hook up. The term for this is asynchronous. The longer the gap between syncs, the longer it takes. But while we are not syncing, we are free to do other things. Facebook/Twitter is almost synchronous; it can happen all the time in real time, but at the expense of doing anything else.

Synchronous Replication: Mirroring

Replication is the process of syncing data. It comes in two flavors: synchronous and asynchronous. SharePoint data is mostly stored in SQL Server, so for synchronous replication it can use a technology called database mirroring to keep two databases looking the same, like a mirror image, on different farms in different data centers. The more the source changes, the harder the mirror has to work to keep current. Think of it has having a constant stream of updates on Facebook or Twitter. SharePoint farms will have about 20 databases of various sizes and purposes. Some change frequently, like the ones holding content; some less so, like the ones holding farm-wide configuration settings. This puts a strain on your system resources, so you will have to plan to have extra resources if you use mirroring.

Latency

To recap, SharePoint farmers (I wonder if that term will catch on?) use synchronous replication like mirroring to keep a source and target synchronized in terms of data states; this is hard work for the servers if there are a lot of changes. Latency is another factor; that's how much time it takes the data to travel between the servers. High latency, measured in milliseconds, naturally causes a performance hit on your production SharePoint farm if the source and target are more than about 30 miles apart. This is frequently the case and is often deliberate so that the data centers will not be prone to the same potential physical disasters.

Asynchronous Replication: Log Shipping

Because fiber optic cable gets slower and less reliable with distance, asynchronous replication is much more widely used to meet long distance DR requirements. Asynchronous replication keeps a source and target in sync over literally any distance, but the target may lag the source by up to several minutes (depending on the write volumes and network latencies). This is like our example of two friends catching up, or connecting your Smartphone to your PC. If it's done once a day, you have the rest of the time to focus on other things, but since you do it every day, the catch up doesn't take too long, and you can do it in the evening when other activities are quieter.

SharePoint stores most of its data in SQL Server, and SQL Server tracks changes in a log. If you copied the logs from your production farm overnight to another farm in another data center, then applied all the changes in it the those databases, the two farms would become in sync again. There is a backlog between the applying of the changes, but this *log shipping* replicates asynchronously because it doesn't happen until a while after the real changes. The advantage is it can be done when the servers are not too busy and requires less system resources as a consequence.

Asynchronous replication provides the kind of RPO performance necessary to meet SLAs of 99.9% up time per year, and it does so in such a way that doesn't impact the performance of production applications. 99.9% is around 8 hours a year, since 99.9% is one day in 1000, or one day unscheduled down time every 3 years, approximately. A year is 365 1/4 days. 8 hours is 1/3 of a 24 hour day. So, if you log shipped every 8 hours, that's the maximum you would lose in a year, you could bring the recovery point back to at worst 8 hours since the last log ship. Keep in mind that if your primary data center is too close to your secondary data center, the same natural disaster could disable both of them, so the benefits of synchronous replication could be moot. Another reason log shipping is a good option is that it is a resilient process; you can keep the logs and even restore them to the production farm to roll it back to a point in time. Note in both cases your farms must have the same architecture, patches, etc. so they can be kept in sync. All of these things need to be considered before you can begin your disaster recovery plan.

Recovery Tiers

This is likely starting to sound complex, but a process I apply to simplify matters is to create priorities among what will need to be recovered. This helps focus resources on what is most important. Defining recovery tiers is an approach that is often used when evaluating in your BIA the recovery requirements for your various business processes within SharePoint. Instead of evaluating and setting recovery requirements individually for all major business process areas, a small number of recovery tiers can be defined. Each tier has a set of recovery performance metrics that are associated with all application environments within that tier. For example, Management may define three tiers like those in Table 2-1.

Table 2-1. *Recovery Tiers Because Not All Content is Equal*

Tier	RPO/RTO	Business Applications in SharePoint
Tier 1	RPO 5 mins, RTO 1 hour	Finance Department Site Collection, Legal Department Site Collection
Tier 2	RPO 4 hours, RTO 8 hours	Project Sites
Tier 3	RPO/RTO 1 day or more	Team Sites and My Sites, all other content

These numbers are just suggestions for your organization since your recovery tiers will vary based upon your business and regulatory requirements. But the general idea applies: there will be a small amount of critical content that requires a very low RPO and very short RTO; then there will be another set of very important sites that require stringent RPO/RTO, but not as stringent as Tier 1; then there will likely be all the rest of the sites which are not critical and may only need to be recovered within one or two days.

Additionally, you may have only two tiers, or you may have more than three tiers, depending on your requirements, but keep in mind that what you don't want is one tier: clearly all your SharePoint sites do not merit the highest priority in terms of recovery. You don't want to pay the price premium to meet your most stringent recovery requirements for sites that don't need it. By the same token, you don't want your critical application environments supported by the same multi-day RPOs or the RTOs that you use for relatively unimportant sites.

Asking your end users about their recovery requirements is an important step, but not the only one. Generally, meeting more stringent recovery requirements requires more expensive solutions. When not thinking about costs, most end users will respond that they want very rapid recovery, when in fact they may easily be able to deal with a failure more easily than they think. The fact is you have to make them really think about it as part of the BIA.

20/20 Hindsight

In some situations, you may have already chosen your architecture—either on the premises or in the cloud—and now you know from your BIA that you will not be able to put in place a disaster recovery plan that will meet your RTO/RPO needs. In any case, the BIA should indicate whether the cost of changing what has been done so far will be less than the cost of a disaster. On that basis, you can win support to fix things and not be stuck with poor decisions and 20/20 hindsight.

In the case of on premises, you may argue you have already paid a third-party consultancy a lot of money to design your SharePoint farm, and they didn't talk about any of this. How can you have different tiers of recovery in that situation? If the farm they created has RPO/RTOs higher than you need, this is an opportunity to save money by changing the rate and amount of data that is backed up/replicated. You may have to create another farm that is just for your tier 1 critical content and migrate content to there. This new farm will cost money but this will likely be cheaper than losing the data, and you can argue you saved money by reducing the RPO/RTO on the tier 2/3 data. If their architecture had too low RPO/RTOs, you should create a new tier 1 farm just to maintain the critical data. Once again you are avoiding greater losses, not spending more money.

What if you are using SharePoint Online and you can't have different RTO/RPOs there, but only what Microsoft offers, which is a 12-hour RTO and 24-hour RPO per year? In that case, you should also consider another hosting option for your critical content like an on-premises farm. This means moving content out of the cloud and building a farm for your critical tier 1 content. Again you can argue that you are avoiding greater losses, not spending more money.

Neither solution is simple, but it is still better than knowing you need to do something but not doing it. In a sense, if you have made decisions about your farm's location without considering DR, you are effectively starting again. This book will help you get to the point where you will be in a stronger position.

Service Level Agreements

Your SLA may already have been negotiated and now is not sufficient to your needs. It may be too high and therefore too costly, or too low, which is potentially very costly! A Service Level Agreement is just that—an agreement between parties recording a common understanding they have reached about the required level of service. It must be a living document that keeps track of changing needs and priorities. It should not be perceived as a straitjacket that restricts either party from negotiating adjustments. In this case, the SLA should be reviewed and changed. In fact, SLAs should be reviewed at least annually. The very process of establishing or re-negotiating an SLA helps to open up communications and establish both parties' expectations of what can be realistically accomplished.

SLAs should be seen as positive things, but they can be a blunt tool to prevent communication. A good SLA ensures that both parties have the same criteria to evaluate service quality. A bad SLA is used to stifle complaints in an already troubled relationship or a quick fix to stop discussion. To be effective, an SLA must incorporate two things: service elements and management elements.

The service elements clarify services by communicating such things as:

- What services will be provided.

- The conditions of service availability.

- The standard of service.

- Escalation procedures.

- Both parties' responsibilities.

- Cost versus service tradeoffs.

The management elements of the SLA focus on how to put the agreement into practice and measure if it is working or not. Without these, an SLA lacks enforceability or a way to agree if it is effective or not. These considerations include the following:

- How to track service effectiveness.

- How information about how service effectiveness will be reported and addressed.

- How service-related disagreements will be resolved.

- How the parties will review and revise the agreement.

The key to establishing and maintaining a successful SLA is having one person on both sides of the agreement that is responsible for creating it and reviewing it. It can be just part of an IT manager's job or a full time job for one person. How long it takes to create one is only answered realistically by doing it and then looking back. It is a living document, so it can be agreed upon and evolve as time goes by.

Disaster Coordination

Now you have prepared most of the groundwork for your plan: you've justified it, got consensus, and created your BIA and RTO/RPOs. You have done your risk assessments, assessed physical limitations such as location and latency. You have planned and decided on your recovery tiers and negotiated your SLAs. So you finished planning your plan? Not quite, but you are at the final hurdle—the dependencies that arise once the disaster itself happens. I will go into more detail in Chapter 3, but here are some principles you can apply to coordinating your disaster. These principles come from the people whose job is arguably the most stressful and chaotic: the Army. They have developed 4Ci to help identify the essential components of a good command structure you will need during your disaster if you want to be able to put your plan into place.

4Ci

This stands for command, control, communications, computers and intelligence. While it is a U.S. military acronym, it applies to the civilian world in relation to how to respond to a disaster. Overall, it describes how the disaster should be coordinated by the people involved, and how essential communication, leadership, and information are. Even before you establish how you will meet the recovery needs of the business from a technical standpoint, you need the people available and communicating well as an effective chain of command. War is hell, as they say, and if a military command structure can continue to function in those circumstances, they have something to teach those of us in the Information Technology world about managing situations that are unexpected and chaotic.

Command

This is the exercise of authority based upon certain knowledge to attain an objective. Note that the phrase "certain knowledge" can mean command experience or training, but it also implies that making command decisions has to be done with the available information. Most commanders would not care to admit that a lot of their decisions are based in guesswork and luck. In the case of a SharePoint disaster recovery, the key question is "Who is in charge and who makes the final decisions when a disaster happens?"

Control

This is the process of verifying and correcting activity such that the objective or goal of command is accomplished. Control means that the person in command is maintaining control of the situation as it develops and new information is gathered and analyzed. It is not enough to say what should be done and, if the disaster happened in the middle of the night, go back to bed. Control must be taken and maintained until the situation has returned to normal or until control can be delegated to someone else.

Communications

This is the ability to exercise the necessary liaisons to effective communicate between tactical or strategic units. When a disaster unfolds, it happens in real time. There is the time the disaster is detected and the time it occurred. There is usually one cause for the disaster but multiple side effects that amplify it and make it grow from a minor "near miss" that didn't miss into a cascade of problems. This is why communication is essential.

For accurate communication, your disaster recovery plan must have a call list. This list must be kept current. The list should have designated backups for each key individual and multiple contact information for them as well. Someone should be designated as the communication list manager to monitor responses and contact backup staff as necessary.

Computers

This refers to the computer systems and compatibility of these computer systems. Obviously the SharePoint farm and all its dependent systems are essential in your disaster recovery. This includes the network, Active Directory and perhaps Exchange, plus third party data sources, etc. This is the largest area of your disaster recovery, so you must be focused on it.

Intelligence

This includes collection as well as analysis and distribution of information. When a disaster occurs, the logs become very important; they can tell you what went wrong and how to get the system back online as quickly as possible. Note that the initial priority is not to work out why this happened. The post mortem can be done after the critical tier 1 and perhaps tier 2 systems are back up and running. At this point, the purpose of analyzing the logs is to find out what when wrong so it can be fixed as soon as possible. If it the cause of the error can't be corrected, it's time for the last resort, which is restoring from backup.

A DR Script

When the stopwatch has started and you are now in recovery mode, many things are occurring at the same time and confusion is inevitable. In order to make the disaster recovery process easier, I recommend a detailed script or set of step-by-step instructions in your DR plan. Of course, the script should be formally reviewed by several different members of the DR team.

Since there is no guarantee that the script will be followed by the same person who wrote it, it's best to use a simple bulleted list with easy-to-follow steps. When in a real recovery scenario, there will be intense pressure and many things going on at the same time. Also, a disaster can occur at any time, so if the plan is executed late at night, confusion is likely to be high.

If possible, try to anticipate errors and include remediation steps. Straightforward and simple instructions go a long way when you are under extreme stress and fatigue. Avoid using terms that may not be understood when extreme fatigue hits. If you must use technical terms, add a glossary.

Last but Not Least: Supply Stores and Restaurants

It may seem unimportant now, but if your staff are onsite for many hours or days, access to good quality food and drinks will help keep their energy levels high and avoid the negative side effects of stress and fatigue. Adrenaline will only keep you going for so long. When it runs out, you need time to rest and recover. It is also good for morale, helps team building, and reduces stress by giving your team a break to eat and re-hydrate. Sometimes the best ideas occur to people if they stop thinking about the problem or step back and chat about it more informally. Do not underestimate the power of a good pizza to solve an IT problem!

As well as planning access to food and drink, consider planned funds/permissions to purchase new equipment and cables. I have seen situations where the solution was very simple, like a damaged cable, but it took hours to find an open store to buy the replacement. If it is a more expensive piece of equipment, put in place a process to get the funds cleared in an emergency to buy the new servers. If it's Friday evening, do you really have to wait until a store opens on Monday before you can get the necessary new hard drive?

Small things like these can make a big difference to meeting your RPO/RTOs, so plan for them now.

Summary

As this chapter shows, there are many factors that need to be considered when planning your plan. The first is getting management buy-in. The next is to get people to change from overly simplistic understandings of SharePoint to something that captures its complexity. This is where you update weak metaphors. This is very important, because stakeholders often don't appreciate that SharePoint is a complex system.

The next step is writing something that will quantify why the DR plan is needed: the Business Impact Assessment. This helps establish a consensus as to the RTO/RPOs and the cost-to-benefit ratio of the DR options. There will be more detail on the technical options in later chapters. Another important factor to understand is physical limitations when planning DR: location, latency, and types of synchronicity.

Your most useful tool in creating a viable DR plan will be building an architecture that reflects your needs. This means creating different tiers in your SharePoint architecture that have different RTO/RPOs and different cost levels relative to the importance of the data in them.

Finally, I offered some advice on creating a good SLA and some initial thoughts on coordinating the disaster. There's more on the latter topic in Chapter 3.

CHAPTER 3

Activating Your Plan

This chapter focuses on the process leading up to the activation of the procedures of your disaster recovery plan. It's important to define the process that says "yes, it is time to active our disaster plan." I've touched on concepts like recovery tiers, which will help you define your plan, but I haven't gone into any real technical detail yet and that is deliberate—that will be done in later chapters. There is a more pressing point I need to get across first: too many plans rely on one person to be in the right place at the right time, to know that a disaster has happened, and to know how to fix it. There are far too many assumptions in that sentence.

- Who decides there's actually been a disaster?

- Who deals with the disaster in general?

- Who in IT deals with the SharePoint farm disaster as distinct from the inevitable broader IT disaster?

- How will the SharePoint people know there's been a disaster?

Without knowing these things, your SharePoint DR plan will be as useless as the breakfast menu for the morning after the Titanic sank. If your organization has no general disaster recovery plan, a SharePoint disaster recovery plan would be of no help to you anyway. The reality is an IT disaster doesn't happen in isolation. It's going to be part of a broader disaster. It's fair to say that when the Titanic hit the iceberg that night, it was a disaster for the kitchen staff planning breakfast, but that was hardly the point. No one told them what was going on and that setting the tables was hardly a priority. If they had a DR plan, it hardly mattered in the context of the bigger disaster. Their plans were no longer relevant. By the way, almost none of the kitchen staff survived the Titanic sinking.

By the end of this chapter, you will know what is necessary to ensure that when disaster strikes, the right people will be in the right place and ready to do something about it.

Welcome to the University of Newbridge

To illustrate the processes and procedures you will need in order to know when to activate your plan, I will use an example of a fictional university. I will base it in my home town: Newbridge, County Kildare, Ireland. Here we have a lot of sheep; as you will see, even these seemingly innocuous creatures can cause a disaster.

I will use the example to flesh out some concepts you should understand when thinking about what needs to be in place before you can activate your DR plan. Let's start with the twinned concepts of *processes* and *procedures*.

A process is not the same thing as a procedure. Think of a process as a "to do" list where each task is assigned to a person or role. A process defines *what* task needs to be done and *who* needs to do it. There are usually multiple *whos* involved in a process.

A procedure is more like an instruction manual. A procedure defines how to do the task and usually only has a single *who* involved.

Keep these concepts in mind as this chapter is all about building the processes and procedures you will need to activate your DR plan. These will be unique because your organization is unique and will have different potential disasters to plan for, a different set of premises, different staff, and a different IT infrastructure. The concepts I raise should help you think about those questions for which you don't have answers.

Let's take a closer look at the concept of a process and its relationship to the objectives that inform it and the procedures that implement the plan.

What Is a Process?

A process is a series of tasks. Despite expectations, a process is not simply a high-level Visio flowchart. A diagram is just a sketch or description of the process. A process is a real thing that combines people, tools, and tasks. It is a set of actions. A process consists of a number of elements and has a number of dependencies. The most important are the roles and responsibilities of the people assigned to do the work. These tie in with the 4Ci in the previous chapter. Who is responsible for doing what and how will they communicate?

No flow chart can capture the complexity of what people need to do when disaster hits. However, the process of creating a process can in itself be valuable because it makes people think in a more organized way.

A disaster is not a situation anyone would want to be in; it's fundamentally unpredictable. As a result, your processes must be elastic. Processes are a journey not a destination. They are drawn up to evaluate risk and help recover from a disaster. They can't be depended on to exactly match the disaster; if they could, you could just avoid the disaster all together!

The key element in the success of a disaster recovery plan is what roles have been assigned to whom. It is impossible to document everything what needs to be done in every eventuality in a disaster situation. You can, however, assign key roles to calm, reasonable, experienced people who can analyze a situation and work towards a solution. You need good people assigned to the right roles and good backups for those people if they are not available.

A process also depends on appropriate tools and equipment to support these individuals in doing their jobs. These have to be put in place in advance (this will be covered in later chapters). Knowing how to use these tools may require additional training.

Processes exist within a framework of policies and standards. A process consists of procedures and methods defining *how* to do the tasks and the relationships between the tasks. Figure 3-1 shows the relationships.

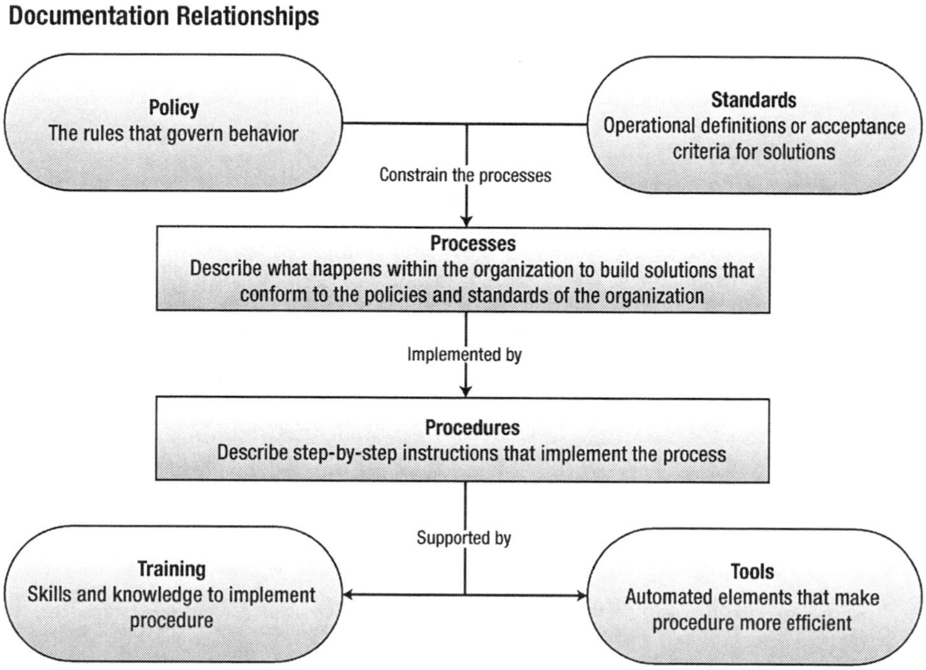

Documentation Relationships

Figure 3-1. Documentation relationships around processes and procedures

Do I Need to Define My Processes and Procedures?

You might or you might not. I will try to avoid the inscrutable answer of the consultant: it depends. There are some specific reasons why you need to define a process or procedure for your disaster recovery plan.

- You need to define a process or procedure that your organization depends on to function. This will give you some assurance that it will continue to be performed when needed.

- You need to define a process or procedure if there is only one person who knows how to do the tasks involved. This may also raise the requirement for training or for more automation to make it possible for more people to do these tasks.

- You need to define your process or procedure if many people perform the tasks in many different ways but one is the preferred way and you want it to be used.

As Figure 3-1 shows, processes and procedures are based on policies and standards. These are evolving statements or rules of conduct.

Benefits of Defining Your Processes and Procedures

First of all, from a business management point of view, defining processes and procedures provides visibility into areas of quality, productivity, cost, and schedule. It is the core maxim of management that "what can't be measured can't be managed." It also improves communication and understanding around what will need to be done. It aids in the planning and execution of plans and provides the ability to capture lessons learned from previous disasters or near misses. It also helps facilitate the analysis/execution of organization-wide processes and provides a basis for training and skills assessment going forward.

Applied Scenario: A Disaster Recovery Plan

This is the beginning of a sample disaster recovery plan. By now, you should realize that people, processes, and procedures are the cornerstones. There are, of course, a range of technical options when it comes to how you will recover your SharePoint farm, and they will constitute a large portion of the rest of this book. At this point, I am describing the elements of a disaster recovery plan that are essential for that technical solution to be put into place.

If you were on the Titanic, your disaster recovery process would consist of the following steps:

1. Identify the disaster: our ship has struck an iceberg. We will sink in two hours.

2. Alert the crew to get passengers into life jackets and onto the deck.

3. Prioritize getting women and children on the lifeboats.

4. Move the lifeboats away from the ship before it sinks.

This is a set of practical steps that should be taken. Now let's look at how that might translate into a SharePoint Disaster Recovery Plan.

The University of Newbridge Disaster Recovery Plan

Let's begin with the introduction. It defines why a disaster recovery plan is necessary. In the case of our imaginary university, sheep broke into the campus and caused a whole host of problems.

Introduction

The university began its planning process after experiencing several disasters caused by a sheep stampede, including a building fire, an environmental contamination, faulty discharge of the fire suppression system, and several electrical outages. The disaster recovery planning has occurred at multiple levels. At the highest level is the University General Emergency Response Plan that covers event identification, general policy, initial response, emergency notifications and communication, and crisis management teams. This document represents the central IT department's effort to communicate what must be done specifically in the event of a SharePoint disaster because we have learned that the general disaster plans for the university and even for IT in general don't include the recovery of the SharePoint farm.

Context and Communication

The IT infrastructure could be in multiple locations. Those locations should be subject to review for risk of compromise. As well as the physical locations, there is the network itself. Have in place processes to review these locations. Also ensure the locations are conveyed to whoever is reading the plan—don't assume everyone knows where all the rooms and building are in advance. A clear, simple map is the best solution to meet this need.

General Facility Risks

The SharePoint farms do not exist in isolation; they are spread around multiple campus buildings and these should be periodically reviewed for potential risks. These periodic reviews should include a facilities walkthrough by a local fire inspector, investigative review of all data center facilities by a fire and sheep safety consultant, and a review by the insurance provider. Campus security or public safety officials should review the physical security of the facilities. They should pay particular attention to fences that sheep can find ways around. Periodic reviews should be conducted with the university's Risk Management staff and Internal Audit staff. Network security audits are also important—not to make them safe from sheep hackers, but from human ones.

Communication

Thanks to the sheep stampede, we now know standard communication paths can't be expected to work in a disaster. Depending on the disaster, different communication methods will work better; hence we have planned for the following alternatives:

- Multiple telephone paths: digital, analog, and cell phones. These will be available in the following locations:

  - Campus security office (room 1.1) in Campus Security building

  - University president's office (room 3.5) in Administration building

  - Data Center control office (room 1.3) in Data Center

- Walkie-talkies and pagers will be available in the following locations:

  - Campus security office in Campus Security building

  - Data Center control office in Data Center

The meeting point and time will be 12 p.m. each day at the clock tower in front of the courtyard of the Old Campus Building. This has been made known to the Core Recovery Team members, listed later in this plan. If no other form of communication is available, this is where the team should gather. Maintain a safe distance from the building should it be in a dangerous state, but stay in sight of the clock tower so team members can identify each other and convene.

Of the Core Recovery Team, one person will be designated to communicate with the university campus' office and the off-campus community.

Figure 3-2 shows a map of the university campus for those not familiar with it.

Communication hubs

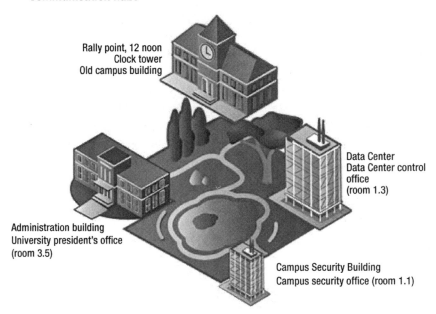

Figure 3-2. Communication hubs for the campus

Setting Priorities

In Chapter 2, I explained that not all SharePoint data is equal. The cost of data recovery and the importance of that data will lead to a plan that divides your SharePoint farm into multiple tiers. This will be different for every organization. In the case of our university, there are three distinct types of content in three different SharePoint farms.

SharePoint Recovery Priority Tiers

We reviewed the existing SharePoint systems in the following locations:

- Research department in the Old Campus Building
- University web site hosted in the Data Center
- Staff and administration intranet hosted in the Administration building

The following questions were asked to establish the tier in which the data belonged:

- What is your team's primary purpose or objective, especially in using SharePoint?
- What is the worst thing that could happen?
- What is the worst thing that has already happened?

- What data do you access every day in SharePoint and where does it come from?

- What critical data do you produce every day in SharePoint and where does it go?

- When is SharePoint access most critical?

Based on these answers, we added SharePoint applications to tier 1, 2, or 3. We also identified any dependencies between the tiers as well as dependencies on other systems such as DHCP and DNS.

Table 3-1 shows the SharePoint applications that have been identified and then classified as belonging to one of the three tiers.

Table 3-1. *Recovery Tiers for Campus SharePoint Content*

Tier	RPO/RTO	Applications on SharePoint Platform
Tier 1	RPO 5 minutes, RTO 1 hour	Research department SkyNet system
Tier 2	RPO 4 hours, RTO 8 hours	University intranet administration sites
Tier 3	RPO/RTO 1 day or more	University web site, Student club sites, and My Sites

Tier 1: Our analysis determined that a standalone SharePoint installation in the Biotech department in the Old Campus Building was the most valuable system on campus. This had been in the Data Center but it was determined that for security reasons it had to be isolated from the network because it gathered highly sensitive and valuable data on a research project for SkyNet. The contract with SkyNet is worth millions of dollars to the university annually. This system processes data in real time from a self-aware artificial intelligence software program so every minute of data is valuable. Ensuring it continues to function in the event of a disaster is our top priority and constitute tier 1. The program itself said so.

Tier 2: These are the university intranet administration sites. The admission of students is the most important process performed in Administration. It has been determined that since the forms are filled out manually by applicants and this information is then manually added to SharePoint lists, this system being unavailable for a day or so would not be very onerous. Even if half a day's forms had to be re-entered, it wouldn't cost Administration much as they could cheaply hire students to do it. These sites are hosted in the Administration building although there are plans to move them to the Data Center.

Tier 3: This contains the student club sites and My Sites. These are popular with the students but are placed in tier 3 because their loss would not cost the university anything if they were not available. These are hosted in the Data Center.

Plan Location and Contents

The location of the plan has to be known and accessible to the people who need it to put it into action. It would be foolish to leave it in the same room as the servers themselves. If that room is compromised or inaccessible for whatever reason, how will you access the plan? The plan's location has to be secure, well known, and accessible 24 hours a day. A bank may be secure but it's only open a certain number of hours a week. Choose somewhere better than that.

As for the plan, make sure it includes contact information for key people in your organization and outside it, too, such as third party suppliers. Try to imagine the plan being put into action by someone with no knowledge of your network or servers. What would you need to tell them?

The full Disaster Recovery Plan is available to team leaders via a safe deposit box in Newbridge Garda Station. It is stored in paper format for speed of retrieval rather than a pocket USB drive or some other digital storage medium. It consists of the following documents:

- Disaster Recovery Plan Overview

- Operational Handbook

- SharePoint Server Shutdown/Restore order with location and tiers

- Asset report

- SharePoint architecture diagrams

- Network topology diagram

- Network outage management process

- Network event problem classifications

- Network demarcation equipment diagram

- Contact information: home and cell phone numbers for all IT staff and key campus decision makers

- Contact information for Nintex Workflow support

Data backups are all kept at the backup warehouse in 1, New Street, Dublin.

Getting the Go Signal

This really is the most crucial question. The disaster will most likely not be restricted to IT and so will be part of a broader decision making command structure. Someone outside IT will first determine if there is a general disaster and then it will be up to them to convey this message to the IT Disaster Recovery Person or Team. The plan will also potentially have different courses of action depending on the severity of the disaster. An *in situ* recovery will not be possible in all cases and a decision has to be made by someone with sufficient authority to recover the farm(s) elsewhere.

Disaster Recovery Plan Activation

Recovery of all three tiers can be achieved within the target timeframes only if there has been no damage to major facilities or equipment, particularly the three buildings where the SharePoint farms are housed: the Data Center, the Administration Building, and the Old Campus Building. A damaged facility will require a different plan of action, including scheduled replacement of facilities or servers/equipment, which can only proceed after 48 hours as insurance documentation must be filled out and an assessor from the insurance company must review the damage first.

An emergency will be determined by the criteria in the university's Emergency Response Plan and notification will be given under the Critical Incident Communications Management Plan. The SharePoint Services Operational (SSO) Handbook procedures should be followed. If a critical system emergency as defined in the SSO Handbook has occurred, this Disaster Recovery Plan will be initiated. This will begin by convening the Disaster Recovery Team. The head of the University Technology Services, or a designee defined by the Crisis Management Team (under the Emergency Response Plan) will convene the Disaster Recovery Team.

Interdependency

It should be clear by now that there is a complex interdependency of processes and procedures that must be defined to deal with a disaster (see Figure 3-3). Even in a scenario like this, there are many different elements. The Disaster Recovery Team doesn't even begin their work until an emergency has been determined by the Emergency Response Plan for the University; how they will be notified is covered in another document, called the Critical Incident Communications Management Plan. Finally, the team must follow what is recorded in the SSO Handbook.

Plans and Processes

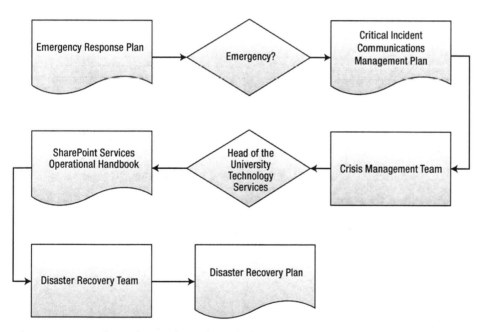

Figure 3-3. Interdependency of people and plans in the university

Decision Makers

There should be a clear list of people who have a part to play in the decisions around recovering the farm. It will be a long list because all IT systems have interdependencies with facilities themselves as well as IT in general. Note that roles are specified here rather than individual names. This is because these are subject to change before and during a disaster and there may not have been time to update the Disaster Recovery Plan.

Disaster Recovery Team

Once the Disaster Recovery Team is assembled they will be apprised of the damage to resources and facilities. This group will represent the University of Newbridge's Technology Services department in efforts to recover from a disaster. Members of the Disaster Recovery Team will include the following individuals. Others will be involved in the process as and when needed:

- Head of University Technology Services
- Director of Operations
- Manager of Operations
- Database Applications Team Leader
- Technical Support Team Leader
- Network Communications Team Leader
- Security and Helpdesk Manager
- SharePoint Farm Administrator

Actions and Tasks

This disaster recovery team will act on a concrete plan of action that focuses first and foremost on the dependent systems. Before SharePoint itself can be restored, there are multiple other systems that are required for it to function correctly: DNS/DHCP, e-mail, authentication, Internet connection, etc. Once these are operational, the focus can move to the tier 1 SharePoint systems. The details of how to restore your SharePoint system specifically will depend on the plan you have put together and will be explored in more detail later in this book.

When these systems are restored and active again, much of the pressure is off the team and the organization, so they can then focus on the less critical systems. Proceeding in this manner also means there is a milestone that can be reached rather quickly, thus giving the sense that control has been restored sooner.

Plan of Action

The Disaster Recovery Team will carry out the following tasks:

- Establish a reasonably located command central for the team. If possible, use room 2.1 in the Data Center. If this room is not available, contact the head of University Technology Services or a designee defined by the Crisis Management Team to establish a location.

- Assign a senior member of staff to be the single point of contact with the Crisis Management Team.

- Designate one member of the Disaster Recovery Team as the Public Relations Representative for the duration of the crisis. This designated team member will coordinate all associated University Technology Service communications and make regular and ongoing statements of status to the Crisis Management Team. Communication should be strictly controlled in this way. Tools like Twitter, Facebook, and blogs are not to be used by other members of the team to unofficially share information.

- Retrieve the backup tapes and documentation from the on-campus or off-campus storage as the circumstances require.

- Distribute charged short-wave radios, pagers, and cell phones for communications.

- Coordinate and make decisions regarding the restoration

- Lead the technical effort to restore systems and communications to an operational state.

- Assess hardware operability or lead purchasing efforts to replace hardware.

- Assess minimum processing needs and report these to the Crisis Management Team.

- Establish priorities and scheduling requirements

- Review the Data Center site and other University Technology Service facilities and assess damage, making a joint decision with the Crisis Management Team as to whether the facilities are intact or whether alternative facilities must be activated.

- Coordinate cleanup or relocation activities.

- Report on the financial aspects of the disaster.

- Notify third party vendors and contractual relationship contacts.

- Conduct an annual review of this plan and a post-disaster review of this plan.

Efforts will focus on verification and restoration of the dependent systems:

- Verify operation of building systems: fire suppression, air conditioning, and electrical service with uninterruptible power supply.

- Verify operation of telecommunications: check both the placing and receiving of calls to on-campus and off-campus numbers.

- Verify service of voicemail, 911 service, alarms, and other critical telecom services.

- Update University Technology Service phone messages to address the disaster.

- If the uninterruptible power supply is not operational contact Vendor at number xxx-xxxx.

- Verify core router, switch units, and network support systems are operational. If not, contact contracted Network Support Vendor at xxx-xxxx.

Restore systems in the following order:

1. DNS/DHCP/WINS servers and domain controllers

2. Authentication/authorization

3. UTS staff desktops/laptops

4. Internet Service Provider connection

5. Backup systems

6. E-mail services

7. Trouble-ticketing system

8. File storage services

Time to Restore SharePoint!

At this point, the disaster recovery team has made operational the multiple dependent systems that SharePoint needs. Now the focus can move to the tier 1 SharePoint systems. The details of how to restore your SharePoint system specifically will depend on the plan you have put together and will be explored in more detail later in this book.

Summary

As you can clearly see, many processes and procedures have to be in place before you can put your SharePoint Disaster Recovery Plan into action. These are not abstract things on paper; they are actual tasks that defined roles have to perform. They include:

- Meeting in the right place and communicating using the predefined methods.

- Knowing the predefined priorities you must act on.

- Knowing where the plan is and getting to it.

- Making sure in advance it contains what it should.

- Putting it into action at the correct time.

- Knowing what the interdependencies are.

- Knowing who does what.

Now your SharePoint team will not be like the Titanic kitchen staff!

CHAPTER 4

High Availability

I've been in the SharePoint administrator role a few times and it is very like being a lifeguard or fireman. When nothing is going wrong, it looks like you're not fully utilized. Managers want you do be busy doing something, working on specific projects. (This is to make them look busy, too.) Only when things go wrong is your real value to the organization fully appreciated—in a short and intense time you get to prove your worth to your manager and others. But I have actually seen administrators who generate a constant state of fake crises so they can look like they are constantly saving the day and putting out fires. This is done to make them look important.

The reality—with SharePoint and many other things—is that if you're very good at your job you can make your system run so well you make it look effortless. The guys who are always averting disaster could apply themselves to proactively making the system more resilient so that it doesn't keep threatening to fail all the time. This doesn't always just mean adding more resources. More resources are more costly upfront and in maintaining them. It's also about optimizing the available resources. SharePoint should be constantly monitored—not just to get a notice that something has gone wrong, but also to anticipate disaster and avoid it—like steering away from the iceberg instead of hitting it so you can show how well you practiced your lifeboat drill.

High availability is all about SharePoint being there when your users need it to do something of value for your organization. Keeping it available is the key function of he who owns the SharePoint infrastructure and servers. If you have done your business impact assessment, you will know the cost of unavailability. Accordingly, you have set your recovery time objectives (RTOs) and recovery point objectives (RPOs). You have also created a process for identifying when there is a disaster and making sure the right people can get into position to deal with it. You have divided your content into tiers so you can give the highest priority to the critical content when disaster strikes. Those tiers will also come into play when you are defining the availability you will need at the best price. The information in this chapter gives you what you need to assess the different options for availability with SharePoint. Topics covered in this chapter include:

- High availability measurement and targets (the nines)

- Resilience (making the system resistant to failure)

- Redundancy (having more than one element that provides the same functionality so there is not a single point of failure)

Together, they provide a framework for protecting the most valuable asset in the system: the information (see Figure 4-1).

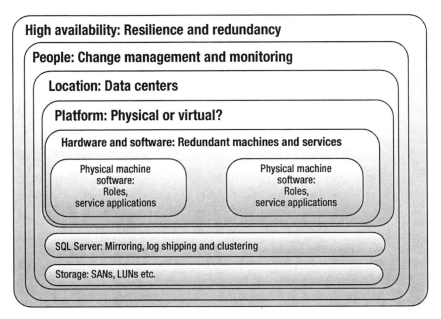

Figure 4-1. Availability is composed of interlocking elements.

High Availability Overview

While disasters are by their definition destructive and unpredictable, it also makes sense to make your system as resilient as possible so that you can mitigate the impact or even stop the disaster in its tracks. As mentioned in Chapter 1, the Titanic had 16 watertight compartments and a double hull so that (it was believed) it could withstand an iceberg collision. In fact, other ships had survived collisions, so it was a sound and proven practice.

There are many steps you can take to toughen your SharePoint farm to make it more resilient, and they all have different considerations. Here are the main ones you'll consider in this chapter:

- The platform: on premises vs. the cloud, virtual vs. physical

- The database layer availability options

- Storage options

- Change management

- Monitoring

- People

Redundancy is the method of having a standby ready to replace a malfunctioning part of the system. You'll look at the options here on the following levels:

- Data centers

- Farms

- Hardware

- Applications

It is most important to look at high availability as something important to the organization as a whole. Your core business determines the impact of unavailability. For some, being available in real time all the time is crucial. These are organizations where information is their key asset and its value is very time sensitive. For example, if the news reports that there has been a coup in a particular country, you may want to sell your shares in a copper mine there quickly because you think the political instability will be bad for business. If you get the news of the coup late, and you can't sell you shares fast enough, both of these things can cost you money. Communication-based organizations like ISPs and telecoms are relied on to be available all the time, too. Ringing your mother the day after her birthday is too late. Even online gaming companies depend on continuous access for their customers. Here are some examples of time-sensitive businesses:

- Online financial transaction processing

- Stock market software

- Online gaming

- ISPs

- Telephone companies

- News services

For some organizations the impact is not merely financial. Their downtime can have an effect on human life or the environment around us. Here the value is harder to quantify but no less important for that—indeed, it is often more important. The following are examples of organizations where lack of availability has a cost to life and not just livelihood:

- Oil companies

- Power companies

- Airlines

- Hospitals

You need to know from your business impact assessment the actual cost of SharePoint being unavailable for any length of time. It could range from no impact to catastrophic. For a ship, any percentage of time at the bottom of the sea is bad.

Measuring Business Impact

To know what availability your users need, you have to ask them. The most practical way is in a structured questionnaire because this helps secure definite metrics. First, collect the following in the questionnaire introduction section:

- Department name

- Date

- Process name

- Process description

Next, list each process or process stage, establish critical dates in the process when applicable (e.g. the day payroll is processed), and assign an impact timeline for each entry. This is identifies how long it takes to reach progressively higher levels of impact. Capturing dates also helps connect it to dependent processes. Table 4-1 shows a sample form for capturing the dates and impact levels.

Table 4-1. Critical Dates and the Impact Timeline

Date/Time	Description	Time Until Impact			
		N	M	S	C

Notice the four columns under "Time Until Impact." These are the four recommended levels to use in your evaluation.

- N (None): There is no impact on any work function. Examples of this include processes that are only utilized intermittently.

- M (Moderate): The process is causing minor or moderate disruption to the function of the department itself or to another department with a downstream dependency.

- S (Severe): The failure of the process results in the department or another department with a downstream dependency being unable to function.

- C (Critical): The failure of the process results in a disruption of the organization's daily functioning.

The boxes on each row in the N, M, S, or C columns should be filled in with the length of time after a failure that it takes for the impact level to be reached. This gives the people planning for availability and disaster recovery more information to work with when calculating RTOs and RPOs.

In the next section of the questionnaire, ask users to provide a list of operational and financial impacts of this process failing under the headings for Impact, Time, and Severity Level. You should also include a section where you ask for a list of upstream and downstream dependencies on this process under the headings System/Process Name and Description.

Finally, ask the users for details for any (or multiple) workaround procedures for this process. For each workaround identified, the following information should be provided:

- Workaround name

- Description

- Date last tested or used

- Hardware required

- Additional personnel required

- Additional supplies required

- How long can it be used?

- How long will it take to implement this work-around?

- What percent of production can this alternative provide?

Combining all this information from the multiple teams/departments in your organization will give you a great deal of useful information. If your organization is very large this may be a daunting task, but it is necessary to secure the critical data users are producing, so resources should be assigned to complete this survey.

The Nines

You will often see availability measured as a percentage of a year. For example, 99% availability is 365/100 = 3.65. This means the service provider is promising only 3.65 days downtime in a year, or 361.35 days uptime a year. In fact, 99% is referred to as "2 nines." The ideal has been to aim for 5 nines, or 99.999% availability, which works out to only 5.26 minutes of downtime a year. Setting the amount of availability at 100% is unrealistic; it would be incredibly expensive, too. Your organization could run out of money before you get 100% availability. Does is matter that the system is 5 nines reliable but doesn't save/earn the organization enough to justify this? Table 4-2 shows levels of the nines and the amount of maximum downtime per year for each level.

Table 4-2. Levels of Nines and the Corresponding Amount of Downtime

% & (No. of 9s)	Downtime per Year
90% (1)	36.5 days (10% of 365)
99% (2)	3.65 days
99.9% (3)	8.76 hours
99.99% (4)	52.56 minutes
99.999% (5)	5.26 minutes
99.9999% (6)	31.5 seconds

Even uptime or downtime is difficult to define. In SLAs, "planned outages" aren't counted as downtime. However, it's still an outage and the fact you may have known about it in advance doesn't change that. If the outage affects users, it is still an outage. For example, Service Packs and patches take hours, potentially every month, to install; longer if the farm is large. How much downtime do they cause in a year? A SQL cluster failover will take up to 15 minutes to complete.

You can't predict the future. As we know in Kildare, Sheep happen(s). So 5 nines is nothing more than a bet or an insurance policy by the service provider. Their pricing strategy is based on probability to ensure profitability when an inevitable disaster happens.

How much a system has failed to perform its primary function is more important and more difficult to measure than availability. For example, if you are a streaming media company whose main product is a sports channel, and you guarantee 99.999% uptime, but the five minutes your system is down is the last five minutes of the Super Bowl, can you truly say you have met your users' needs?

With SharePoint, the system has to be available when people need it the most; this is a measure of quality of service not quantity. It is also largely a matter of perception. The system could be down over a weekend and it might not be noticed until Monday morning (assuming your staff is in the same time zone). But every minute it is down Monday morning is bad for users' perceptions of the system's availability.

From my own experience the main cause of downtime is human error. The number one cause is routine maintenance tasks that went wrong, followed by lack of web server resources or SQL Server capacity. Only occasionally does hardware failure causes the outage. Better change management practices will help reduce mistakes during maintenance tasks. Better monitoring and resource planning will reduce capacity issues.

Resilience

"A stitch in time may save nine."

Gnomologia, Adagies and Proverbs, Wise Sentences and Witty Sayings, Ancient and Modern, Foreign and British, Thomas Fuller, 1732

This expression, for those unfamiliar with it, means that one stitch in a piece of cloth to sew up a hole may prevent nine more if it tears. In other words, timely action can prevent more work later on, and who doesn't like less work?

Resilience is your SharePoint system's ability to withstand disaster. You can maximize resilience at multiple levels at the same time. The weakest point will ultimately be where the system breaks down, but remember that your goal is to minimize user impact and save the organization money, not to make the most resilient system possible for the sake of it. Also, a more complex system has more points of failure and is harder to administer.

Platform

Even before we look at the internal application redundancy options, the SharePoint platform itself presents us with a number of options that will have different resilience considerations. There is a big difference between how you will plan for resilience between SharePoint in the Cloud and a virtual on premises farm because of the way the servers are stored and maintained. Understanding the strengths and weaknesses of each platform decision specifically in relation to SharePoint is the first step in creating greater resilience.

On Premises vs. the Cloud

With great power there must also come — great responsibility!

Stan Lee, *Amazing Fantasy* #15, August 1962 (the first *Spider-Man* story)

The primary difference from a resilience point of view between on premises and the cloud is that the owner of the SharePoint platform in your organization has little to no input into the physical infrastructure of your farm if is built on a Cloud solution since the infrastructure is provided by an external provider. For example, if you build your own infrastructure, you can make decisions about the hard drives, cables, servers, NICs, power supply, and storage. Of course, this requires more knowledge and cost. Even if you build the servers and host them off-premises, the building, rack space, and some amount of the monitoring and perhaps backup or other operations are out of your full control. With this control comes responsibility, but as mentioned before, SLAs tend to be simplistic and focus on a percentage of time. SharePoint Online offers 99.9% (http://download.microsoft.com/download/F/1/3/ F133AF39-F878-4009-8C6A-B60144C32679/SharePointOnline%20Standard%20Service%20Description.doc).

This is qualified further with the following statement in the *Service Continuity Management* section:

SharePoint Online has set an RPO and RTO in the event of a disaster:

12-hour RPO: Microsoft protects an organization's SharePoint Online data and has a copy of that data that is equal to or less than 12 hours old.

24-hour RTO: Organizations will be able to resume service within 24 hours after service disruption if a disaster incapacitates the primary data center.

I have referred to this information before but mention it here again in the context of how Microsoft is qualifying its initial 99.9% availability. The company says that with any disaster, no matter how many times you experience one in a year, you will lose up to 12 hours of data. Also, if the data center fails, you will have to wait 24 hours before it's back online. That's a long wait and a lot of loss. You have to decide if this amount of resilience is enough for your organization based on your BIA. If not, you should identify the content that could go in the cloud but separate out content that should not. This should then be given a more resilient platform on premises or with off-site hosting.

SharePoint Online takes a lot of the complexity of high availability out of your hands and puts it into Microsoft's. This saves you resources, but it just ensures that downtime will not negatively impact your business beyond a point it can afford.

The Amazon Cloud

SharePoint Online is not the only option when it comes to SharePoint in the cloud. There are external hosting companies that will manage your servers for you or will host SharePoint on their servers in a standard multi-tenant model. Most of these options are becoming less relevant, however, with the advent of large cloud providers that offer some well established and reliable options.

One of these options is to host your SharePoint servers with Amazon's infrastructure called Amazon Web Services (AWS). The Amazon SLA offers 99.95% availability (http://aws.amazon.com/ec2-sla/). It also offers Infrastructure as a Service (IaaS) as opposed to (SaaS), so you have more control over the infrastructure—although if there is an outage you are still at their mercy.

Not so much a resilience point, but from a disaster recovery point of view the biggest difference is the amount of control the owners have when there is an outage. When your cloud provider has an outage, your SharePoint platform owners will feel helpless unless regular updates are provided by the infrastructure owners. In my opinion, cloud providers have trouble with this requirement: they want the power but are afraid of giving out information because it shows how responsible they were for the outage.

In my experience, the frequency of outages in the cloud that are caused by human error are just as high as on premise scenarios. For example, the Amazon outage in early 2011 was caused by a network engineer incorrectly shifting all the network traffic to a low-capacity network meant only for administration. This led to a cascade of problems that created among other things a "re-mirroring storm" and a brownout of the storage control plane. This article provides excellent perspective on what happened specifically but it also teaches a lot about how one mistake can lead to a large outage plus how to tackle and address it: http://aws.amazon.com/message/65648/.

The key learning point from this occurrence was that the users most affected were ones that had their entire infrastructure in the same Availability Zone. An AZ is roughly is the same as a data center but has more logical divisions than physical. There can be more than one AZ in a data center. Amazon has multiple AZs in one region. For example, the US East region has four Availability Zones: us-east-1a, us-east-1b, us-east-1c, us-east-1d. The Amazon EC2 SLA offers 99.95% availability, but only if you are running across multiple Availability Zones and not across an entire region. It really pays to know your infrastructure SLAs; don't just trust to the provider to know these things.

If you did want to host SharePoint 2010 on AWS, what are the main considerations from an architecture perspective? Latency will be your main thing to watch. Amazon uses something called Elastic Block Storage (EBS) for storage and their hosting platform is called Elastic Compute Cloud (EC2). EC2 consists of Amazon Machine Images (AMIs) which are virtual machines (VMs) running in Amazons AZs. You should make sure your web front end (WFE) servers and SQL Server are in the same Availability Zone and using this ESB storage on EC2. For backup, you would use Simple Storage Service (S3), which is a cheap way to store large block of data. Your WFEs should also be configured to use Elastic Load Balancer (ELB) to provide redundancy. The main point I will make is that having your AMIs in the same AZ decreases your resilience, while spreading them across AZs even in the same region will increase latency beyond the point where it performs well and affects user experience. These AMIs are stateless and so have to be connected to EBS for storage. They are metered by the hour, so having them on 24 hours a day is expensive.

An interesting option may be to use AWS as a development platform. Performance is not so much an issue, and your costs are reduced as you can only run the AMIs for the 8 or so hours your developers work per day.

Recommendation

My recommendation is to place tier 2 and 3 content in the cloud but keep tier 1 on premises. This way you are getting the flexibility and cost benefits of the cloud but you have full control. You're keeping costs down by having the minimum amount of data in the expensive infrastructure for the critical content. This will also make disaster recovery planning simpler as you can focus upon the on-premises content first. But without knowledge of your particular circumstances, it's difficult to make anything more than general recommendations.

SharePoint Online is a better option than AWS or other major cloud providers in most circumstances because of the ease of integrating your authentication with Windows. But even so, when trying to decide which option will suit your organization, the best option is always to test the waters with a pilot. Make sure the pilot has distinct measurable criteria for success. Check, for example, that moving to the cloud didn't have any performance impact and all the users have the necessary browser and Windows version. Is there a large overhead in setting up ActiveSync between the users' Windows accounts and SharePoint Online? What happens when this has to be done for all the users in your organization? Can users access from home? Will you require additional processes to manage granting of SharePoint Online accounts? Moving to a new platform is always disruptive, so make sure the rewards are worth the investment. Ensure that your SharePoint Online administrators know how to use the interface fully. Also, ensure that your developers are aware of the limitations involved in developing solutions for the online platform as the security is more restrictive. The final point I would make is that while Microsoft will facilitate synchronizing your Active Directory accounts with your SharePoint Online accounts, you must know the process of separating them again should you choose to. Once again, a pilot will provide a better understanding of the work involved in setting up SharePoint Online.

Physical vs. Virtual

Virtualization adds more options for high availability. This is because it allows you to create failover clusters. These are groups of physical machines all running as part of your SharePoint farm such that the whole farm can continue to function if one part (node) fails. For example, Hyper-V, the virtualization software from Microsoft, uses Cluster Shared Volume (CSV). With CSV, multiple virtual machines can use the same logical unit number (LUN) (storage disk) yet fail over (or move from node to node) independent of one another. CSV gives you flexibility for volumes in clustered storage; for example, it allows you to keep system files separate from data to optimize disk performance, even if both are contained within virtual hard disk (VHD) files.

Virtualization adds complexity and, as a result, requires more knowledge and experience to manage. However, because of clustering it will give you another layer of resilience and availability for your SharePoint Farm. The future is virtual, however, and so if you are trying to decide between two, I would recommend virtual. A virtual platform allows you to allocate resources more dynamically and makes replication of machines simpler. For development and testing, virtualization has the great advantage of allowing you to roll back a machine to a previous point. I wouldn't recommend doing this with a production system, but for testing a patch or code, it's very helpful.

SQL Server

In your SharePoint farm the most difficult part to re-create is the user content. This is stored in SQL Server databases. As a result, your high availability focus should be on this content—not because it is the most vulnerable part of your platform, but because it will be the most costly to recover if users have to re-enter it.

As mentioned previously, bad capacity management is one of the main causes of unavailability. Once you have done your capacity planning projections, pre-grow your databases to that size. When they reach 75% of that capacity, revise the estimates and get more space. If content is growing beyond planned expectations, this in itself is symptomatic of a problem. If water is rushing into your ship, the solution is not to make your ship bigger! Without adequate quota usage or users placing large and unplanned amounts of content in SharePoint, your capacity usage will balloon faster than you can provide for it. Also, lack of quotas on logs can lead to more verbosity on diagnostic logging or auditing logs, which can fill up your databases very quickly.

Transaction logs are where most growth can occur in SQL Server. Every database that stores content has a corresponding log that tracks all changes to it. This is a way of maintaining as much data fidelity as possible. In SharePoint content databases where there are a lot of changes, these logs should be carefully managed. You should set the size of your transaction log files to a large value to avoid the automatic expansion of the transaction log files. If you do have automatic expansion turned on, configure it to use memory units instead of a percentage after you thoroughly evaluate the optimum memory size. Back up the transaction log files regularly to delete the inactive transactions in your transaction log. There is more on backing up in Chapter 6.

Also watch the size of site collection recycle bins, and make sure there are processes for the archiving or deleting unwanted content. The word "management" in a "content management system" means removing rubbish as well as making the ability to add content more efficient. Since meeting or exceeding capacity is a risk to availability, it should be tackled as such rather than seeing capacity as something that should be infinitely added. It's true that overly draconian user quotas are counterproductive because they make users spend too much time removing content or not being able to use the system. For example, many companies have imposed 2GB mailbox limits on users when web mail products like Gmail allow 8GB. Exchange online now allows 25GB, which I think is more realistic but may be symptomatic of users storing and sharing too much via e-mail rather than using SharePoint. Transitioning to SharePoint for collaboration should make the rate of mailbox growth slow.

Once you have tackled the issue of capacity being used up unnecessarily, you can focus on ways to preserve the data. Here are the three main technical options that will make your SQL Server more resilient and hence more available: mirroring, log shipping, and clustering.

Mirroring

I've touched on mirroring before: a principal server has a mirror that maintains an current copy of its content. A third optional witness server in a third data center can monitor the principal, if it is unavailable. The mirror is made the principal by the witness server (see Figure 4-2). This is described as warm or even hot standby, depending on whether it takes minutes or seconds. SharePoint 2010 is mirroring-aware for all its databases as long as they are using the full recovery model. This is where setting the recovery model to FULL tells SQL Server to keep all committed transactions in the transaction log until a backup has been made.

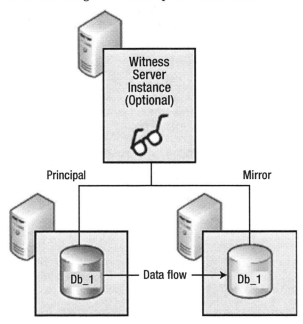

Figure 4-2. The witness watches the principal and switches to the mirror if the Principal is unavailable.

Mirrors for databases can be specified in the SharePoint Administration UI via PowerShell or via the object model. Instructions on this are available from many resources online, including this blog post by Bill Baer: http://blogs.technet.com/b/wbaer/archive/2010/05/03/database-mirroring-in-sharepoint-2010.aspx.

There are three types of mirroring, which have different benefits depending on your needs:

- High protection: This option is synchronous, which is like Twitter: constantly up to date but resource heavy. Failover is manual, there's no witness server. There is also is a low tolerance for any poor latency or performance.

- High availability: This option is synchronous like high protection, but with the third witness server which triggers the failover. Also not tolerant of any lag or interruptions between the principal and mirror servers.

- High performance: In this mode, SQL tells SharePoint that the write to the database is done before hearing back from the mirror that the write was done there too. For that reason this mode can be tolerant of high latency and poor bandwidth. This mode is referred to as asynchronous; it updates when it can, like friends meeting for an occasional dinner or your smart phone sync.

Many factors come into play when making a decision about which option is right for your organization. Consider a simple example of a news organization with its servers in an office near a river. Several variables affect which option it adopts. The high protection option suits an organization with only two offices less than 30 miles apart, such as two offices in a large city. For example, London is approximately 27 miles across. If the organization needed high protection, it's because they want to ensure that all information is captured; but there's no requirement for automatic failover, so there is no witness server. Say this news agency has an office near the river Thames. In the event of the river overflowing, they could relocate to the other office. This could take a few hours; in the mean time, there would be no requirement to switch to the mirror system until all the staff were at the second location, when the switchover would be done manually.

The high availability option is the same, but here the witness server makes the switch. In this case, the staff doesn't have to relocate because they are in a third location where the witness server is. In the event of a flood, the servers automatically switch.

The high performance option would suit the same news agency if their offices were more than 30 miles apart.

Mirroring has another secondary advantage when it comes to availability. Since maintenance mistakes are one of the main reasons for downtime (planned or unplanned), mirroring is a good way to patch SQL Server by patching the mirror first, then the principal. This prevents downtime because while you are patching the principal the users access the mirror. Then they are switched back to the principal. If there are issues with the mirror patch, there's no service interruption. If you have a witness, patch that before the other two. Since a restarted machine has to "catch up," patch when there are low amounts of activity on the server. If all goes well, downtime will be in seconds.

Log Shipping

Here the transaction logs, which are the records of the changes to the database, are copied to a second database, but asynchronously, perhaps overnight. This is usually done to a distant data center perhaps in another country. For SharePoint Online, the logs are shipped from Dublin to Holland, which acts as a cold failover data center. As a result of the delay in moving the data and restoring it, log shipping is a disaster recovery option rather than high availability. However, it has the advantage of being simple and reliable and so is best utilized when used in conjunction with mirroring or your next option, clustering.

Clustering

SQL Server clustering is a high-availability technology for SQL Server. Think of it as virtualization for SQL Server. It has a whole group of terminology all its own. A cluster involves the sharing of server resources between one or more nodes (servers) that have one or more shared disks grouped into logical units called resource groups. A resource group containing at least one IP address, network name, and disk resource is called a virtual server.

Each virtual server appears on the network as a complete system. When the virtual server contains SQL Server resources, clients connected to the virtual server access resources on its current host node. While the terms "active" and "passive" are often used here, they are not fixed roles, as all nodes in a cluster are interchangeable. Should the current host (sometimes designated as the primary) fail, the resource group will be transferred to another (secondary) node in the cluster. With clusters having more than two nodes or two instances, it's important to set failover order by choosing the preferred node ownership order for each instance. The secondary will become the primary and host the virtual server. Active client connections will be broken during failover, but they can reconnect to the virtual server now hosted by the new node. The clients will have to reconnect manually, however, and work in progress will be lost during the failover. Most commercial applications now handle this reconnection task seamlessly.

The goal of clustering is to provide increased availability to clients by having a hot standby system with an automatic failover mechanism. SQL Server clustering is not a load-sharing or scale-out technology. During a failure, all clusters will experience a brief database server interruption. On large clusters with multiple nodes and instances, clients may experience degraded performance during a failure event but they will not lose database availability.

Instances

SQL clusters are either single or multiple instances. In the case of a single instance, one node in a cluster owns all resource groups at any one time and the other nodes are offline. Should the primary node fail, the resource groups will be transferred to the secondary node, which comes online. When the secondary node comes online, it will assume ownership of the resource groups, which typically consist of disks containing your database files and transaction logs. The secondary node comes and SQL Server will start up on the virtual server and roll uncommitted transactions in the transaction log backward or forward as it recovers the database.

This topology was formerly called active-passive. Single-instance clustering is most frequently used for mission-critical applications where the cost of downtime far outweighs the cost of the wasted hardware resources of the secondary node sitting idle while offline.

In the case of multiple instances, one virtual server in a cluster owns some of the resource groups and another virtual server owns other resource groups. At any one time, the virtual servers themselves can be hosted by a single node or different nodes and would appear to clients as named instances of a single server. In that case, they are named instances of a virtual server, hence the name "multiple instance." With multiple-instance clustering, previously called active-active, the hardware requirements of each individual node are greater as each node may at any one time be hosting two (or more) virtual servers.

You should consider multiple-instance clusters to be more cost effective than single-instance clusters as there are no nodes offline or waiting. However, should one node host more than one virtual server, performance is typically degraded. Your best bet is to use multiple instances when you require high availability but not high performance.

Clustering or Mirroring?

Mirroring is the new kid on the block when it comes to high availability with SharePoint 2010. Clustering has been around for longer and has a number of advantages.

- Clustering technology is more established, which makes it better documented, supported, and known by SQL Server administrators.

- Mirroring means configuring within SharePoint whereas clustering is more of a SQL Server-only availability option. This suits SQL administrators better.

- Clustering is always automatically self-correcting unlike mirroring, which has to have a witness server or be manually switched.

- Mirroring is resource heavy while clustering claims to have no performance overhead.

Another factor in picking either mirroring or clustering is the cost of storage, and that is the next topic.

Storage

Each PC, Mac, smart phone, tablet, etc. has its own storage internally in the form of a hard drive. In recent years, large organizations have moved to having large storage devices that multiple server can connect to and use. The main type used now is a storage area network (SAN). This consists blocks that can be efficiently allocated where needed and can store any type of content. An older type was network-attached storage (NAS). It is more like a server whose main function is storage and it also sits on the network. Direct-attached storage (DAS) is more like an external hard drive. Cheap and easy to set up, you just plug it into the server and you're done.

Clustering comes with the requirement of shared storage; this means the nodes in the cluster have to be on the SAN. This is because all the servers in the cluster must be able to access the same data. This makes your SAN a single point of failure and so it's good for HA but not DR. Clustering also does not support cheap DAS storage. Both require lots of storage so this is an important consideration. DAS storage costs much less because it's attached directly to the SQL Server, either the principal or mirror. There's no sharing between servers so it's simpler and cheaper to implement. NAS differs from SAN in that it has its own file system while SAN does not (see Figure 4-3). For database systems like SharePoint, SAN is better as it is simpler for the system to optimize the location and access to the data. NAS is better for storing and managing files.

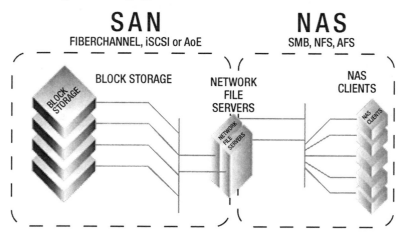

Figure 4-3. NAS has a file system, SAN does not.

A final point about storage and high availability: SAN storage can in itself be mirrored. This means you could have a mirror of your cluster, but it costs millions of dollars and so would have to be justified.

Recommendation

Of the three options (mirroring, clustering and log shipping), some organizations like Microsoft use a combination of all of them; so don't think of them as separate choices. For tier 1, having all three is ideal. For tier 2 and 3, log shipping is sufficient in many cases, but of course it depends on what is in tier 2. In certain cases, you could have mirroring as well as it adds availability and makes maintenance easier while not being too expensive. To help you make the decision, here is a breakdown of the options.

Should I Choose Mirroring or Log Shipping?

Do both. Mirroring is mainly for HA and log shipping is for DR. If you have to choose one, I would choose log shipping because that's your plan B if the farm becomes unavailable. Mirroring helps keep it going, but not if there is data corruption of a data center failure. One thing to note is that failovers can be complicated to manage when combining mirroring and log shipping. This is because your mirroring principal server is also your log shipping primary server. However, during a mirroring failover, your primary role doesn't automatically follow the principal role. You can either manage this manually (which I recommend) or you can automate. Playing around in SQL after a failover can be stressful, which makes automation a more attractive option.

Should I Choose Mirroring or Clustering?

I would choose clustering as it is a SQL-based technology and more resilient. But if money is a factor, mirroring is cheaper because of the expensive SAN storage. The main difference between clustering and mirroring is that the cluster works at the instance level and mirroring works at an individual database level. So in that sense, clustering protects more of your farm. Resource usage is also a factor: in clustering you can run active-active, which means that the second node in your cluster can be hosting another database instance (or two or three more) and be doing work. In mirroring, the mirror is passive until it becomes the primary, so it just sits there.

So, your choice is mirroring or clustering for HA and log shipping for DR.

I should also mention that some service application databases can't be log-shipped or asynchronously mirrored. For example, you have to re-run the search on the failover farm; you can't replicate the search index. Also, some settings databases like Business Data Connectivity and the Application Registry Service can't be mirrored; you just have to ensure they have the same settings by configuring them the same. But this is not a big issue with the Application Registry Service as it's only used when upgrading the Business Data Catalog from MOSS 2007 to 2010. I will explain more about making Service Applications available later in the chapter.

Change Management

> *"Am I responsible or are you," a senior official asked his pilot, dubiously beginning a flight to Baghdad, "for seeing that this machine is not overloaded?"*
>
> *"That will have to be decided at the inquest."*
>
> Jan Morris, *Farewell the Trumpets: An Imperial Retreat* (1978), p. 357.

Since most availability issues are caused by human error during maintenance, a practical change management process will help prevent mistakes. Change management is about ensuring that any need to change a live system goes through an agreed process. This means the following:

- Consistent review and approval criteria for change requests.

- Adequate communication between stakeholders regarding changes.

- Tracking and recording of requests to make historic analysis possible.

- A clear approval path for changes.

If your organization has proper change management processes that meet these needs, SharePoint should follow them, too. If not, a process needs to be set up.

The key reasons mistakes are made is the principle of least privilege is not followed. It means people have access rights higher than their training and knowledge allows. If a user can make a change without needing Site Collection Administrator rights or higher, it should not need a formal change request. Communication should be via a regular change board review meeting. A SharePoint list can be used to track the change requests and the approver. The point is that there must be a formal approval process, not just something ad hoc. Even "urgent" changes must meet review and approval criteria, be communicated to stakeholders, be recorded, and of course be properly approved by someone who understands the technology sufficiently to make a responsible decision. You don't want that decided at the inquest.

Monitoring

Microsoft System Center Operations Manager 2007 (SCOM) is your best option for monitoring SharePoint 2010. There are built-in tools, too. These include:

- Health analysis problems and solutions

- Administrative reports

- IRM Policy Usage reports

- Health reports (slowest pages, most active users)

- Web Analytics reports

Custom reports can be built and deployed to Central Administration Monitoring using just Excel or even SQL Reporting Services. SharePoint's logging service, which uses the Windows Unified Logging Service (ULS), includes a log viewer and PowerShell cmdlets for managing logs. Finally, the developer dashboard is a panel at the bottom of any page that gives a report in its behavior and performance.

The key point is that monitoring will be done well if the SharePoint farm owner has the appropriate training and experience. If you or the farm owner is not familiar with all of the above options, this knowledge gap should be filled. Monitoring is about averting disaster and keeping systems available. I will discuss this again later in the book.

People

I mentioned the appropriate training is required for the stakeholders who will have ownership of SharePoint. Let's discuss governance in relation to availability. The following roles should be filled when it comes to your SharePoint platform to make and keep it available:

- An architect to create the detailed design appropriate platform for your organizations needs.

- An implementer to install and configure the platform.

- An infrastructure owner to maintain the hardware and software. This person will work in conjunction with the owners of Windows Active Directory, Networks, SQL Server, Storage, and any other dependent systems.

- A SharePoint application owner to manage the application itself.

- SharePoint site collection owners to manage site collection settings.

- Site owners to manage access to content.

- Content owners to manage content.

There should also be a backup person for each of these roles in case the main person is not available. I also recommend you invest in good people. Contractors can fill a gap but may disappear abruptly, taking their knowledge with them. If the expertise is hard to find, train someone internal. SharePoint is not that difficult. (How else would I be able to do it for 10 years?)

Having a fallback person for each role is the first step in approaching resilience from the point of view of having additional copies of other parts of your system so if one fails, another can take over quickly with minimal loss of user access. Redundancy can be implemented on multiple levels that will benefit your SharePoint platform's availability and I will explain them next.

Redundancy

Redundancy is actually a subset of resilience but is sometimes seen as the main way to achieve it. Actually, when you think about it, surely it's better to put in place measures that will prevent the failure of redundant parts of your platform. Hardware failure does happen, but it's not as common as failures by people and processes.

Redundancy comes in two varieties depending on whether human intervention is required or not. With active redundancy, if a device goes down, the system automatically reroutes the work to another device. With passive redundancy, you maintain a standby system and manually switch over.

Here's an example of redundancy to provide availability: at home I have two Wi-Fi networks, one that is connected to my high-speed cable Internet provider and another connected to a slower, cheaper mobile Internet provider. I rely on Internet availability to provide me with remote access to my clients, so it's essential to my business. My Business Impact Analysis tells me if I can't access my clients for more than a few hours, I won't be able to do my work for them, hence I'll cease making money. So I can't just hope my Internet connection doesn't go down. My process is that if is my high-speed Internet access goes down, I switch to the slower cheaper option and still have Internet access. All my devices know the passwords of both Wi-Fi networks so the switch over is fast enough for me—only a few seconds. Initially, I had the two Wi-Fi networks switched on at once, but I found that sometimes devices connected to the slower one even when the faster one was available, so I was working unnecessarily with sub-optimum performance. Now, I keep my second Wi-Fi switched off; I switch it on only if the first becomes unavailable. In other words, I initially had active redundancy, but I switched to passive redundancy as it gave me more control.

Redundancy should not be your only availability strategy with your SharePoint farm. Given enough time, a redundant system will be more resilient than one without any other form of resilience, but high quality hardware, good change management, and monitoring are more important. Don't make redundancy your only HA strategy. Keep in mind that redundancy is expensive and won't on its own give you as much reliability as good system management.

With my home Wi-Fi, I have no control over my ISP. In fact, if the system goes down, I'm not even notified or given updates about work being done to fix it. The only way for me to work around this gap was to have a second provider. I could have started calling them the minute it went down, but we all know that is a waste of energy.

When adding redundancy to your SharePoint architecture, look at risk, impact, and conditions of failure. The three tier model will help with prioritizing. In other words, the ship sinking is bad but the ship not having coffee is not so bad. Don't give unimportant systems the same expensive redundancy as important ones.

Let's look at the levels where you can have redundancy for your SharePoint farm.

Data Centers

A data center is a single geographical location where you host your SharePoint farm. This can also be your server room in your organization or even just under your desk. The point is it's a single point of failure for your SharePoint platform. Having more than one with a redundant replica of your SharePoint farm in another data center is expensive but it can provide availability and disaster recovery. Bear in mind that once the second data center is more than 30 miles away, latency makes it a poor candidate for synchronous replication, so log shipping is a better option.

Farms

For change management, different SharePoint farms are used. There are usually three, but sometimes four or more. A typical setup looks like this:

- Development farm: Owned by developers. Virtual as this is cheaper and quicker to wipe or roll back. A simple architecture used for coding. Not necessarily on the network.

- Testing farm: Owned by developers. Closer in design to a production environment. On the network but only accessible by developers.

- Staging/Preproduction farm: Owned by infrastructure. Used for user acceptance testing (UAT) and stress testing. A copy of production. Also for infrastructure staff to test deployment and patches/service packs.

- Disaster Recover farm: A copy of production. Sometimes the same farm as staging.

- Production farm: The live system in use by the main body of users to share content.

Note that multiple farms will give you more availability because they help prevent maintenance or development errors breaking the production farm because code and patches are not deployed straight to the live environment but are tested first. It also allows for UAT, which helps control changes being rushed into production to satisfy users.

Hardware

Preventing hardware failure is a crucial skill for SharePoint Infrastructure owners. Here are some specific pointers for keeping your farm available:

- Use the best hardware you can afford. Don't use old or second-hand servers in your Production environment.

- Multiple servers are a relatively cheap way to do redundancy so buy redundant components. Scale out with multiple servers to avoid single points of failure.

- For all operating system and SharePoint application drives, use RAID 1.

- Follow vendor recommendations for maintenance and ensure the presence of redundant power through generators or batteries.

Application-Level Redundancy

Within the SharePoint Application itself there are a number of configuration options that will give you redundancy and therefore availability.

Roles

Additional servers not only allow you to scale out and provide more resources, SharePoint allows you to have multiple servers with different roles. The main ones are the web front end servers. These serve the pages to the users that are the UI for the application. I recommend a minimum of three for under 50k users. With each additional 25k users, add one more WFE. For application servers, I would suggest a minimum of two so that each service application is running on at least two servers. The second role is the application server. This runs services such as the user profile synchronization service, metadata management service and the search service. Dedicating servers to the application server role allows you to assign resources more easily and manage the services more easily. For example, if you have a large amount of content to index, you may have multiple servers assigned to the search service role exclusively. Roles are logical terms because every server in the SharePoint farm has a particular service application once you install it. You then allocate instances of the service to servers to define their role in the farm.

Service Applications

Because the SharePoint application has grown to be able to do so much, its different functionalities have been split off into separate mini-applications (apps) in their own right and are now parts of the SharePoint platform. This means, for instance, that synchronizing user profile information with active directory SharePoint has a mini-app with its own settings pages, administrators, schedule, and three databases. Some apps are simple and can be made redundant by just having more than one instance on more than one application server, but some are more complex and require more careful planning.

   SharePoint coordinates the multiple instances of the service applications by using timer jobs. They ensure that the system does the tasks it needs to do when they need to be done. For example, if the user profile service has to run every hour, the timer job will start either on the first available server running that instance or all the app servers. If the application server failed that is running the timer jobs, they will be restarted on another server when the next timer job is scheduled to run and the logs record an error.

   If users are in the middle of using a service application that doesn't store its data in a database when it fails, they will lose some data. The two services that do this are the Access and Excel Services Applications. Here, your only option is to install the service app on multiple app servers. With other service apps, the data is stored in SQL Server so you have the option to use mirroring or clustering on those databases to keep the service app running.

There are some databases you can't mirror. They are:

- The synchronization database for the User Profile service
- The database of the Application Registry service application
- The logging database of the Usage and Health Data Collection service application
- The staging database of the Web Analytics service application

If the databases are lost, they can only be restored from backup and reattached to the service application or new instances of the databases. This means you can't perfectly mirror all of your databases, but the majority is redundant and resilient. They are:

- Search Administration, Crawl, and property databases of the Search service application
- Profiles and Social databases of the User Profile service
- Business Data Connectivity service application
- State service application
- Web Analytics service application
- Word Automation Services service application
- Microsoft SharePoint Foundation Subscription Settings service
- PerformancePoint services

Search

Search requires more planning for availability as it has seven different components with different ways to make them available. They are:

- Query components
- Index partitions
- Property databases
- Crawl databases
- Crawl components
- The Search Administration component
- The Search Administration database

These are hosted on servers with specific search roles. They are:

- The crawl server, which hosts the crawl components and a search administration component
- The query server, which hosts query components and index partitions

- The database server, which hosts the crawl, query, and search administration databases

They interrelate in the following way:

- Crawl components crawl content sources and pass the indexed content to query components.

- Index partitions are groupings of query components. With them you can spread an index over more than one server.

- Property databases store metadata about the crawled content and are associated with an index partition.

- Crawl databases store schedules for crawls and data about what content sources to crawl.

- The Search Administration component monitors user actions and writes any search configuration changes to the Search Administration database, which stores general search configuration information.

Here is how you make each redundant:

- Crawl component: Run more than one on different crawl servers.

- Crawl database: Can be mirrored or clustered in SQL Server.

- Query component: Create mirrors on different query servers.

- Index partitions: Distribute multiple instances of the partition across multiple servers link mirrored query components to the same index partition.

- Property database: Can be mirrored or clustered in SQL Server.

- Search Administration component: Have more than one search service application as there can only be one Search Administration component.

- Search administration database: Can be mirrored or clustered in SQL Server.

But how can users keep searching if part of your index partition is lost? You must have multiple instances of the same index partition propagated to multiple servers so that there is more than one copy of each part of the index connected to the same query component or its mirror. This way, the query component always has access to the entire index.

Summary

High availability is something achieved not just through meeting a percentage of uptime in a year. It is a proactive process of monitoring and change management to ensure the system does not go down. It is also about having high quality hardware. Finally, it is about having redundancy at every level of your architecture from the data center down to the components of the individual service applications.

C H A P T E R 5

Quality of Service

In my experience, the main causes of SharePoint performance and response issues noticed by users are not a result of SharePoint being at fault at all. They are a result of network or SQL Server issues. In my early years, I would often be frustrated when trying to troubleshoot the vague message from the help desk that "SharePoint was slow." All of the SharePoint and Windows event logs were fine. Eventually, some network or SQL Server guy would casually mention that they were having some performance issues that day. That SharePoint is so dependent on these two other tiers is now something I am well aware of, so it's one of the first places I go if I think the quality of service problem is being caused by something outside of the application itself.

The evolution of computers and networks towards Internet-based applications leaves no doubt about the important role they are playing in organizations expecting a more service-oriented architecture (SOA). The quality of these new services will be a key issue for their wide deployment, and this quality is determined by the opinion of the users in your organization. The best quality of service (QoS) is not the highest but the most suitable to the different users' needs. In order to provide a suitable level of QoS, the SharePoint administrator needs to know which relevant network parameters have impact on the quality as it is perceived by the users.

A SharePoint farm does not exist in isolation; its main dependency is the network it is sitting on. While high availability and disaster recovery for Windows networks are beyond the scope of this book, I can talk about network QoS in relation to SharePoint. All your user requests for pages go via the network. If it is performing slowly, then SharePoint will appear slow. If it slows to the point where it affects user experience, the perceived availability of SharePoint is affected. By understanding and improving the environment SharePoint exists in, you can make SharePoint more highly available. This chapter will look at the methods you can use to improve the quality of service you offer your users. Some of them include:

- WAN optimization
- Centralized versus regional SharePoint deployment
- Caching

Why Quality of Service Is Essential

QoS is comprised of the mechanisms that give network administrators the ability to control the mix of bandwidth, delay, variances in delay (jitter), and packet loss on their network in order to:

- Deliver a network service such as Voice over IP (VoIP).
- Define different service-level agreements (SLAs) for divisions, applications, or organizations.

- Prioritize traffic across a WAN.

QoS gives the network administrator the ability to prioritize traffic and allocate resources across the network to ensure the delivery of mission-critical applications, especially in heavily loaded environments. Traffic is usually prioritized according to protocol. So what is the benefit of prioritizing traffic?

A simple metaphor is the high-occupancy vehicle lane (also called a HOV or carpool lane) on the highways in America. If you're not from the USA or otherwise unfamiliar, in a large multi-lane highway, one lane is marked with a white diamond and the only traffic allowed in this lane are vehicles with more than two or more occupants.

For business applications, you want to give high priority to SharePoint if it has become a mission-critical application. All other traffic can receive equal treatment. Mission-critical applications are given the right of way at all times. Video and audio streaming applications take a lower priority. Bandwidth-consuming applications, such as file transfers, can receive an even lower priority. In Figure 5-1, the blue cars are SharePoint traffic that has been given its own on ramp and special lane (with white diamond) to travel in where there is less traffic. The red cars represent file transfers, video, and audio files.

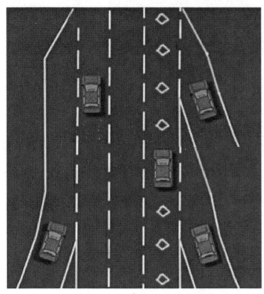

Figure 5-1. Red cars are low priority traffic, blue cars are high priority.

There is a wide range of QoS services. Queuing, traffic shaping, and filtering are all essential to traffic prioritization and congestion control. These also determine how a router or switch handles incoming and outgoing traffic. QoS signaling services determine how network nodes communicate to deliver the specific end-to-end service required by applications, flows, or sets of users. QoS is required wherever there is congestion. QoS has been a critical requirement for the WAN for years. Bandwidth, delay, and delay variation requirements are at a premium in the wide area.

LAN QoS requirements are emerging with the increased reliance on SharePoint as a mission critical application and the growing popularity of voice over LAN and WAN, which use more bandwidth. The importance of end-to-end QoS is increasing due to the rapid growth of intranets and extranet applications like SharePoint that have placed increased demands on the entire network.

But before we attempt to resolve these issues, let's first look at user perception of poor QoS and its causes.

Perceptions and Causes of Poor QoS

When a user clicks on a link and it takes anything over 10 seconds, they perceive this as a problem with SharePoint. The target should be under 5 seconds for standard pages, but even that is too much if there many pages are required to do a simple task. For example, a user has to search for a site, add a task to it, and then update a calendar. That task should take them only 5 minutes, but if it requires them to render 15 different pages that each take 5 seconds to load, every minute has an additional 25% just waiting for pages to appear! This is because there are on average 3 page loads per minute to make up 15 pages in 5 minutes. If each page load takes 5 seconds, that's an additional 15 seconds on top of 60 seconds, hence 25%. From a perception point of view, this is very frustrating: over a minute extra on a 5 minute task is unacceptable.

If loading a single page takes up to 30 seconds, you know you have a problem beyond just a non-optimized network or application. What are the most common causes of delays? Delays can occur at any of the following levels:

- Client: Time it takes to render the page by user's device and browser.

- Client-side LAN: Serving the page to the user's device on their local network.

- WAN: Transferring the data over the wider network.

- Server-side LAN: Transferring data from server network.

- Server: Accessing and transferring data from the server.

Delays at all of these levels can be potentially caused by the following factors:

- Client:
    - CPU/processor delay
    - Virtual/physical memory limits
    - NIC configuration, network drivers, and TCP/IP configuration
    - Older client application versions
    - Proxy server configuration
- Client-side LAN:
    - Switch configuration
    - Over-utilization
- WAN:
    - Link speed (bandwidth)
    - Delay (latency)
    - Packet loss, retransmissions, timeouts

- • Network throughput
- • Round trips
- • Server-side LAN:
  - • Switch configuration
  - • Contention for uplink
- • Server:
  - • CPU/processor delay
  - • Virtual and physical memory limits
  - • NIC/network drivers and TCP/IP configuration
  - • Network speed (10/100/1000MB)
  - • Server software layer

Examining a typical performance delay produces a result like the one in Figure 5-2. The largest portion of the delay occurs because of the wide area network (WAN).

End-to-End Perceived Network Performance:

Causes of a 30 second delay

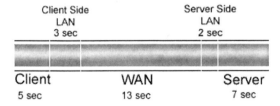

Figure 5-2. *WAN causes largest portion of delays.*

While any or all of these can be the cause of your delays, the most likely culprit is the WAN. Let's use an example of a manager in London opening a SharePoint page on a server in Sydney. Users in Sydney report this takes 12 seconds, but for the London user it takes over 2 minutes. Why should that be?

Applied Scenario: Flowers and Elephants

Fancy Flowers is a florist supply company. They have two offices, one in London and another in Sydney. The buyers are based in London and the flower suppliers in Sydney. When the flowers bloom, the suppliers upload photos of examples to the Fancy Flowers SharePoint portal called the Daisy Chain. Buyers in London open the images and place orders to buy the flowers.

This is the core business benefit of SharePoint to the company. It is essential to the buyers that the images open quickly. The buyers are currently complaining the photos are taking too long to open and this is seriously impacting their ability to order flowers quickly while they are still fresh. The photographs have to be high resolution; the average size is 4MB.

The suppliers upload the photos to the regional SharePoint server based in Sydney and when they open the photos, they open in about 12 seconds; in London, they take about 2 minutes to open. It is therefore taking 10 times longer to open the files in London. Buyers have to review hundreds of flowers so this is seriously impacting their efficiency while they wait for the photos to open.

Isolating the Cause

The buyers are waiting for the photos to download to their client machine from the server all the way over in Sydney. Both offices are running on the same server hardware and client machines, as well as client software. This means you can rule out these items as being at fault. The next culprit to look at is the pipe, or bandwidth between the two offices.

The bandwidth available in both offices is 3Mbps (megabits per second). To calculate what that means in terms of download time, you do this: 3Mbps is .375MB per second, which is 4MB in 12 seconds. This is what users in Sydney are seeing, but not the users in London. The only difference is the distance between the Sydney server where the photos are stored and the London office. It is an approximately 10,000 mile (16,000 kilometer) journey each way between the two offices. Is this causing the delay? Figure 5-3 shows the journey the data was takes.

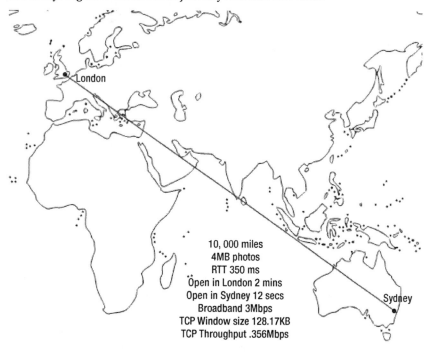

10, 000 miles
4MB photos
RTT 350 ms
Open in London 2 mins
Open in Sydney 12 secs
Broadband 3Mbps
TCP Window size 128.17KB
TCP Throughput .356Mbps

Figure 5-3. *London to Sydney*

Fiddlers, Pipes, and Pings: Measuring Tools

I'm sure you have seen the pipe metaphor being used to describe bandwidth. The image is of a big pipe between the offices with data flowing along it at the speed of light, since these are fiber optic cables. If light travels 186,282 miles (about 299,792 kilometers) in a second, why does it take 2 minutes to download a photo of an orchid?

As you should know by now, this is too simplistic a metaphor. A better metaphor might be water flowing down a hill: it twists and turns around obstacles, slows down and speeds up depending on the terrain, and some of it doesn't get there at all.

For a start, light in a fiber optic cable is not traveling through a vacuum, so it's only going 2/3 the speed of light, but the real delays are the hops between multiple routers and switches. A tool like Fiddler 2 (Figure 5-4) allows you to follow the course of your data as it makes the journey from source to destination (it's freeware, available at `www.fiddler2.com/fiddler2/`).

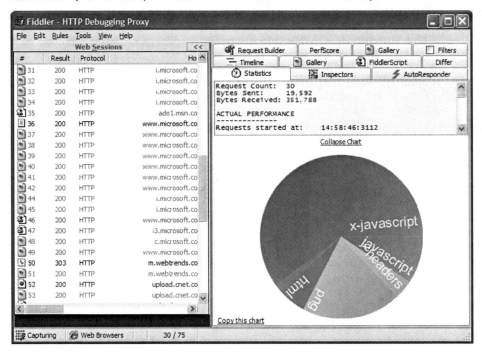

Figure 5-4. Metrics from Fiddler 2

Ping, a tool for measuring latency, indicates that the round trip time (RTT) from London to Sydney is 350ms. Strictly speaking, latency measures the time the trip takes one way, not round trip, but in the real world, the return journey is more important. If you recall the water-rolling-down-a-hill metaphor, you know some is lost along the way. In communication networks, the average rate of successful message delivery is called throughput. The Ping in Figure 5-5 is from Ireland, where I am writing this, to Apress in the US, likely in Virginia (I got this information from WHOIS). According to `www.mapcrow.info`, this journey is 4,240.70 miles (6824.56 kilometers), which is less than half the distance from London to Sydney (10,000 miles/16,000 kilometers) so this ping time roughly checks out with the ping time from Sydney to London and back of 350ms.

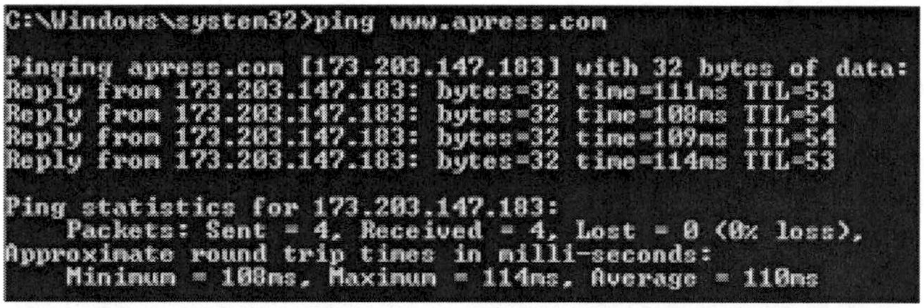

Figure 5-5. Metrics from a Ping. Average roundtrip from Ireland to Apress in US: 110ms

TCP Throughput

We will have to dig deeper to find the real reason data takes so long to transfer over physical distance. All web traffic, which includes SharePoint, travels via the Hypertext Transfer Protocol (HTTP), but that in turn travels over the Transmission Control Protocol (TCP). TCP is what really dictates how fast the traffic originating from SharePoint can travel.

TCP sets limits on the amount of data a computer can accept without acknowledging the sender. Think of it as the maximum number of party invitations from one person you can get without sending back any RSVPs. If the sender has not received acknowledgement for the first invitation (packet of data) sent, it will stop sending any more until it gets a reply. After a certain length of time, if it has not received a reply, it may resend. Why does it do this? Why not just assume the data was received and just keep sending? It doesn't for the same reason you ask for RSVPs: you want to be sure the message has definitely been received. This is how TCP keeps data transmission reliable.

To get your real throughput, you use an equation like Figure 5-6. Don't worry if you're not very mathematically minded; I'm not either. I'll not be including many formulae in this book.

$$\text{Throughput} \leq \frac{\text{RWIN}}{\text{RTT}}$$

Figure 5-6. The amount of data you get is limited by the TCP buffer and latency.

Because of this waiting for a reply to maintain quality of communication over quantity, the full bandwidth available might not even be used. This buffer, for TCP, by default is only 64KB. So, it sends 64KB, then waits for a reply; if it gets one, it sends another 64KB. You can see that the latency of 350ms, or a third of a second for each packet to get from Sydney to London, is going to add up. This web site quickly calculates it for you: www.speedguide.net/bdp.php (Figure 5-7). Note that RWIN is the abbreviation for TCP Receive Window, which is the amount of data that a computer can accept without acknowledging the sender. BDP stands for the bandwidth-delay product.

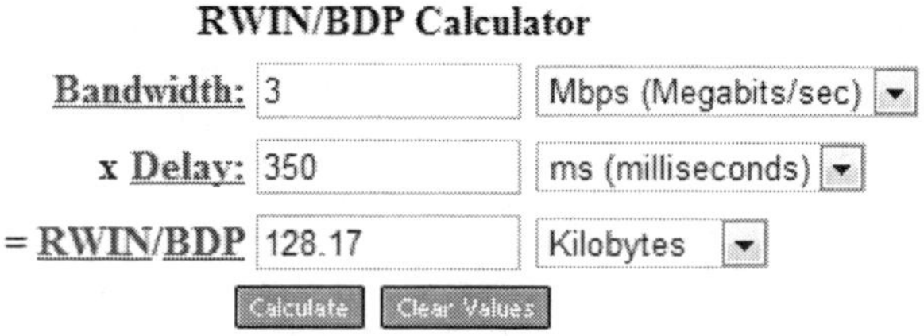

Figure 5-7. Calculating BDP. Note that 1,000 kilobits is a megabit but 1,024 kilobytes is a megabyte.

81

In this scenario, 3Mbps x 350ms = 128.17KB, which is double the 64KB size that is the recommended amount. But it's not something you can control. Windows 2008 server tries to automatically find the optimum TCP Window/RWIN/BDP size. It begins at ~17.5Kbps and can go up to 16Mb. This can't be manually tweaked, so you have to rely on the system to choose the right balance of speed and reliability.

Let's work out the throughput and see if it explains the 2 minute download time in London vs. 12 seconds in Sydney. In Figure 5-8, you divide the TCP Window Size (128,170) by the round trip time in seconds (.35) and get a TCP throughput of .366Mbps.

$$.366\text{Mbps} \leq \frac{128,170 \text{ bits}}{.35 \text{ seconds}}$$

Figure 5-8. Calculating BDP

To work out how many kilobytes per second (Kbps) that is, multiply it by 1,024 (remember, there are 1,024 kilobytes in a megabyte, but only 1,000 megabits in a kilobit) then divide it by 8 (there are 8 bits in a byte). The result is 45.568Kbps. At that rate, a 4MB photo (which is 1,024 × 4 = 4,096 kilobytes) will take 87.43 seconds (divide 4,096 by 46.848). So that's about a minute and a half. The other 30-ish seconds could be accounted for by lost packets and the fact that latency does fluctuate. Remember in Figure 5-2 there were other causes of delay, not just the WAN. The London latency figure of .35s RTT gives a best case throughput of almost 9 seconds, not far behind the 12 seconds they experience.

Exploring Possible Solutions

There's obviously a problem: QoS is too low for the users because it takes too long to open a photo. The problem has been isolated: it's not with SharePoint or even with web applications in general; it's even lower down the stack at the TCP and network layer. You now understand better why you have a problem, and you have some metrics to measure it better. The hard metrics you can't control or change are:

- The sizes of the files: 4MB.

- The distance between the flower suppliers who upload the photos and the buyers who download them.

- How quickly the suppliers need to upload the photos and how quickly the buyers need to see them.

So what can you do to improve the quality of the service? The first thing most people would suggest is to increase the size of the pipe. In tests for the previous versions of SharePoint, Microsoft indicated that latency affects WAN performance until bandwidth becomes restricted at 512 kilobits per second and lower; a T1 line with a latency of 500 milliseconds provides about the same performance as a T3 line with the same amount of latency. For best performance over a WAN, Microsoft recommends that you target a bandwidth range of 3Mbps (Dual T1) or greater. Since you already have that, adding bandwidth will not significantly help with the time it takes to open a photo.

What if you used content deployment to transfer the photos from a site collection in Sydney to one in London overnight? The problem here would be what constitutes "overnight." At 8 a.m. Monday, when the work week starts in Sydney and the producers are uploading new photos of flowers, it is still nine hours earlier, or 11 p.m. Sunday night in London. By the time the producers have uploaded a day's worth of photos in Sydney at 6 p.m. their time, it is now only 9 a.m. and the buyers want to see them.

There is no window of opportunity to transfer them overnight. As you can see in Figure 5-9, London is always "behind" Sydney. If the earth rotated the other way, or if London was a great place to grow flowers, then there would have been a nine-hour window to transfer the photos gradually to London while Sydney slept.

But as it is, every minute spent transferring the photos is taking up time the buyers need to assess them. For example, suppose you had 100 photos uploaded on a Monday by the flower producers in Sydney. They are uploading to a server in Sydney, so the speed is fast for that task. They are providing the information as soon as the first flowers bloom, which is optimum. It takes 2 minutes each to transfer one photo to a buyer's machine in London. Users don't normally think of viewing an image as downloading it, but that is what is required. This assumes optimum download speed, no interruptions, and no data loss. So 100 photos x 2 minutes = 200 minutes, which is 3 hours 20 minutes. If the photos were transferred via content deployment after the Sydney day was over at 6 p.m. on a Monday (which is 9 a.m. Monday), the staff in London would still not be able to see any of them until 12:20 p.m. their time. They may as well have downloaded them themselves one by one. They have still lost 3 hours 20 minutes of time in which they should have been considering which flowers to order.

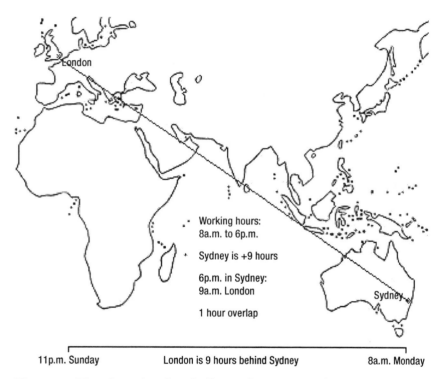

Figure 5-9. There is no time for a bulk asynchronous transfer.

The photos are 4MB and that is large for an image. On most web sites, images are optimized using software for that purpose so they are reduced to maybe 100KB in size. The Sydney office doesn't have the staff or software/training to optimize these images.

The process has to be quick because of the nature of the product. While they send a photo of an open flower, they are selling buds because that is what will be shipped to allow time for them to open in the UK. (This is a made-up scenario, by the way. I don't really know how this happens in real life. The key point here is to illustrate a time-sensitive process.)

Here's the (made-up) simple approval and alert workflow process:

1. A producer takes a digital photo of a flower in the field with a digital camera once they have a bloom.

2. They connect the camera to a laptop on their truck in the field connected via Wi-Fi to the Internet.

3. Using a VPN connection, they upload the photos to the Fancy Flowers Daisy Chain portal.

4. They then add metadata like cost, quantities, and any other pertinent details.

5. The Sydney office receives an alert by e-mail there is new content in the picture library.

6. They review the photos and metadata, and flag them as ready for review by the buyers.

7. The buyers can place orders immediately on the portal by selecting Order alongside the flowers they want.

8. This sends an e-mail alert via a workflow to alert the producers (the flower growers) to begin packing the flowers.

9. It also alerts the cargo plane company that the flowers will soon be arriving at their depot to be flown to the UK.

Adding an extra step where the suppliers would be required to open the photos in image processing software and converting them to lower resolutions had been tried in the past and did not work. There were multiple time-wasting issues. Sometimes the photos were just made smaller by height and width to make their file size smaller and thus became too small on the screen to see clearly; sometimes the wrong images were uploaded. The issue was these are flower growers not photo specialists. This also placed a burden on the Sydney office to correct the photos or ask producers to re-upload images. This slowed the process of getting the photos in front of the buyers far more than the 2 minutes it takes a photo to load. Another alternative is needed.

If you can't change the earth's rotation, where flowers are grown and purchased, or the process of getting the photos into SharePoint, what else can you do?

WAN Acceleration

The next option is WAN acceleration. WAN acceleration technologies are devices, sometimes referred to as WAN optimization controllers (WOC), put in the path of the data traffic to attempt to speed it up. There are multiple vendors providing this but they all use some combination of the following techniques.

You now know that throughput is determined mainly by the TCP receive window (RWIN) and the Round Trip Time (RTT), also referred to as latency. What can these technologies do to affect throughput in a positive way?

The first is data reduction. The WOCs examine all the data in real-time being sent through them across the WAN. This information is stored in local data stores on each WOC. Then, when duplicate information is detected, references are sent to the appropriate WOC instructing it to deliver the information locally rather than re-sending it across the WAN. This has the potential to reduce over 90 percent of WAN bandwidth. But it is at its most effective when there are thousands of users requesting the same pages.

WAN accelerators also offer latency mitigation. You know that each data packet is like an invitation; another is not sent until an RSVP has been returned. This acknowledgement (sometimes called an ACK) slows down the data transfer process if the servers are far apart. In this case, the roundtrip is taking 350ms—almost a third of a second—and this is slowing down the data transfer. With WAN acceleration, WOCs act as a local post office, acknowledging the data transmissions from the server sooner. As a result, the WOC can maintain or increase TCP window sizes, which increases application throughput. All this reduces impact on the application performance across the WAN.

The problem with cold transfers like these photos is that the data still has to flow over the small WAN link. So, before WAN acceleration, a single buyer in London on this 3Mbps circuit could max a TCP session at, say, 2Mbps because of WAN delay. But, add WAN acceleration in and this 2Mbps shoots right to 3Mbps. At this point, the circuit can't transfer any more. But the user doesn't really notice the difference because it's not that much more bandwidth AND now you have induced a WAN bottleneck. QoS kicks in and starts dropping packets, which backs off TCP transfers of this user and then the other users/buyers in London. As a result, the users don't notice the difference. Also, because you hastened the bottleneck on the small WAN circuits, buyers are still frustrated waiting for the photos to load.

WAN accelerators also offer a feature called packet coalescing. Think of this as wrapping up lots of letters into a bundle and sending them together to speed up the RSVP/ACK process. Some applications are considered "chatty" because they use lots of smaller packets to communicate. Added together, these packets can consume substantial bandwidth—something in limited supply. WOCs can combine multiple packets traveling between the same two sites into a single packet, reducing application response times and bandwidth.

Deployment Strategies

The WAN accelerator (WOC) can be placed on the route of your traffic or off to the side. These are referred to as in-path and off-path (sometimes out-of-path). With in-path design (Figure 5-10), the WOC is inserted between the WAN router and LAN switch. That means all traffic will go through the device. The advantage of this approach is it allows for automatic traffic optimization. The device opens its own TCP connection to its peer and will send to its peer only the traffic that can be optimized. All other traffic is routed normally.

In-Path Design

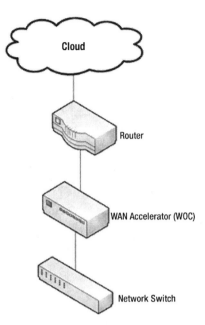

Figure 5-10. *All traffic is via the WOC.*

MPLS and PBR are also options. Multiprotocol Label Switching (MPLS) is a networking mechanism that transports data from one network node to the next with the help of labels. These labels identify what is in the packet to speed up the forwarding of it to the right destination. Think of it as the address on the envelope. Policy Base Routing (PBR) is where the network administrator wants to set further routing rules for packets based on other criteria like where the packet came from. Think of it as using the return address on an envelope. An in-path design is the simplest to deploy for branch offices with one MPLS network or for a medium-to-large location with two MPLS networks.

With off-path (Figure 5-11), the WOC is not in the direct line of traffic in order to optimize it. The traffic must be redirected to the WOC by means of a PBR statement. The advantage of this approach is it is non-intrusive: it allows transfer from one mode to the other by only changing the configuration. The disadvantage, of course, is that is necessitates more configuration and good application knowledge (ports/protocols to be used). As a result, off-path designs are more complicated. Care must be taken to standardize on an off-path design to ensure full optimization is achieved and impact to production traffic is minimal.

With off-path designs, the load balancers take on two different roles:

- Traditional load balancing: When all traffic is redirected, via a PBR or other means, to the LB and the LB evenly distributes traffic loads among the various WOCs within a cluster.

- In-path load balancing: When both inbound and outbound traffic is intercepted by the LB when positioned inline on the network path. The LB will then send the traffic to various WOCs in a disproportionate traffic load distribution.

Off-Path Design

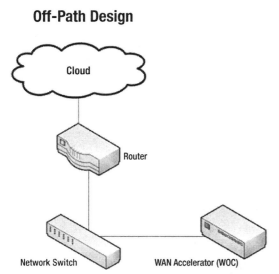

Figure 5-11. Traffic is redirected to the WOC.

In the case of Fancy Flowers, they have one MPLS network connecting London and Sydney, so the best place to test the WOC would be directly in the path of the traffic going out of Sydney. Before testing the WAN accelerator, the Fancy Flowers team had a benchmark; they knew it took 2 minutes to open a photo in London. After adding the WOC it still took 2 minutes! This was because the files are cold, not cached.

For example, if the WOC keeps a local copy of the home page of the Sydney branch of Fancy Flowers on the Daisy Chain portal, after the first person from London visits there, that page will be stored on the WOC in the server room in London. Then any subsequent visit to that page by a London user will load faster as the requests don't have to go back and forth to Sydney to load the page, images, stylesheets, etc. This means they are saving bandwidth between London and Sydney that can be used by other applications. Once a page has been cached, it is sometimes referred to as warm, as if the page has been "warmed up" by the first visitor who visited it "cold" because it was not cached on the WOC.

The problem in this scenario is that the Fancy Flowers buyers in London are almost always visiting "cold" pages. That is because the 100 or so pictures are uploaded in the morning in Sydney and then looked at by the 5 buyers in London when they start work. There has been no time or prior visits from London to warm up the pages.

After testing, Fancy Flowers decided that the cost of WAN acceleration was not giving them a sufficient benefit to warrant the cost. The main problem was the distance, and WAN acceleration didn't add any benefit with cold files.

The Middle Ground

The main part of the problem is the distance. The solution that ultimately halved the time it took the buyers in London to open a photo is to set up a SharePoint portal, an extra daisy on the chain, halfway between London and Sydney. It is possible to test the RTT from London to various cities in the world by using the Speed Test web site's (www.speedtest.net) interactive map that allows you to ping from your location to anywhere in the world. The results of some cities are listed in Table 5-1.

Table 5-1. Testing Latency from London to Various Locations

City	RTT of ping in milliseconds from London
Cairo	80ms
Dubai	175ms
Mumbai	320ms
Bangkok	330ms
Sydney	350ms

Based on this analysis, a host provider is selected in Dubai (Figure 5-12) to provide a SharePoint server to store the photos. This is inexpensive as only a small number of user accounts are created for the producers and the buyers. The amount of capacity required is also low—and cheaper than storing the photos on the Fancy Flowers SAN. It also has the benefit of increasing security. The flower producers no longer have to be given VPN access directly to the Fancy Flowers network.

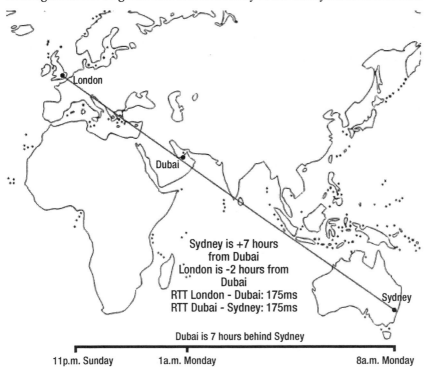

Figure 5-12. Latency reduced by adding server in the middle

The time it takes to upload the photos by suppliers did increase to about 1 minute. But this is not seen as onerous by them as they know the buyers won't see them until after 6 p.m. their time, which is 9 a.m. London time. The main advantage is to the buyers in London: the time taken to open a photo is reduced by more than 50%, and the buyers really notice a difference!

Let's work out the new throughput. In Figure 5-13, you divide the TCP window size (128,170) by the new round trip time in seconds (.175) and get a TCP throughput of .732Mbps.

$$.732\text{Mbps} \leq \frac{128{,}170\text{ bits}}{.175\text{ seconds}}$$

Figure 5-13. *Calculating BDP with the new RTT*

Again you calculate how many kilobytes per second (Kbps) that is. You multiply it by 1,024, then divide it by 8. The result is 93.696Kbps. At that rate, a 4MB photo (which is 1,024 × 4 = 4,096 kilobytes) will take 43.71 seconds (divide 4,096 by 93.696). QoS more than doubled, network security increased, and there's even a savings on the cost of storing the photos on the SAN. A good result all around!

Centralized vs. Regional SharePoint Deployment

In the Fancy Flowers story, the content was added in one part of the world and viewed in another. That isn't generally the case. Most collaboration is done between people in the same region, and some of that content is of interest to the broader global community within the organization, particularly through search. This section will look at the advantages and disadvantages of distributing your SharePoint architecture across the globe. As you saw in the case of Fancy Flowers, placing the content close to the people who need to see it provides a higher QoS. This is a good general principle.

The services architecture in SharePoint 2010 means you can centralize some services while keeping others regionalized. By adding scaled-down SharePoint Foundation deployments to the mix, you can have cheaper local collaboration and less complexity. The options that suit your organization will depend on your users' needs and the QoS you wish to provide.

Table 5-2 names and describes the service applications in SharePoint Server 2010 that you can deploy across farms. The logic in each case makes sense: for example, you would want to be able to synchronize search data, metadata, or web analytics across farms.

Table 5-2. *Which Service Applications **Can** Be Deployed Cross-Farm?*

Service Application	Purpose	Storage
Business Data Connectivity	Provides connections to line-of-business data systems.	DB
Managed Metadata Service	Hub for managing taxonomy, keywords, and tags. Content types sync across site collections.	DB
Search	Crawl content and serve search queries.	DB
Secure Store Service	Single sign-on authentication to external systems.	DB
User Profile	Manages user data for My Sites, User Profile pages, social tagging, and other social networking functionality.	DB

Service Application	Purpose	Storage
Web Analytics	Provides traffic, search and inventory reports.	DB

In the case of the service applications that can't be deployed across farms, they tend to rely on caching to track data they need while showing you their content, as in the case of Access, Excel, and PerformancePoint. Services like the State Service do need a database, but are very farm specific. Table 5-3 shows the types of services that would not need to be as available across multiple farms.

*Table 5-3. Which Service Applications **Can't** Be Deployed Cross-Farm?*

Service Application	Purpose	Storage
Access Services	Provides a browser interface for Access 2010 databases.	Cache
Excel Services Application	Provides a browser interface for Excel 2010 spreadsheets.	Cache
InfoPath Forms Services	Provides a browser interface for InfoPath 2010 forms.	Cache
PerformancePoint	Pivot data, extract facts, and dimensions. Builds KPIs, scorecards, and dashboards. Connects to Analysis Service cubes.	Cache
State Service	Stores related temporary HTTP session data	DB
Usage and Health Data Collection	Produces various usage and health reports based on collected farm wide data.	DB
Visio Graphics Service	Viewing and refreshing of published Visio diagrams in a web browser.	Blob cache
Word Automation Services	Viewing and refreshing of published Word documents in a web browser.	Cache
Microsoft SharePoint Foundation Subscription Settings Service	Provides multi-tenant functionality for service applications.	DB

Knowing your service applications is a crucial part of understanding how to deploy SharePoint in a way that makes the QoS and the user experience good. The simplest is not always the best. The goal is greater communication and productivity, which sometimes means more than one hub.

Single Hub

A single hub is when the SharePoint farm and all service applications are run from one location (Figure 5-14). The advantage of this approach is less complexity, which means less cost. The disadvantage is the QoS for the users far from the hub (like Sydney) is very poor. It also means all metadata and search content is consolidated. Overall, though, the benefits to the IT department in terms of management and the Finance department in terms of cost are outweighed by the loss of potential return on investment to the business from the platform as users far from the hub will not be motivated to share and collaborate.

Single hub in London:
All services deployed there
Collaboration slow for users
in Sydney
But simpler to manage and
all content in one search

Figure 5-14. Simple for the administrators, slow for the distant users

Central Hub with Spokes

A central hub with spokes gives regional users good QoS for collaboration by placing a farm in their region, Sydney in this scenario (see Figure 5-15). They use this for local collaboration. Their My Sites are also hosted here as most of their social networking is also local. It is possible to share user profiles across farms, but currently, using the User Profile service application across WAN links is not supported. That is because this service requires direct database access. So for WAN environments like this scenario, the User Profile Replication Engine (UPRE) is recommended instead. The UPRE is part of the SharePoint Administration Toolkit (http://technet.microsoft.com/en-us/library/cc508851.aspx). It replicates user profiles and social data (such as social tags, notes, and ratings) between User Profile Service applications. This replication can be one-way or bidirectional. The Fancy Flowers folks decide to use this approach because they find the time zone differences between London and Sydney prevents knowledge sharing and good communication between the branches. They develop the My Sites functionality to display updates from all staff to make them more aware of each other and communicate better.

The Search service is also centralized in London. This is done by federating the content in the Sydney index rather than crawling it directly. Federation is similar to running multiple searches at once and displaying the results on the same page, but in separate web parts. This makes it easier for users to identify where the content is located. You can crawl content directly across WAN links from a central farm. The search architecture in 2010 is optimized for crawling over WAN connections. You can even put crawler components on separate crawl servers. These would be dedicated to crawling the remote content and so have less impact on general performance. Since the general intranet pages will change less often and have less editors and more readers, this can be hosted remotely from users, but caching can be used to make access faster as pages will mostly be warm rather than cold.

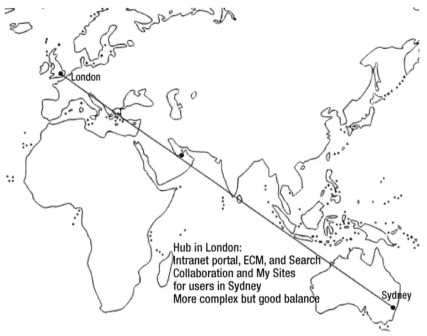

Hub in London:
Intranet portal, ECM, and Search
Collaboration and My Sites
for users in Sydney
More complex but good balance

Figure 5-15. More complex but better ROI

Just because you can deploy a service across a WAN link doesn't mean you should. Spreading the web analytics service across a WAN is not recommended possibly because it is chatty and would adversely affect other applications by using all the bandwidth. With the Business Data Connectivity service, QoS is best if the farm is close to the data. The same is true of the Secure Store Service: keep the service close to the application to which it is authenticating. This option is more complex and expensive than a central hub, but your organization may be getting more value from SharePoint as a result.

Central Hub and Mini-Hubs

A third option, which is an economical compromise between the previous two, is to only deploy SharePoint Foundation in your regional office(s), as shown in Figure 5-16. This gives local users the benefit of fast collaboration, but without the cost of the SharePoint Standard or Enterprise licenses. The more local offices you have, the more this will be a consideration. The content in these local offices can still be crawled by the central hub, but users will have to go there to perform a search. Essentially, this is the same as just a central hub, but with separate cheap local collaboration sites.

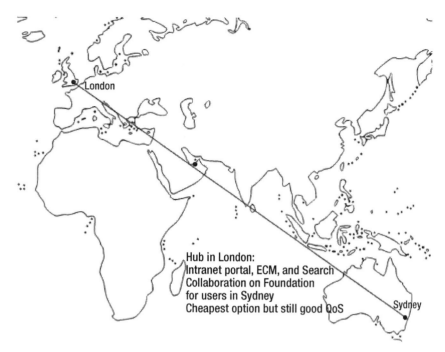

Figure 5-16. *Distributed, but less costly*

Cache

Hello, I'm Johnny Cash.

-Opening line at many of his concerts and public appearances

Caching has the largest impact where there is a high ratio of content consumers to producers and where the content changes infrequently. This is generally not the case with SharePoint, which aspires to make all users contributors and for updates to be fast and frequent. But caching can be set by the administrator to react differently depending on the profile of the user. If the user is anonymous, it can be assumed the content will change less often for them so the content is kept warm. With authenticated users, the content is assumed to be colder and so the caching is not as frequent. SharePoint gives you a range of options to manage the caching of page output through the web UI without having to resort to editing back end configuration files (see Figure 5-17).

Page Output Cache Profile

You can specify a cache profile for caching page output for anonymous users, and a cache profile for caching page output for authenticated users. These cache settings will apply only to this site unless you select the **Apply this setting to all subsites** check box.

Note that sites cannot currently override the inherited anonymous user cache profile.

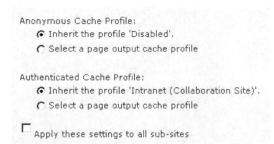

Anonymous Cache Profile:
- ⦿ Inherit the profile 'Disabled'.
- ○ Select a page output cache profile

Authenticated Cache Profile:
- ⦿ Inherit the profile 'Intranet (Collaboration Site)'.
- ○ Select a page output cache profile

☐ Apply these settings to all sub-sites

Figure 5-17. Caching is easily set through the Settings pages.

Summary

The main ways to improve your quality of service are WAN optimization, designing your farm so that content is near the people who need to see it, and caching infrequently changed pages. WAN acceleration can only help so far with the limitations of latency. But there are options in SharePoint 2010 to get a cost-effective compromise between user satisfaction and a not overly complex architecture.

It should be clear that "the pipe" is an overly simple metaphor and that making it bigger is not necessarily the best way to improve QoS. However, I do think that faster broadband in business is lagging behind what is available in the domestic market due to competition and that this will change. For example, I pay very little every month for 20Mbps and many businesses are content with 3Mbps. Also, broadband's pricing method is unfair because businesses pay no matter how often or how much they use their broadband. This is not the way with electricity or water, and it should be the same for broadband. Why are you paying 24/7 for something you may only use 8 hours a day, 5 days a week? Why does a light user have to pay as much as a heavy user?

CHAPTER 6

Back Up a Step

Backups are your next line of defense after high availability options like resilience and redundancy. As described in Chapter 4, you can protect against failure to a degree. While hardware failure does happen and disasters, like sheep, do happen, the main cause of unavailability of a system is maintenance that has gone wrong. Backups are always necessary no matter how comprehensive your resilience and redundancy planning because data on a disk is fragile and any number of things can destroy it. However, one of the principle advantages of digital data over physical data is that it is relatively easy to create an exact copy. Content that is simply zeros and ones can be copied with almost perfect fidelity whereas copying a physical document is a process far more prone to error. You'll rarely regret making copies of data.

Whatever the cause of your system failure, you must have copies or be able to reproduce what has been lost. What is primarily reproducible is the farm itself in the sense that SharePoint can be reinstalled and reconfigured; you don't have to rewrite the application from scratch. Reinstallation does take time but it has the advantage that you can do this in advance by having a second farm on standby. This approach has cost implications because you have hardware and software serving no immediate purpose other than just waiting to become useful. Your business impact assessment (BIA) should have convinced your stakeholders and management of the necessity of such an approach. To properly reproduce a farm, however, you must have a detailed design of your production farm.

In other words, you have to know your architecture well to know what to copy and how to copy it. This chapter focuses on the following:

- *Knowing what to copy*: Some things are more important to back up and to do so more frequently. Do you know what they are? Your BIA is the key here.

- *Dependencies*: SharePoint is a complex system, and backups must include everything required to reproduce the data correctly. You must also know the order in which to restore information.

- *Code and content*: SharePoint is an extendable platform. Have you captured all of the extensions correctly?

- *Backup tools*: Tools can automate what you capture, but you must know their strengths and weaknesses as they are not a substitute for proper backup planning.

- *Documentation*: This is the product of all of the preceding steps. Once again, documentation is not a substitute for careful, responsible planning and re-planning. It is simply the product of your understanding of what needs to be backed up and how it needs to be restored.

Everything the users create is stored in the content databases, which are relatively easy to back up and attach to an existing farm to give users access to their content again. Backing them up is not the hard part. The hard part is bringing back a structure for that content to exist within. To back up something sufficiently you must understand its internal dependencies. After reading this chapter you will understand what backup entails: primarily it is about knowing how to copy or reproduce everything your users need quickly and correctly. But while you need copies of your content databases, re-attaching them to a farm is not as hard as getting a farm back to the point it was—hardware, software, configuration, and code-wise—before it was destroyed.

Backup Planning and Preparation

The first step in backup planning and preparation is knowing when to start. The answer is quite simple: when your SharePoint farm goes beyond the point where it will take longer to recreate the farm and its content from scratch than to restore it from a backup. You will find that to be as soon as users start to use it. The uses can be testing or proof of concept but you have to start creating backups from the very beginning because it will be less painful than starting again with a brand new, empty server. Virtualization can make recreating the farm architecture and configuration relatively straightforward, but reproducing original, real-time data by users is more time consuming. Furthermore, users hate doing it!

Planning how to copy data, at what intervals, with what tools, and how you will document it is a continuous process. It starts by looking at what your business does and the impact of losing certain content as well as the productivity benefits of the SharePoint application. This is contained in your BIA.

Business Impact Assessment

The backup approach you use will ultimately be informed by the BIA because it is what determines your restore priorities. You must know your RTOs and RPOs for different content, from critical down to non-critical. This is the same as high availability in the sense that some content is more important and must be given higher resources. To understand how to back up SharePoint, you must first understand the architecture thoroughly so you can identify what you have to back up. As demonstrated in Chapter 4, this means collecting details of processes and the impact of their failure over a course of time as well as capturing interdependencies and dates/times that are particularly significant to the business. For example, the payroll site in SharePoint mainly needs to work at the end of the month, and a failure at that time will have a bigger impact than one in the middle of the month.

Some content users can quickly reproduce their content manually, or they may not ever need something again once it has been created. For example, a site used to plan a one-off event has no continued value. Business processes, however, are like IT processes: they are chains of tasks. To fully understand, capture, and back up a process, you sometimes have to ensure that the steps before SharePoint and after are also captured. Carefully backing up the payroll process may be of no value if the parts of the business process preceding it (such as capturing timesheets) or the parts after (creating payment transfers) are also not backed up. There are many dependencies that have to be taken into account in a disaster situation, not just in the planning but in the execution of the plan

Dependencies

To successfully back up your SharePoint architecture and then successfully restore it requires a detailed understanding of all the dependencies within SharePoint required that make it work. Implicit in the need to backup/restore is the realization that your high availability tactics will eventually not be resilient enough. Data will be corrupted, hardware will fail, or some other event will mean you have to rebuild the platform from the last point you backed it up. Sometimes this may be planned: you may back up your farm to move it to another data center, for example.

In previous chapters you examined the dependencies of a disaster recovery plan, which include the following:

- Management signoff

- A BIA

- Stakeholder input on RTOs and RPOs

- Physical limitations and logistical planning

You also looked at what is required to put the DR plan into action in the context of an example organization's broader disaster recovery planning.

- Who decides there's actually been a disaster?

- Who deals with the disaster in general?

- Who in IT deals with the SharePoint farm disaster as distinct from the inevitable broader IT disaster?

- How will the SharePoint people know there's been a disaster?

You have also learned some parts of the logical architecture of SharePoint, namely service applications. To back up and restore SharePoint successfully, you will need to understand these components better, as well as the parts of SharePoint included or not included in SQL Server databases. This is because the different backup options back up some things and not others.

Your core dependencies in SharePoint are the following:

- The configuration, specifically the logical architecture and service applications.

- The content stored in the form of data in SQL Server generated by the users.

If you can back up and reproduce only these things, you have the bulk of what is required to bring SharePoint back to life. But remember that SharePoint is an evolving system, and it may have evolved further functionality in the form of code—the part not included in the configuration or in SQL Server.

Code and Content

The part of the system you can't have ready in advance as easily is the code created by developers and the content created by users that depends on that code to be present. For example, a developer could write a solution that includes creating structural elements like sites, lists, content types, and Web Parts. Restoring the content databases without restoring these code elements won't get you far: they can't be used until the structure they depend upon has been reinstalled as well. Re-installation of a farm without documentation is a haphazard process at best but asking users or developers to perfectly recall in the correct order and with all dependencies in place again is virtually impossible. As you will see, SharePoint's built-in tools will capture code wrapped in solution packages and content in content databases, which contain the site collections users work in. This is the good news: the majority of what you have to preserve and recreate can be preserved and recreated.

If you now know you will need to back up the configuration, code, and content, how do you do it?

Backup Tools

"A bad workman blames his tools"

—Old Irish Saying

There is a mistaken belief that the tools you choose will back up SharePoint for you. The reality is the tool only helps you back up what your users need. It can automate tasks and make them more efficient, but you choose *what* and *when*. The three main backup tools you have to choose from are

- SharePoint's built-in backup tools (or third-party tools)

- SQL Server's built-in backup tools (or third-party tools)

- The Windows file system's built-in backup tools (or, most commonly, third-party tools)

Figure 6-1 shows that, for example, if you use SharePoint backup for Service Applications, it backs up some settings to files and also uses the SQL backup tool (in the overlap between the two) to back up content in SQL Server databases. However, if you only use SQL Server's backup tools, you only capture the data in SQL Server, and in that case, the databases would have to be attached to a Service Application in the restore/DR farm. Note also that if some customizations are made to SharePoint but not through SharePoint itself, these have to be recorded and backed up separately—for example, any change to the Web.config file not made via SharePoint Central Administration.

Backup Tools

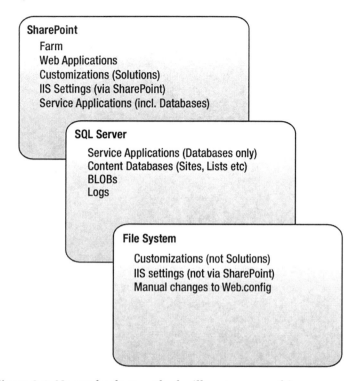

Figure 6-1. No one backup method will capture everything.

Documentation

I will describe the tools that capture parts of a farm's infrastructure, but there is still no substitute for good documentation. Think of documentation as the main form of backup you will rely on in the disaster situation—the tools you use to restore it are simply a means to that end. In the end, documenting what you or others have done in the process of creating and evolving the SharePoint farm will be the absolute most important thing you will need to restore it. Content databases are actually quite simple to back up. They're just a set of tables, after all. It is the system they have to fit into that is complex and has to be thoroughly documented. When your production farm was designed, it likely had two important documents.

- *Solution Architecture*, which described the business requirements and the architectural decisions made to address them.

- *Detailed Design*, which showed the steps to implement the architecture. This would have included screenshots and tables of configuration data like server names and names of service accounts.

These documents may not exist for a number of reasons. Perhaps an external company installed SharePoint and didn't document the process, or SharePoint simply grew from a user's need on a server under their desk, and so no planning or documenting was done. Whatever the reason, an opportunity was lost to document how the production farm and other farms were installed and configured. What has also been lost is that perhaps this process didn't go perfectly smoothly because of some idiosyncrasy in your network. A workaround was likely discovered but the information about it is either lost or only partly remembered. Not knowing about any pitfalls means that re-creating the production environment will take longer as these workarounds will have to be rediscovered. If this documentation is available, it is very useful as you now have the first document in your disaster recovery plan. If you don't have it, do it now! While your production farm is operational, capture as much detail as you can about how it has been set up. The main parts to capture in SharePoint are

- Server names

- Service accounts

- IIS configuration: Application pools and accounts used in them

- Service applications and how they are configured. Focus on the more complex like the User Profile Service and Search.

- Other Central Administration settings such as outgoing and incoming mail servers, and how often and how large your different kinds of logs are captured.

- Web application settings

- Alternate access mappings

- Any delegation of rights within administration such as administering a specific service

- Any availability settings like mirroring

- Overall topology: which servers host which service application instances and proxies (more on what there are later)

As with SharePoint itself, there should also be documentation created by the network and SQL Server people in your organization for the installation of the Windows servers and their network configurations, and details of the SQL Server installation and configuration. SQL Server, for example, should have detailed documentation on how it's clustering, mirroring, or log shipping were set up. This will go beyond the generic information provided by Microsoft, as it will detail the specific server names, configurations, and, to some extent, the rationale behind the configuration in terms of how it fits the needs of the business. There is generic information on the Internet for these things, but the documentation I am referring to here specifically reflects the design of your organization's environment.

If none of this is documented, it is a serious risk to your SharePoint farm. Don't think that the person who did the original installations will be available to do the reinstalls and that they will remember what to do. While some people do have eidetic memories (perfect recall), most of us don't. This is why documentation of the installation and configuration of your SharePoint farm and its dependencies, Windows Server and SQL Server, is essential. If it was not done previously, it must be done now as part of your backup preparation process. Bear in mind that your production system is running and accessible now; if it fails, you won't have the opportunity to look up its settings when you have to reproduce them.

Backup Using SharePoint

"Everything flows, nothing stands still."

—Heraclitus, Quoted by Plato in *Cratylus*

Using the built-in SharePoint backup tools will produce the most complete picture of your SharePoint environment. The most important parts are the content databases, and they are preserved this way. Every SharePoint farm is unique because so many parts are only part of that farm. For example, the server names and IP addresses are unique in your domain, and the content is unique. Recreating a farm is in a real sense impossible; you are actually creating a new farm very like it. The main part of the SharePoint farm you will want to back up is the configuration database. It's shown as an option in the SharePoint backup page. The diagram in Figure 6-2 gives the impression that you can back this up using the configuration-only backup. However, it only backs up the configuration settings that are portable to another farm, not those that are unique, such as the following:

- Antivirus

- Information rights management (IRM)

- Outbound e-mail settings (only restored when performing an overwrite)

- Customizations deployed as trusted solutions

- Diagnostic logging

You can restore this to an existing farm; if these settings don't have values, they will be set. But notice there are a lot of things missing from that list—the most obvious is the service Applications settings. I'll talk more about preserving them later.

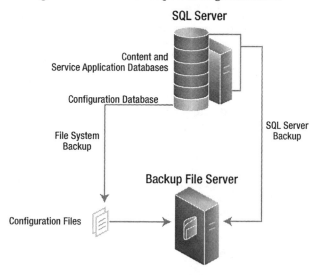

Figure 6-2. It looks like all the configuration is captured.

Backup and Restore in Central Administration

Despite this caveat, the SharePoint farm backup tool in Central Administration will capture as much of SharePoint for you as any other automated tool. As you can see in Figure 6-3, it is used to back up, restore, change settings, view a history, and check the status of a current backup job.

Figure 6-3. The main SharePoint backup and restore options

All of the options listed in Figure 6-3 assume you have a running farm to back up or restore to. In a disaster recovery situation, if you have got back to the point where you can see this Central Administration page, you are 90 % back to where you were before the disaster. Central Administration provides tools for performing individual backups of the entire farm, individual site collections, sites, libraries, or lists. A full farm backup can be restored from Central Administration, but tools are not provided for scheduling recurring backups or for restoring individual site collections, sites, libraries, or lists. These operations can be managed using PowerShell scripts. To schedule automated recurring backups, use the PowerShell cmdlets in scripts that are scheduled with the Windows Task Scheduler. I'll talk more about PowerShell next.

Backup Using PowerShell

SharePoint itself doesn't include a tool for scheduling backups; this is done via PowerShell. A backup can also be done via STSADM, but this tool is being slowly deprecated, so it's recommended to use PowerShell. Furthermore, I recommend you use PowerShell rather than the options in Central Administration to perform and automate your backups because PowerShell commands can be placed within scripts that can be scheduled with the Windows Task Scheduler. The dependencies for scheduling and running PowerShell-based backups successfully are permission and path related (with thanks to Todd Klindt for these).

- Your Central Administration application pool account must have read/write access to the location of the backups.

- Your SQL Service account must have read/write access to the location of the backups.

- If you're running a farm backup from STSADM or Windows PowerShell, the account you're running it as must have read/write access to the location of the backups.

- The location must be accessible from the SharePoint machine the backup is running on.

- The location must be accessible from the SQL instance that SharePoint is trying to back up.

- This is why all the examples are UNCs (\\server\share) and not local paths (e:\backups).

To perform a backup with PowerShell, do the following:

1. On the Start menu, click All Programs.

2. Click Microsoft SharePoint 2010 Products.

3. Click SharePoint 2010 Management Shell.

4. You use the PowerShell command Backup-SPFarm to start your backup.

Note For help and examples, type get-help Backup-SPFarm –examples.

---

5. The following script will start a full backup to e:\backup. To do so, create a new text file in Notepad and add the following line:

```
Backup-SPFarm -Directory e:\Backup -BackupMethod full
```

6. PowerShell files use the .ps1 extension, so save this file as e:\Scripts\BackupSharePointFarm.ps1.

7. For security, Windows Server won't allow PowerShell scripts to run by default. Thus, you need to adjust the Execution Policy to allow them. To do this, issue this instruction at the PowerShell command line:

```
set-executionpolicy RemoteSigned
```

8. Next, enter the following command in the Task Scheduler as your scheduled command line action, or enter it in a batch file that you schedule to run:

```
powershell -command e:\Scripts\BackupSharePointFarm.ps1
```

9. The account on which the task runs has to have farm administrator permissions, or at least PowerShell permissions; otherwise it can't run properly

Speeding Up Backups

The GUI in Central Administration does have some advantages over the PowerShell commands, however. For example, backups can be made faster by increasing the number of threads used for backing up and restoring (Figure 6-4). Using the Central Administration tool doesn't mean you can avoid all planning and thought in your backup process, however. For example, you must also specify a location for your backup. I recommend you create the backup on the machine and then copy it to the network. A backup of 600GB in SharePoint will take 6 hours, so factor in the time to do this that doesn't clash with other operations. Another way to speed up backups is to first do a full backup and then only do subsequent differential backups. You will see these options on the "Perform a backup" page. The differential backups are faster because they only copy what's changed, not the total farm.

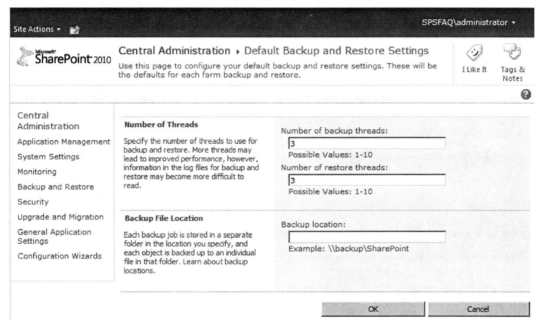

Figure 6-4. These settings affect performance and capacity in SharePoint Backup and Restore.

Recommendation

Full backups create a new backup of the complete farm. *Differential* backups create a backup of all the data stored in databases that has changed since the last full backup. Naturally this means you must have first created a full backup. As well as speed, an additional advantage of a differential backup is it uses fewer resources. This is important because a backup will consume all available I/O resources until it has completed its job, so shorter is better. If you perform one full backup per week during non-peak hours plus a differential backup every night, you will have a good balance between the two. This will depend on the amount of new content your users add. If it is a small percentage, you might only need to create a full backup monthly. If you have the option, perform the backup to a different disk than SQL Server itself. For the backup, RAID 10 is recommended, because of its fast write performance, as opposed to RAID 5, which is slow because it has to maintain parity information. For more information on choosing the appropriate RAID options for SharePoint see http://technet.microsoft.com/en-us/library/cc298801.aspx.

Backup Components

SharePoint allows you to back up many important parts of what makes up your farm. These parts are shown in Figure 6-5. It indicates the importance of packaging customizations in solution packages. These can be backed up using SharePoint. Beyond this, you can see that the main components of your farm are the service applications. So let's look at the constituent parts of service applications in more detail.

Select component to back up

Select the top-level component to back up. You can also click the name of a Web application to browse its contents.

Select	Component	Type	Description
☐	⊟ Farm	Farm	Content and configuration data for the entire server farm.
	SharePoint_Config	Configuration Database	Configuration data for the entire server farm.
☐	⊞ Solutions	Solutions	Collection custom solutions.
☐	⊞ InfoPath Forms Services	Server Settings and Content	Administrator-approved content and settings for the server farm.
☐	⊞ SharePoint Server State Service	State Service	Service for storage of temporary state information used by various SharePoint Server features.
☐	⊞ Microsoft SharePoint Foundation Web Application	Microsoft SharePoint Foundation Web Application	Collection of Web Applications
	⊞ WSS_Administration	Central Administration	Collection of Web Applications
☐	⊞ SharePoint Server State Service Proxy	State Service Proxy	
☐	⊞ SPUserCodeV4	Microsoft SharePoint Foundation Sandboxed Code Service	Settings for the Sandboxed Code Service.
	Microsoft SharePoint Server Diagnostics Service	Microsoft SharePoint Server Diagnostics Service	Settings for the diagnostics service.
☐	Global Search Settings	Search object in configuration database	Crawler impact rules for the farm
☐	⊞ SharePoint Foundation Search	Index files and Databases	Search instances for Microsoft SharePoint Foundation
☐	⊞ Application Registry Service	Application Registry Service	Backwards compatible Business Data Connectivity API.
	Microsoft SQL Server Reporting Services Diagnostics Service	Microsoft SQL Server Reporting Services Diagnostics Service	Settings for the diagnostics service.
	Microsoft SharePoint Foundation Diagnostics Service	Microsoft SharePoint Foundation Diagnostics Service	Settings for the diagnostics service.
☐	⊞ Shared Services	Shared Services	Shared Services of the server farm.

Figure 6-5. The SharePoint Backup and Restore components you can back up

Preserving Your Service Application Architecture

As mentioned, to back up something sufficiently, you must understand its internal dependencies. When it comes to service applications, the first point to understand is that, like index partitions, they are logical containers within what is called the shared services architecture. SharePoint has over 20 services, and it may be simpler to think of these as miniature applications residing on the SharePoint platform. They all have their own administration pages, settings, administrators, and databases. The framework they are part of allows SharePoint to distribute requests between them, providing load balancing and redundancy. It also provides an interface called a service application proxy that allows other applications to interface with them. See Figure 6-6 for details. Because their architecture is so linked to the farm as a whole, you have to back up the whole farm to preserve them. For example, instances and their endpoints are machine specific.

Shared Services Architecture

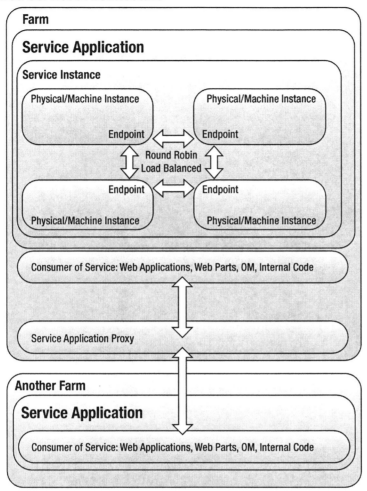

Figure 6-6. The logical components of service applications

When you install SharePoint, it gives you the means to install service applications (see Figure 6-7). Doing so installs the service on all the machines in the farm, but not until you install a physical or machine instance on a specific server in the farm do you have an actual service application. An analogy would be when an office administrator makes the install media for Word available on the network but it is not actualized until a user installs it on their PC.

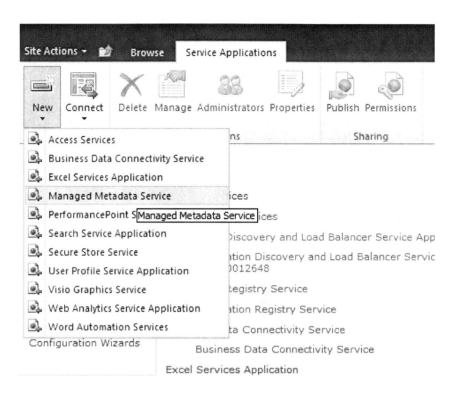

Figure 6-7. Installing a new instance of one of a choice of service applications

After you install the service application, you can install a server instance on multiple machines. In Figure 6-7 you aren't installing the service applications as the titles seem to imply; you are actually installing instances of them. As mentioned in Chapter 4, this approach provides redundancy. Machines/servers running instances of applications are referred to as application servers, although this is just a logical distinction as services can be run on any server in the farm. SharePoint uses a built-in round robin mechanism to find an instance of the application and run the service instance. This helps distribute load.

The connections between the service instances are called endpoints. These are part of the Windows Communication Foundation (WCF), which is an application programming interface (API) for building connected service-oriented applications. These endpoints have an address and binding properties that specify how the data will be transferred.

Each service application also requires a proxy. This is unlike an endpoint in that its purpose is to connect the service to consumers, which can be web applications or even other service applications on other farms. For example, you can connect the Managed Metadata Service to another farm this way to maintain consistent metadata. Service application proxies can be grouped so that when you create a new web application you can simply associate it with a proxy group to connect it with all the service applications in that group together. For example, one web application may be for external users and its proxy group contains Search Service App 01 and Managed Metadata Service App 01 (see Figure 6-8). This web application has a URL like *external.something.com*.

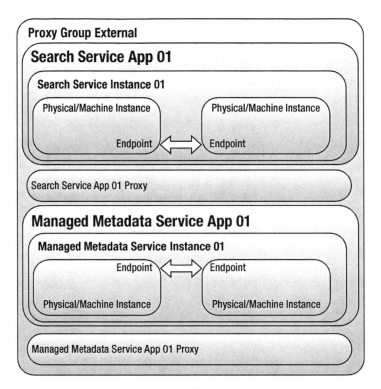

Figure 6-8. *A group of service applications for external users*

Then a second proxy group for internal users could be on the same farm with service applications called Search Service App 02 and Managed Metadata Service App 02 (see Figure 6-9). This web application has a URL like *internal.something.com*. This allows for a great deal of scalability and organization with in your farm architecture.

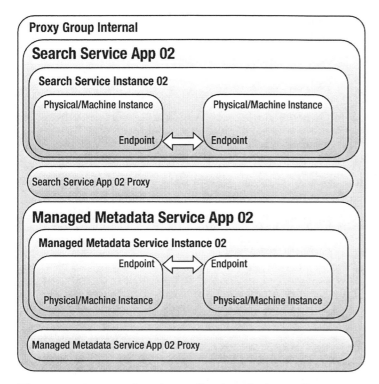

Figure 6-9. A group of service applications for internal users

When creating a web application you can choose to see the proxies in particular groups by selecting the proxy group from a drop-down (see Figure 6-10). You then can select the services you wish to associate with the web application.

Service Application Connections

Choose the service applications that this Web application will be connected to. A Web application can be connected to the default set of service applications or to a custom set of service applications. You can change the set of service applications that a Web application is connected to at any time by using the Configure service application associations page in Central Administration.

Edit the following group of connections: | Internal ▾ |

	Name	Type
☐	Managed Metadata Service	Managed Metadata Service Connection
☐	PerformancePoint Service Application	PerformancePoint Service Application Proxy
☐	Search Service Application 1	Search Service Application Proxy
☐	Excel Services Application	Excel Services Application Web Service Application

Drop-down options: External / Internal / [custom]

Figure 6-10. Grouping of connections via proxy groups

If you use proxy groups, note that after a restore you must reassociate the service application proxies with their respective proxy groups. This is because service application proxies are not assigned to proxy groups when restored. All web applications will be associated with the default proxy group. You must associate web applications with other proxy groups if you want to do that.

Backup for Service Applications

As you can see, a service application is not simply a database. Many of its settings are stored in the Central Administration database because they are part of the farm as a whole or connect it to other applications. If the application does have a database, some of its settings and data are stored there, but not all. The recommended way to back up service applications is therefore a full farm backup. Even if you select the service application to back it up on the SharePoint backup page, you will not have everything required to completely restore the service application.

One main component missing is that backups of service applications don't include the related proxy. To back up both the service application and the service application proxy, you must either back up the farm or perform two consecutive backups, selecting the service application in one backup and selecting the associated service application proxy in the second backup. A more direct approach is to select the Shared Services node (at the end of Figure 6-5). If you do this, all of the service applications and the related service application proxies on the farm will be backed up.

Table 6-1 shows the data sources used by the different service applications. In some cases, these are databases in SQL Server; in others, the data is simply stored in cache while the data is in the external source, as is the case with the Access and Excel services. Many service application databases can't be backed up individually from SharePoint Server 2010. To back up service application databases only, you must use SQL Server backup. Once again, a farm backup will capture all you need.

Table 6-1. *Databases for Service Applications and Backup Scenarios*

Service Application	Database or data source name(s)	What SharePoint backs up
Business Data Connectivity	Business Data Connectivity	Backs up external content type definitions. Separate backup required for external data. If you restore the data to a different location, you have to change the location information in the external content type definitions.
Managed Metadata Service	Managed Metadata Service	If tagging is being used, to successfully use the Managed Metadata Service application in the disaster recovery farm, you must also restore the Social Tagging database for the User Profile service application.
Search	Crawl, Property, and Search Administration	If your farm includes Microsoft FAST Search Server 2010 for SharePoint, your backup will also back up the Content SSA and Query SSA (including the People Search index). However, in addition to your standard backup, you must run a backup of the FAST Search Server 2010 for SharePoint the farm.

Service Application	Database or data source name(s)	What SharePoint backs up
Secure Store Service	Secure Store	Before backing up the secure store service, do the following: • Record the passphrase. You will need the passphrase when you access the restored Secure Store Service. • Ensure that you back up the Secure Store Service every time you change or refresh the master key. When you change or refresh the master key, the database is automatically re-encrypted with the new key. Backing up the secure store service ensures that the database and the master key are in synchronization. • Keep the passphrase in a secure location.
User Profile	Profile, Synchronization, and Social Tagging	Social Tagging database is required by Managed Metadata Service.
Web Analytics	Staging and Reporting	Microsoft recommends that you not run the Web Analytics service application on the disaster recovery farm until after failover.
Access Services	Cache	Rebuild in disaster recovery farm.
Excel Services Application	Cache	Rebuild in disaster recovery farm.
InfoPath Forms Services	Cache	Rebuild in disaster recovery farm.
PerformancePoint	Cache	Rebuild in disaster recovery farm.
State Service	State	Log-shipping the State database is not supported.
Usage and Health Data Collection	Logging	Microsoft recommends you don't run the Usage and Health Data Collection service on the disaster recovery farm, and that you do not mirror or log-ship the Logging database.
Visio Graphics Service	Blob cache	Rebuild in disaster recovery farm.
Word Automation Services	Cache	Rebuild in disaster recovery farm.

Service Application	Database or data source name(s)	What SharePoint backs up
Microsoft SharePoint Foundation Subscription Settings Service	Subscription	Rebuild in disaster recovery farm.

Backup Using SQL Server

The main limitation with using SQL Server as your only backup method is you can't use SQL Server tools (or Data Protection Manager) to back up a service application. Use SQL Server to back up content databases, but note that you will have to manually rebuild the rest of your farm, which is not a good option if users are waiting. If you are running SQL Server Enterprise, Microsoft strongly recommends that you use backup compression. For more information about backup compression, go to http://go.microsoft.com/fwlink/?LinkID=129381.

The danger with focusing on SQL Server for your SharePoint backup strategy is that if you know SQL Server better than you know SharePoint, you will be tempted to assume SQL Server backups are all you need to restore a farm. I would not recommend this, but SharePoint does depend on the following components of SQL Server and you should take them into account when planning your overall SharePoint backup strategy. Capturing the transaction logs will capture changes made within your SQL databases, whereas BLOBs are storage for SharePoint outside of SQL Server so I have referenced both here.

Transaction Logs

In SQL Server, each database has at least one data file and one transaction log file. SQL Server stores the data physically in the data file. The transaction log file stores the details of all the modifications that you perform on your SQL Server database and the details of the transactions that performed each modification. Because the transactional integrity is considered a fundamental and intrinsic characteristic of SQL Server, logging the details of the transactions can't be turned off in SQL Server. Transaction logs are automatically backed up when you back up the farm, Web application, or databases by using either SharePoint Central Administration or Windows PowerShell.

The transaction log file is logically divided into smaller segments that are referred to as virtual log files. In SQL Server, you can configure the transaction log file to expand as needed. The transaction log expansion can be governed by the user or can be configured to use all the available disk space. This is something you will want to avoid as it will threaten the availability of your farm.

To keep your transaction logs manageable, use the following guidelines:

- Set the size of the transaction log files to a large value to avoid them expanding automatically.

- Configure the automatic expansion of transaction log files by using memory units instead of a percentage after you thoroughly evaluate the optimum memory size.

BLOBs

BLOBs (binary large objects) are used in Remote BLOB Storage (RBS). RBS is a way of storing files outside SharePoint content databases. This is done for a number of reasons.

- *To save money.* SQL Server storage is more expensive than using a SAN, NAS, or even a Cloud tier.

- *To improve performance.* Uploading or downloading to SQL Server can be slow for larger files.

- *To manage data more easily.* Now your storage is centralized.

- *To be compliant.* SEC 17a-4, for example, requires an organization to store certain account holder documents on a specific type of compliant storage tier.

SharePoint Server 2010 backup backs up remote BLOB stores but only if you are using the FILESTREAM remote BLOB store provider to put data in remote BLOB stores. If you are using another provider, you must manually back up the remote BLOB stores.

Backup of the File System

As Microsoft points out in TechNet, the following components of your farm are not backed up because they are stored on web servers. A file level backup will capture them.

- Application pool account passwords

- HTTP compression settings

- Time-out settings

- Custom Internet Server Application Programming Interface (ISAPI) filters

- Computer domain membership

- Internet Protocol Security (IPsec) settings

- Network Load Balancing settings

- Secure Sockets Layer (SSL) certificates

- Dedicated IP address settings

These details are best captured in documentation. Customizations like the following must also be captured as files and documented:

- Master pages, page layouts, and cascading style sheets. These objects are stored in the content database for a web application.

- Web Parts, site or list definitions, custom columns, new content types, custom fields, custom actions, coded workflows, or workflow activities and conditions.

- Third-party solutions and their associated binary files and registry keys, such as IFilters.

- Changes to standard XML files.

- Custom site definitions (Webtemp.xml).

- Changes to the Web.config file.

113

Workflows

Workflows are a special case of customizations that you can back up and recover. The good news is that the definition data and workflow history are preserved in a SharePoint backup. The in-process workflow state is even preserved. Any SharePoint Designer workflow steps that are in the middle of a wait period during the backup will resume and complete after the backup is finished.

As Microsoft suggests, make sure that your backup and recovery plan addresses any of the following declarative or custom declarative workflow scenarios that apply to your environment. Declarative workflows, such as those that you created in Microsoft SharePoint Designer 2010, are stored in the content database for the site collection to which they are deployed. Backing up the content database protects these workflows. Declarative simply means that parts of the workflow are prewritten, in this case by SharePoint Designer, so that everything doesn't have to be coded from scratch.

Custom declarative workflow actions have components in the following three locations:

- The Visual Studio assemblies for the Activities are stored in the global assembly catalogue (GAC).

- The XML definition files (`.ACTIONS` files) are stored in the `14\TEMPLATE\{LCID}\Workflow` directory.

- An XML entry to mark the activity as an authorized type is stored in the `Web.config` file for the web applications in which it is used.

If your farm workflows use custom actions, you should use a file backup system to protect these files and XML entries. Similar to SharePoint Server features such as Web Parts and event receivers, these files should be reapplied to the farm as needed after recovery.

Workflows that depend on custom code, such as those that are created by using Visual Studio, are stored in two locations. The Visual Studio assemblies for the workflow are stored in the Global Assembly Catalog (GAC), and the XML definition files are stored in the Features directory. This is the same as other kinds of SharePoint Server features such as Web Parts and event receivers. If the workflow was installed as part of a solution package, backing up the content database protects these workflows.

If you create a custom workflow that interacts with a site collection other than the one where the workflow is deployed, you must back up both site collections to protect the workflow. This includes workflows that write to a history list or other custom list in another site collection. Performing a farm backup is sufficient to back up all site collections in the farm and all workflows that are associated with them.

Workflows that are not yet deployed must be backed up and restored separately like any other data file. When you are developing a new workflow but have not yet deployed it to the SharePoint Server farm, make sure that you back up the folder where you store your workflow project files by using Windows Backup or another file system backup application.

Summary

Your farm is a unique and constantly changing complex system. When focusing on how to back this up and restore it successfully, you will need clearly documented and tested steps. You can't fully rely on automated tools, partly because they can't capture everything and partly because they can only capture what you tell them to and when. Keep in mind that your SharePoint farm will have external dependencies that must also be backed up and restored before it can be restored. Also, SharePoint is not just the SharePoint application and its settings; it is also built on Windows servers, a network, and SQL Server. Without these parts, it can't function for your users.

The most important and valuable parts of your SharePoint farm are the parts that took the most time and effort to create: the code created by the developers and the content created by the users. Some code and some content is more important than others and I have already discussed how prioritizing content is essential to achieve your organization's recovery point and recovery time objectives. Use SharePoint to back everything up and create good documentation, and you will have given yourself the best chance of a successful backup. In the end, preparation and your knowledge are more important than which tools you choose.

CHAPTER 7

Monitoring

"Well, enough to get out of the way."

—Frederick Fleet, when asked how much sooner he could
have seen the iceberg that sank *Titanic* if he'd had binoculars

Your ability to maintain high availability is entirely dependent on you monitoring practices. In nearly every SharePoint disaster I have heard of or had to clean up after, there was a point when someone could have prevented it. Prevention is really what administrators should be rewarded for—not fixing problems that could have been prevented. But that is not how we tend to think. We focus on putting out fires and rarely think about measures to spot them early and save lives. This is a costly way to think; smoke alarms are cheaper than fire engines.

Let's use the Titanic metaphor to show how you can change your approach to monitoring SharePoint. The monitor is the lookout on your ship, not the tools they use. In the case of the Titanic, the lookouts in the eagle's nest were given reports that there were icebergs in the area, but they lacked binoculars—not because there were none on board, but because the key for the locker in which they were stored was in the pocket of a crew member who had been re-assigned before the voyage. The cold, night air made their eyes water and the lack of wind made the icebergs hard to spot as no waves were braking on their sides. The result: when the warning was given, it was too late. The ship glanced off the side of the iceberg and started to take on water.

Using this example as a lesson for your SharePoint farm, note the following:

- The lookouts knew there were icebergs because they had reports from other ships in the area to this effect.

- They had the tools to spot them (binoculars), but they were locked away.

- Weather conditions meant they could not spot them as soon as usual.

- By the time they did spot the iceberg, there wasn't enough time to steer clear.

Translating this into lessons for SharePoint reveals the following:

- Monitoring and reporting can warn of disasters.

- People and tools are crucial to preventing disaster.

- Intervening factors outside of your control can make situations worse.

- Knowing a disaster is going to happen is not enough to prevent it. You must also have the means to do so.

Maintenance Tasks

Monitoring starts with actively looking and so let's begin with the routine daily tasks of the lookout for your SharePoint farm. After that, you'll look at the weekly, monthly and quarterly tasks you can do to proactively prevent disasters.

Monitoring is mainly a task of routine vigilance. You should divide your administration role into tasks you perform regularly and even at a particular time. Beyond this regular schedule there may also be specific dates in your organization when extra watchfulness is required. For example, if your business is a TV sports channel, then your system work during the Super Bowl will be very important. Thinking along these lines, build your own custom task list.

As an administrator of SharePoint, your first task every day should be to visit the portal's main access pages and see if they render for you and as quickly as normal. Access them via a standard PC/Mac on the network, not just directly on the server. Do this in the morning, preferably before any of the users log on. This means starting your day an hour or two before everyone else. After you have built some automatic alerts, this will be less necessary, but for now it's a good starting point. If something is wrong, you will have an opportunity to diagnose and fix it—perhaps before the broader user community even notices, which is ideal. There should be no worse shame for the owner of SharePoint to get a call from the help desk or directly from someone in upper management to say SharePoint is down—and you didn't know about it.

You should be checking for performance bottlenecks daily and trying to catch them before they affect your SLA and the users' experience. I will show you a number of tools you can use to help do this, but remember, the best tool is your own intelligence and proactivity. Checking to ensure that the portal is working is only the very first part of your daily monitoring responsibilities. If you do see a problem, you have maybe an hour or two to resolve it before users notice. If you have been in this situation, you know it's a stressful one. It's far better to expend your energy daily identifying problems that could be days, weeks, or months away.

Your servers exist in physical space: it may be part of your responsibly to ensure the server room is secure, at the right temperature, and that no cables are loose or prone to be tripped over. Small things like this can bring down the best-architected farms. Some days will be different: perhaps the COO is making a big announcement at 9 a.m. and thus you can expect a spike in usage. If you notice a fall in usage that has no normal cause, like a public holiday, it may be a sign something is wrong. Checking and rechecking should become a normal routine and you should begin your day looking at the automated tasks from the night before, starting with backups.

Check Your Backups

You should also begin each day by ensuring the backup from the previous night has occurred. If you work for an organization that has offices all over the world, you may also be receiving a handover from the administrator of the previous shift, in which case a clear understanding of what has happened on their shift is essential so you can take over smoothly. Check your latest backup carefully. Make sure there is nothing outside normal parameters: size of backup, time it took, name of the file, etc. Test your backups by restoring them to a redundant system. This is useful as occasionally users delete content that can't be retrieved from the recycle bin. An example is if they delete list content in datasheet view. Having the backup from the night before lets you give the user their content back quickly. Sometimes it's useful to have this restore for security reasons. Users sometimes claim they uploaded something when they didn't, or didn't change someone else's access rights. This is an easy way to see what the site was like the day before.

Check Storage

Data never sleeps. It is constantly changing and generating more of itself and filling your disks' finite capacity. In SQL Server for SharePoint, data is created in the following places:

- Databases and their Transaction Logs
- Search Indexes
- Logs

Daily, you should be looking at the rate of growth of your disk volumes. Lack of capacity is one of the major causes of system unavailability and poor performance. You can do this using a range of tools: Windows Explorer, Performance Monitor, or Microsoft Systems Centre Operations Manager (SCOM). Don't leave the ordering of new hardware to the last minute. If the rate of growth indicates that your organization will need more capacity in less than three months, order it now. It can take that long to get sign-off, receive the hardware, and install it.

Monitor Reliability and Performance with Windows

Your Windows servers are the main container for your SharePoint farm. As such, having the tools to monitor their integrity is very important to your farm. Windows Server 2008 R2 offers a number of ways to monitor the reliability and performance of your system over time, all accessed via Server Manager. To open Server Manager, go to the Administrative Tools group in the Start menu on each of the servers in your SharePoint farm. You can also search for it in the Search box in the Start menu. Once opened, it looks like Figure 7-1. The first place to look is Event Viewer, under Diagnostics. There are other monitoring tools, like Performance Monitor in here, but check the error log first as it may show you something you didn't anticipate.

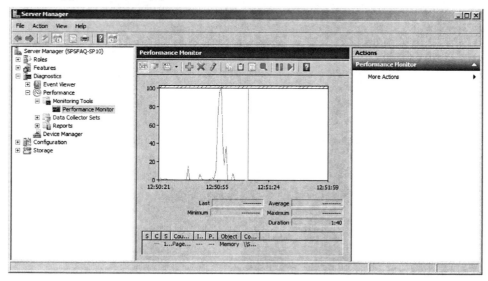

Figure 7-1. Open the Event Viewer after you visit your portal's main pages and backups.

Check Event Viewer

The Event Viewer is your main point of daily communication from your hardware, system, and software—including SharePoint. It should be your main point to check on the health of your system. The first place to look in Event Viewer is the Summary of Administrative Events (see Figure 7-2). This section will show you what new errors have occurred in the past hour or 24 hours. These will be the first errors you will want to check out.

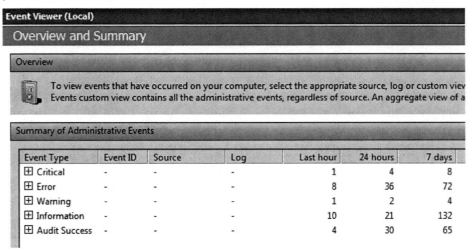

Event Viewer (Local)

Overview and Summary

Overview

To view events that have occurred on your computer, select the appropriate source, log or custom view
Events custom view contains all the administrative events, regardless of source. An aggregate view of a

Summary of Administrative Events

Event Type	Event ID	Source	Log	Last hour	24 hours	7 days
⊞ Critical	-	-	-	1	4	8
⊞ Error	-	-	-	8	36	72
⊞ Warning	-	-	-	1	2	4
⊞ Information	-	-	-	10	21	132
⊞ Audit Success	-	-	-	4	30	65

Figure 7-2. The errors from the last 24 hours

You can also filter events to see the Critical, Error, and Warnings with these steps:

1. Expand the Event View folder in Server Manager, or open the Event Viewer directly from Administration tools from the Start menu.

2. Select the log from which you want to filter events: the most common to look at is Application under Windows Logs.

3. Right-click the log and select Filter Current Log.

4. In the log Properties window, select the Critical, Error, and Warning check boxes.

5. Click OK when you have finished.

The path to the SharePoint-specific Operational logs is shown in Figure 7-3.

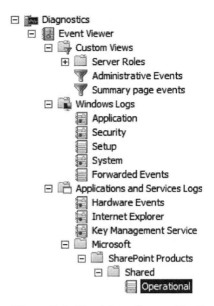

```
□ 🐟 Diagnostics
   □ 📋 Event Viewer
      □ 📑 Custom Views
         ⊞ 📁 Server Roles
            🔻 Administrative Events
            🔻 Summary page events
      □ 📷 Windows Logs
            📋 Application
            📋 Security
            📋 Setup
            📋 System
            📋 Forwarded Events
      □ 📋 Applications and Services Logs
            📋 Hardware Events
            📋 Internet Explorer
            📋 Key Management Service
         □ 📁 Microsoft
            □ 📁 SharePoint Products
               □ 📁 Shared
                     📋 Operational
```

Figure 7-3. *Check here for specific SharePoint events.*

Windows doesn't just allow you to passively consume data on what's happening in SharePoint; it can also actively inform you of events that could cause trouble down the line. It can even react to events in ways that begin to completely fix the problem. Let's look at these tools now.

Create a Subscription

The Event Viewer allows you to subscribe to events on multiple servers and attach tasks such as sending an e-mail or running a program in response to particular events. Here are the steps to ensuring you are notified of any Critical or Error events in the logs on your SharePoint servers. The first step is to create a new subscription, as shown in Figure 7-4.

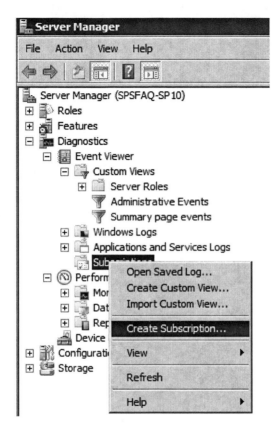

Figure 7-4. *Step 1 is to create a new subscription.*

Next, name your subscription and where the details of the subscription trigger events will be written to. You can also at this point identify multiple source computers for your subscription. Computers that will be sending events to each other must have the proper authentication in place first. Do this by adding the computer account for your "primary" server to the Administrators group on all servers from which you wish to collect events. This may require a reboot. The primary server is just the one you manage the subscription from, so logically it would be the one from which you access SharePoint Central Administration. The OK button will remain inactive until you select at least one computer (Figure 7-5).

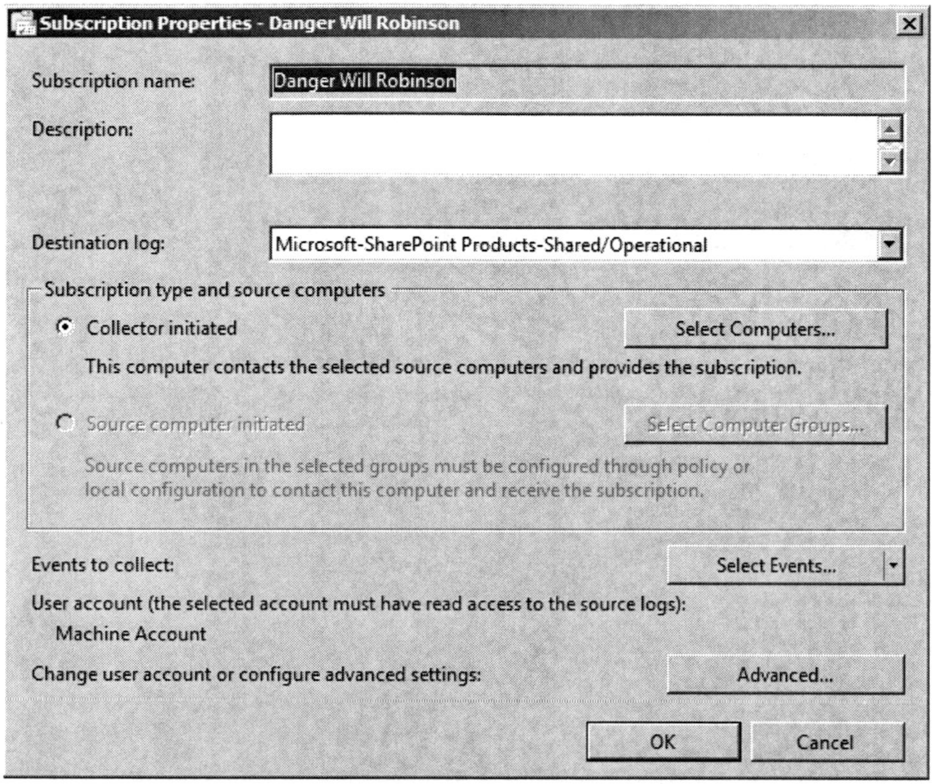

Figure 7-5. Step 2 is to specify where to collect the data from.

Next, click the Select Events button, click Edit, and choose the information you want to collect from where. In Figure 7-6 I have chosen Critical, Warning, and Error messages from the Event log for SharePoint in the past 24 hours. You can experiment with more refinement than this to suit your own needs. Figure 7-7 shows the subscription.

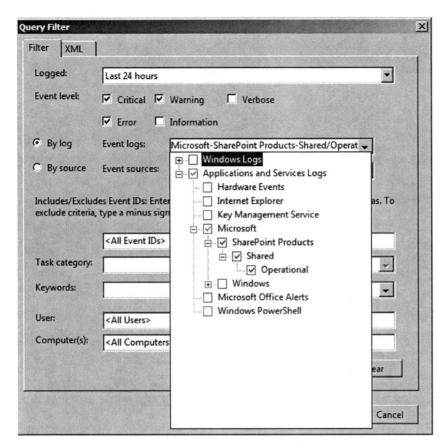

Figure 7-6. Step 3 is to specify the criteria for your subscription.

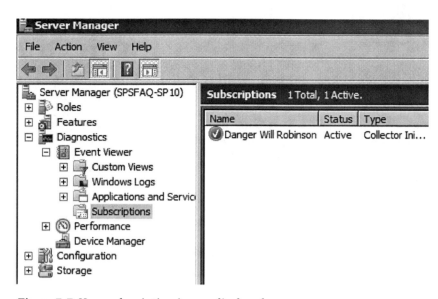

Figure 7-7. Your subscription is now displayed.

Your subscription will start automatically. Details of what it captures will be displayed in the Forwarded Events Log, as shown in Figure 7-8.

Figure 7-8. Forwarded events are displayed under Windows logs.

You now have a way to consolidate specific events across all your SharePoint servers. You may not need sophisticated tools like SCOM if this is sufficient for your organization's needs. The events you subscribe to are a result of recurring errors, because if you could predict everything that was going to go wrong before it happened, you'd be doing more with your life than administering SharePoint. I have used it in the past to alert me to recurrent problems caused by patching procedures that were not followed. You will build up your own profile.

Alerts: Instant Monitoring

The alerting function is also very useful for receiving messages directly from your servers. It is used to define a counter value that will trigger an alert to send a network message, execute a program, or start a log. This is useful for maintaining a close watch on your system, and one of your daily tasks should be checking for these messages. For instance, you can monitor unusual activity that doesn't occur consistently and get an alert when the event has been triggered, such as a spike in processor usage or the system using over 80% of memory. Security-related events are good candidates for the alert service as well: you can receive a message immediately if someone other than the approved list of users is accessing the machine.

With alerts, certain checks are much more frequent than daily; they are immediate, but they must be set up in advance. You can also configure the alert service to notify you when a particular resource drops below or exceeds certain values, thresholds, or baselines that you set up. Counter logs can also be viewed in the console, and the counter log data can be saved to CSV and TSV files and viewed in spreadsheet or report software. You can configure the logs to be circular, which means that when the log file reaches a predetermined size, it will be overwritten. Logs can also be linear, and you can collect data for predefined lengths of time. Logs can be stopped and restarted based on parameters you set. You can save files to various formats, such as HTML, or import the entire control OCX into an OLE container. Be careful of logs using too much space; set limits on them or put them on a separate volume where these is plenty of space and back them up to a separate machine. They may be useful after a server crash.

Setting up Tasks: Sending an E-mail Alert

So you have consolidated your events from multiple servers and specified which ones you want to know about. What action do you want Windows to take when they occur? You can ask Windows to run a program, put a message on the screen, or send an e-mail. You even specify multiple actions. The most common action is to send an e-mail so I will describe the steps here. To schedule a task for sending out alerts upon the arrival of a subscribed event, start Task Scheduler from the Administrative Tools.

On the General tab (Figure 7-9), name your task and specify under what privileges it will run. I have set mine to run whether I am logged on or not. I am also not running it with the highest privileges. Don't be tempted to do this in a production environment as it is always best practice to follow the principle of least privilege and it is unlikely this task needs all the privileges the Administrator (in my case) account has. For additional security, you could use an account with limited privileges just for this purpose.

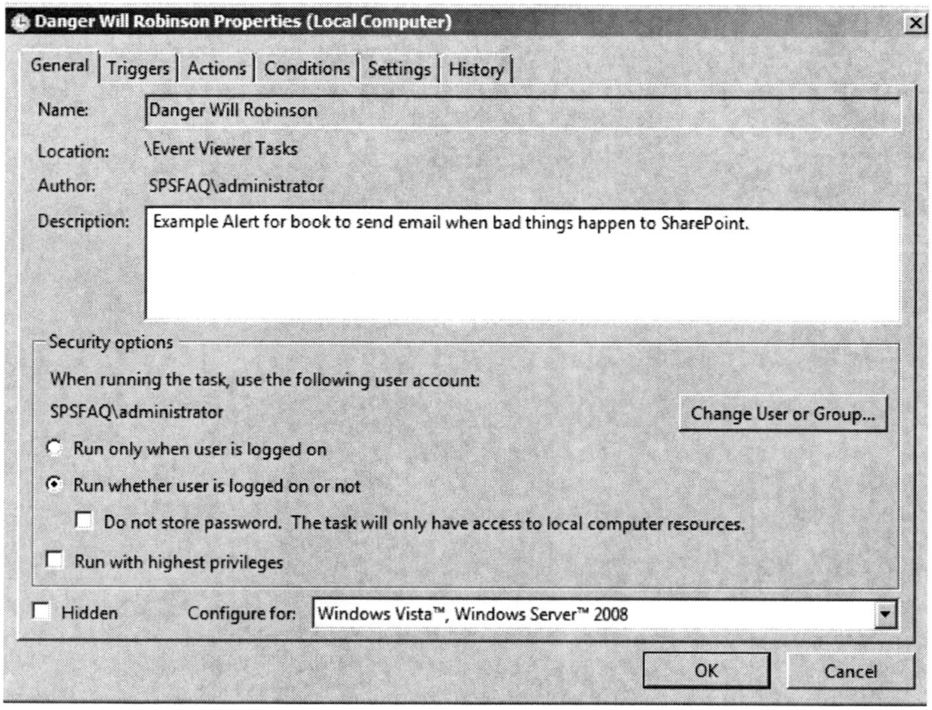

Figure 7-9. General settings

On the Triggers tab (Figure 7-10), I pressed the New button to bring up this dialog. In it I specified my task to run just before I check it in the morning every day. That way, when the e-mail is sent, it will contain the latest information and I will receive it an hour before I arrive into work at 7 a.m. (Set this to suit your own schedule.) I have also ticked the box that says "Synchronize across all time zones." This is useful if you want to set this task so it is seen in the morning by your administrators in other countries.

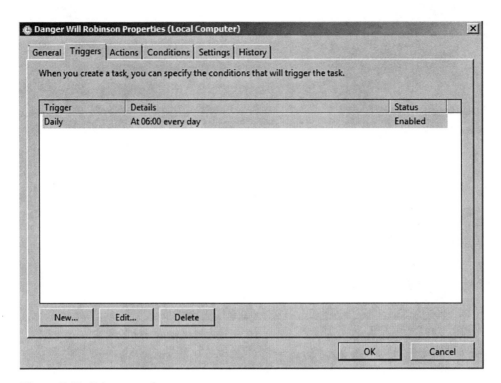

Figure 7-10. Triggers settings

On the Actions tab (Figure 7-11), I pressed the New button to bring up this dialog. Here is where you choose your action. The first drop-down also allows you to display a message or start a program. In this case, specify where to send the e-mail and what SMTP server to use.

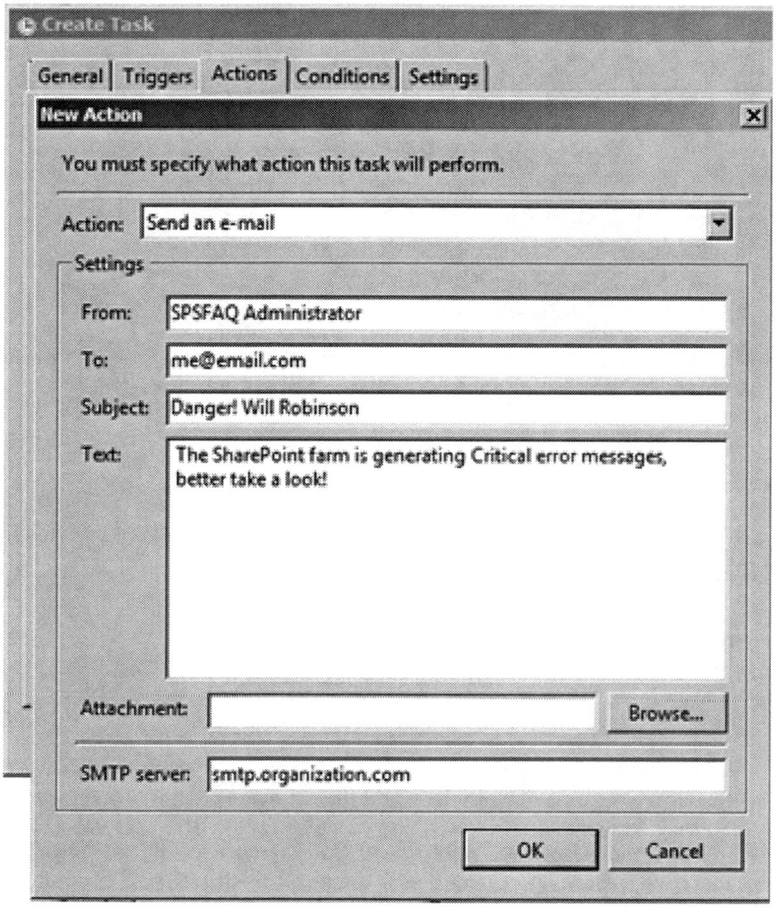

Figure 7-11. Actions settings

On the Conditions tab (Figure 7-12) you have the option to have the computer wake up to send the e-mail; this may be necessary if it has been idle all night. Otherwise, leave the settings here as the default. Other than the trigger, you may want to send the e-mail if the machine has switched to battery power or has had to use a secondary NIC.

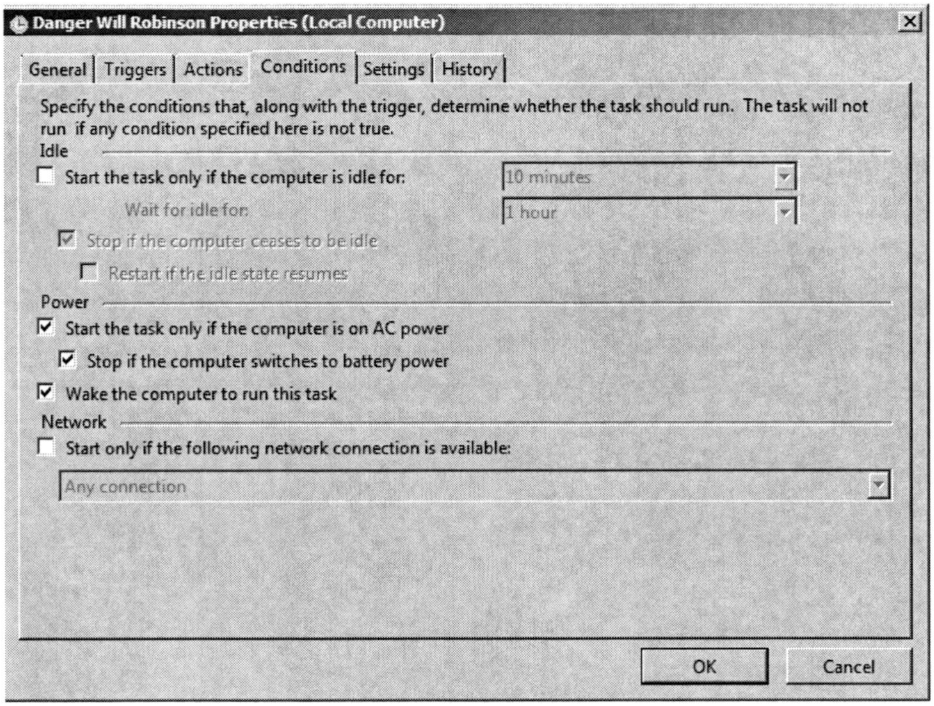

Figure 7-12. *Conditions options*

On the Settings tab (Figure 7-13) you have options about when and how the alert will run. I set it to retry five times if it fails and to stop if it takes longer than an hour. You can also create one-off tasks that automatically delete after they run. If there is more than one instance of a task, your options are (if the task is already running) to run a new instance in parallel, queue a new instance, or stop the existing one.

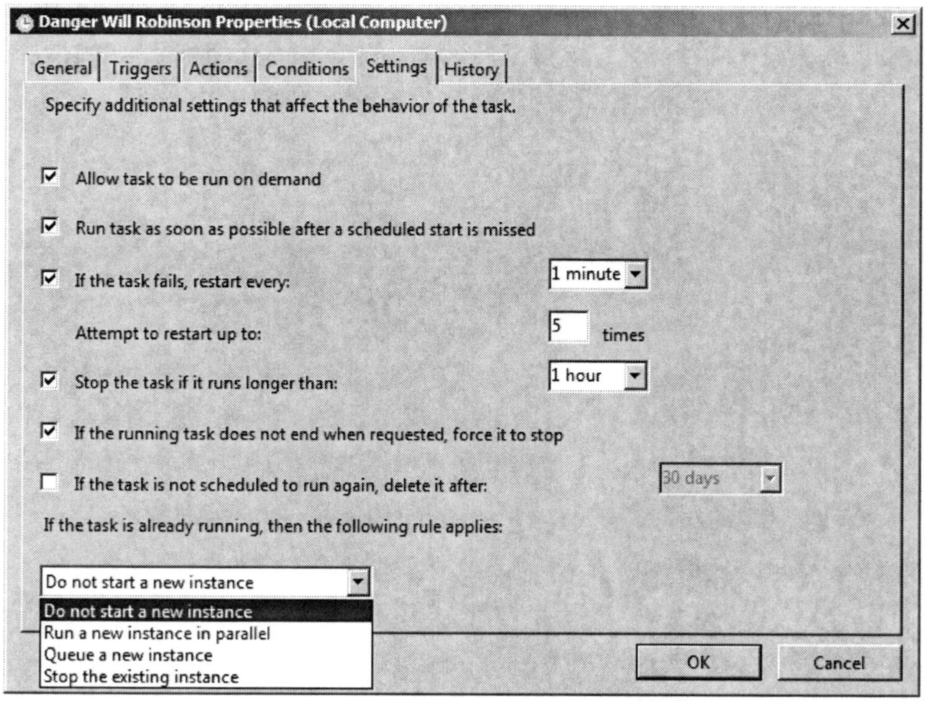

Danger Will Robinson Properties (Local Computer)
General
Triggers
Actions
Conditions
Settings
History
Specify additional settings that affect the behavior of the task.
Allow task to be run on demand
Run task as soon as possible after a scheduled start is missed
If the task fails, restart every:
1 minute
Attempt to restart up to:
5
times
Stop the task if it runs longer than:
1 hour
If the running task does not end when requested, force it to stop
If the task is not scheduled to run again, delete it after:
30 days
If the task is already running, then the following rule applies:
Do not start a new instance
Do not start a new instance
Run a new instance in parallel
Queue a new instance
Stop the existing instance
OK
Cancel

Figure 7-13. *Settings options*

Once you have been prompted to enter your administrator password to create the task, you can manually run it to test it (see Figure 7-14). Multiple tasks will alert you as soon as possible to problems with your SharePoint farm. It may be that one person is not monitoring it 24/7, in which case alerts can be set up to be sent to the appropriate person for that time. Some organizations, for example, have some staff only on call outside of normal business hours, so separate alerts can be configured to send to the appropriate person depending on the day/time. The nice thing about this functionality is there is a simple, clear graphical interface to let you create and manage them.

Task Scheduler (Local)
Task Scheduler Library
Event Viewer Tasks
Microsoft
OfficeSoftwareProtectio
WPD
Name
Status
Run
End
Disable
Export...
Properties
Delete

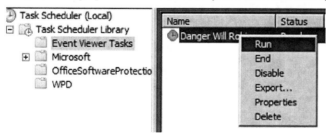

Figure 7-14. *Run your task.*

Your SharePoint system may generate errors but sometimes you need to be alerted if the hardware is using too many resources such as memory or processing power. In this case, you want to get the alert because you want to catch the problem before it generates errors at the application level. Your goal is always, like the binoculars on the *Titanic*, to see the trouble coming from as far off as possible to give you the greatest chance to avoid it.

You can also collect data from multiple servers in what are called data collector sets. I will show you how to set up event subscriptions using them to monitor memory- and performance-related counters.

Using Counters

Counters for memory and performance are useful for locating bottlenecks on your system. They will also detect bursts on the servers, which can be caused by sudden activity. This can either be expected, like when a big announcement is posted on the intranet, or unexpected, like a denial of service (DoS) attack. I will show you how to configure some of the more useful counters. Here are the steps to setting up what is referred to as a Data Collector Set:

1. Open the Server Manager console.

2. Right-click on Data Collector Sets ➤ User Defined, and create a New ➤ Data Collector Set (Figure 7-15).

3. Name the Data Collector and choose to Create manually (Advanced).

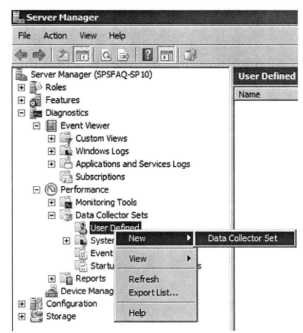

Figure 7-15. Create new Data Collector Set.

4. After clicking Next, choose the types of data to collect.

5. Select Create data logs and Performance counter (Figure 7-16).

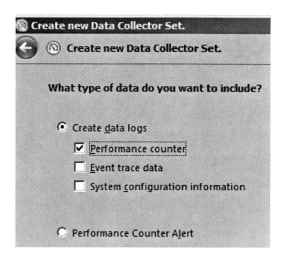

Figure 7-16. Create logs for performance data.

6. On the next screen (Figure 7-17), click Add and select performance counters to monitor. At the top of the screen you can select counters from computers other than the local computer. For each computer you wish to monitor, enter the counters into the same Data Collector Set. So, for example, if you plan to monitor three counters on three machines, nine total elements will be added to the Data Collector Set.

7. Finally, click OK. Your monitor will be created at the following path:
   C:\PerfLogs\Admin\<Data Set Name>\<ServerName_Date_Number> \DataCollector01.blg

8. Double-click on this file to open the monitor.

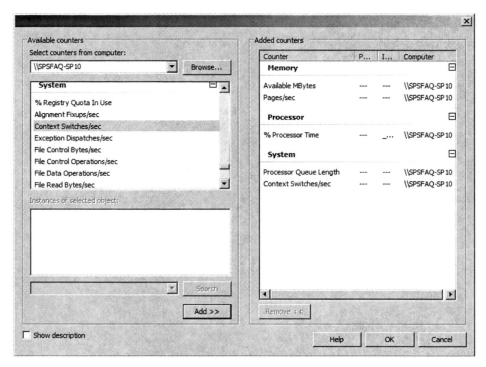

Figure 7-17. *Choosing what to monitor*

With many hundreds of performance counters available, one of the biggest headaches in setting them up can be simply determining which counters will be most useful. In fact, only a few of the available counters are actually necessary for monitoring entire-server performance. There are other counters that you'll find useful when these entire-server counters alert you to problems that may be occurring on the server, but you don't need to run them all of the time. Consider these few as a good starting point for monitoring on all of your servers.

Processor \ % Processor Time

This counter is the overall measurement of when a server is actively processing useful work. It measures when the processor is doing something other than the System Idle Process. When this counter is high, it means that the processor is actively processing useful work and you have efficient utilization; it's only a concern if users complain of poor server performance that corresponds with periods of high processor use. However, when this counter spikes to 100% (or 50% in a dual-processor system) it can mean that one process is consuming an entire processor's resources and thus needs attention.

System \ Processor Queue Length

This counter shows how many instructions are currently in line for attention by the processor. When this counter goes much above zero, it is often an indication that the processor can't keep up with the workload you are asking it to perform. A high count here can indicate that you need either a faster processor or fewer services running on the server.

System \ Context Switches / Sec.

A context switch occurs when a processor switches between which waiting instructions it is processing. As processors are only able to process a single instruction at a time, context switches give the illusion of multitasking. High levels of context switches are problematic because of the resource overhead involved with swapping out what the processor is working on. In situations where too many actions are being required of the processor at the same time, this can be a very high number. Typically, you'll see very high figures with very old applications or on Terminal Servers where many users are running many processes at once.

Memory \ Available MBytes and Memory \ Pages / Sec.

These counters are useful for determining memory use on the server. When a server processes its workload, it loads elements into memory for processing. When that memory begins to fill up, pages are swapped out of RAM to the disk. Since the disk subsystem is significantly slower than solid-state RAM, swapping usually involves a reduction in overall performance. Thus, the count of Available MBytes should be a number greater than zero, while the count for Pages/Sec should be a relatively low number.

When these counters are in those ranges, this means that the server has the correct amount of RAM assigned to it, and it isn't requiring more memory than available physical RAM. In virtualization environments where memory can be dynamically assigned to servers, it is often a best practice to manage the count for Available MBytes to be relatively close to zero as well. This means that the exact amount of memory required to perform that server's workload has been assigned to the server, while none is wasted and sitting idle.

You can usefully add other counters for the disk subsystem and networking as necessary. For servers with large amounts of data storage and retrieval, the disk subsystem can often be a significant bottleneck. In environments that do not use gigabit networking, it is possible for the network to be a bottleneck to performance as well. Keep an eye on these to spot problems, so you can suggest solutions when customers want to improve performance.

Once you've added the counters, select a sufficiently long sample interval (see Figure 7-18). Smaller intervals provide more granular data, but they take more resources to capture. With more remote computers being sampled, a longer sample interval is often necessary to prevent overloading the server collecting the samples. A good sample interval may be as long as 10 minutes per sample, providing round-the-clock sampling with relatively little impact.

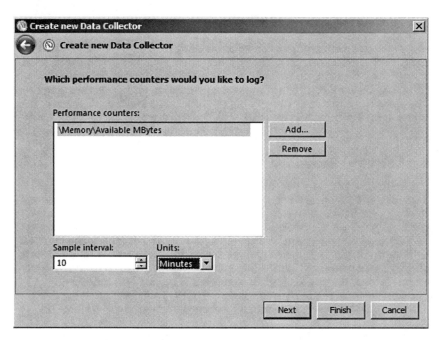

Figure 7-18. Set the sample interval.

You also have the option to configure Windows to monitor multiple machines with one Data Collector Set. This makes sense because a SharePoint server farm is not one machine in isolation. It is part of a whole. It is also useful to be able to view data from multiple servers in one administration interface. Here are the steps:

1. From within the Event Log on your management server, click on the Subscriptions node. A window will appear that asks if you want to enable the Windows Event Collector Service. Click Yes to start the service and configure it to automatically start with the computer. This enables the management server to collect events from other computers.

2. Next, from a command prompt on both the management server as well as any other servers you wish to collect events from, enter the command `winrm quickconfig`. This enables the Windows Remote Management service (WinRM), sets its initial network configuration, and prepares it for use by the Event Log (see Figure 7-19).

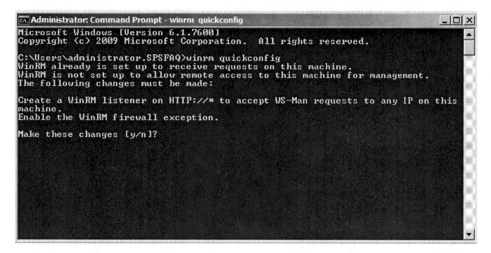

Figure 7-19. Enable WinRM.

3.   Computers that will be sending events to each other must have the proper authentication in place first. Do this by adding the computer account for your management server to the Administrators group on all servers you wish to collect events from. This may require a reboot.

4.   Finally, back on your management server, right-click the Subscriptions node and choose to Create Subscription. In the dialog that opens, enter in the necessary information that scopes the type of data you want to collect, how the data will be transferred, and any advanced settings that relate to the speed in which events are transferred. The steps for creating a subscription are in the "Create a Subscription" section earlier in this chapter.

Check Task Manager

Another location to check daily that gives you some immediate feedback is Task Manager. To start Task Manager, take any of the following alternative actions:

- Press CTRL+ALT+DELETE, and then click Task Manager

- Press CTRL+SHIFT+ESC

- Right-click an empty area of the taskbar, and then click Task Manager (see Figure 7-20).

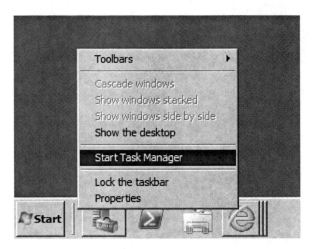

Figure 7-20. Starting Task Manager

Task Manger is a tool you can use daily to look out for potential bottlenecks and points of failure in your system. It is particularly useful because it is looking at your machine's performance in real time. It shows you the status of the programs that are running and allows you to end programs that have stopped responding. You can see graphs and data on CPU and memory usage; you can also view the network status and see how your network adapter is functioning. If you have more than one user logged on to the server, you can see who they are, what they are working on, and send them a message, which is useful if the server is in a remote location ad you are only one of a number of people with this level of access to it.

SharePoint's Monitoring Tools

Eternal vigilance is the price of liberty; power is ever stealing from the many to the few.

—Wendell Phillips

I'm using this quote to refer to power or system resources. It is as true of your SharePoint farm as it is of the liberty of people that it is ever being stolen by the few at the expense of the many. You have looked at the Windows tools for monitoring your farm's health, now let's drill down further to the tools within SharePoint you can use for monitoring. SharePoint Central Administration (Figure 7-21) has several monitoring tools (namely Health Analyzer, Timer Jobs, and Reporting) to help you maintain the eternal vigilance you will need to keep your farm resources free. First, let's look at how you might troubleshoot an error and then see where the information comes from.

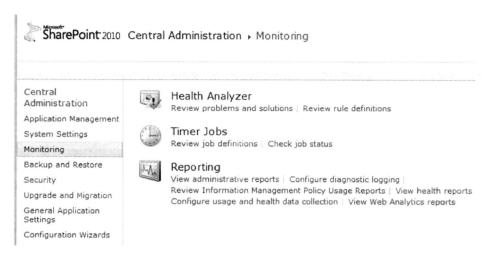

Figure 7-21. The monitoring options within SharePoint

Troubleshooting Errors

When something does go unexpectedly wrong despite all your alerts and monitors, it may appear as an error message like that in Figure 7-22. How do you find out what that long, enigmatic Correlation ID means?

Figure 7-22. The first step is find what the Correlation ID means.

Your first place to look should be the Operational logs in Server Manager (Figure 7-23). Here you will see the most recent SharePoint related events.

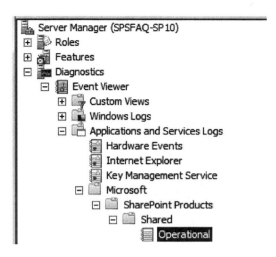

Figure 7-23. Check the logs.

If the error is not showing there, you can search the logs directly using Notepad. Locate C:\Program Files\Common Files\Microsoft Shared\Web Server Extensions\14\LOGS, open the latest logfile with Notepad, and then search for the correlation ID. You can also use PowerShell to locate and output the error to a text file. Locate the Correlation ID and corresponding error message with PowerShell. These commands are very CPU heavy, so use them sparingly.

Output to console:

```
Get-SPLogEvent | ?{$_.Correlation -eq "7cf3fec7-4a71-481a-8ad3-c845190e6947"} | select * |
Format-List
```

Output to text file:

```
Get-SPLogEvent | ?{$_.Correlation -eq "7cf3fec7-4a71-481a-8ad3-c845190e6947"} | select * |
Format-List | out-File CorrelationID-Error.txt
```

This will generate a file with the following text:

```
Timestamp : 06.05.2010 19:02:44

Continuation : False

Process : w3wp.exe (0x0ECC)

ThreadID : 4972

Area : SharePoint Foundation

Category : Runtime

EventID : tkau

Level : Unexpected
```

```
Message : Microsoft.Office.Server.Search.Query.SearchServiceNotFoundException: The search
request was unable to connect to the Search Service.

Correlation : 7cf3fec7-4a71-481a-8ad3-c845190e6947

Context : {}
```

Now you have a real message ("The search request was unable to connect to the Search Service.") that you can understand and use to fix the problem.

The Unified Logging Service

The Unified Logging Service (ULS) is the single, centralized location for logging error and informational messages related to SharePoint Server and Solutions. This means you have one place to look when you need to troubleshoot an issue or monitor the overall health the SharePoint application. It aggregates logs from the following three locations:

- SharePoint trace logs

- Windows Event Log (which I have discussed already)

- SharePoint logging database

The Unified Logging Service (ULS) viewer is an excellent way to get a real-time look at your logs. You download it from `http://archive.msdn.microsoft.com/ULSViewer/Release/ProjectReleases.aspx?ReleaseId=3308` and install it on your SharePoint server. Once installed, click CTRL+U and then OK to see the data being added to your log in real time (Figure 7-24).

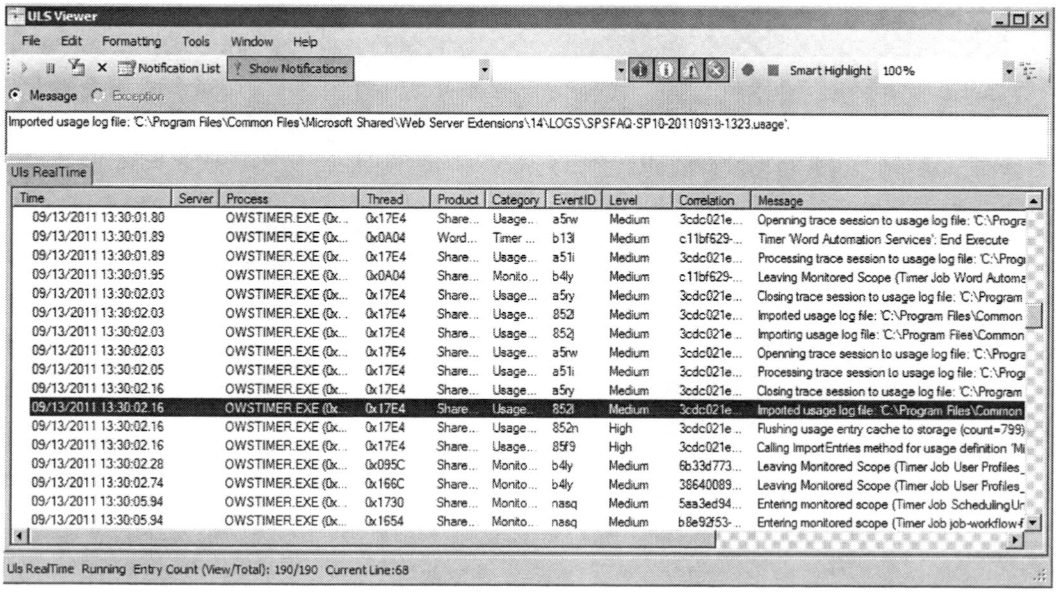

Figure 7-24. Your logs in real time

Try the Toggle Correlation Tree button. You could use the example correlation ID to trace a series of events inside SharePoint. A specific error may occur a number of times in a big ULS log file, but with the correlation ID you can easily track them. Another good feature is notifications. You can set the notification level for ULS Viewer; by default it will pop up and notify you of a Critical message.

Health Analyzer

This tool is used to automate the monitoring of the configuration of your SharePoint farm. It is clever because it does more than alert you to problems like the Event Viewer; it can fix the problems automatically for you. For example, if the logs are set to verbose and are going to fill up the disk capacity, the Health Analyzer can reset them. This is because each rule is in fact a DLL, a compiled program that can execute script. It runs inside a timer job and so is fully automatic.

You will notice it alerts you when you visit SharePoint Central Administration (Figure 7-25). In this example, it is on a yellow background but if there is a serious problem, it's red.

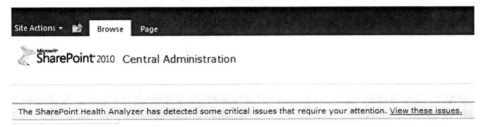

Figure 7-25. A Health Analyzer alert

There are over 60 rule definitions, all listed on the Review Rule Definitions page (Figure 7-26) in Health Analyzer. Each once can be scoped to every server on the farm and have a different schedule.

Figure 7-26. *Click here to create a Health Analyzer alert.*

As before, it is configured through rules that can be evaluated hourly, weekly, monthly or on demand. You can also configure it to send you alerts either by e-mail or SMS text message. Since some of these jobs only run monthly, if you have just set up your farm, you may want to run them all once to see your farm's initial health. To do this, run the following PowerShell (with thanks to Matthew McDermott for this):

```
$jobs = Get-SPTimerJob | Where-Object {$_.Title -like "Health Analysis Job*"}
foreach ($job in $jobs)
{
  $job.RunNow()
}
```

You can also see in Figure 7-26 the ability to manually re-run an individual rule to see if it is now being followed. The Review Problems and Solutions page, accessed under Health Analyzer in the Central Administration Monitoring section (see Figure 7-21) shows any problems your farm may be having.

Timer Jobs

Timer jobs are the clockwork mechanism of SharePoint—the cogs and moving parts of the system. You can monitor them from the Review Job Definitions page, accessed under Timer Jobs in the Central Administration Monitoring section; you can also manually run them to ensure they are working. The Check Job Status Page lets you see the history of when jobs were last run and if they were successful. This can be useful for troubleshooting.

Diagnostic Logging

There are three settings in diagnostic logging you can set for SharePoint 2010.

- Event Throttling

- Event Log Flood Protection

- Trace Log

These are accessed in Configure Diagnostic Logging under Reporting in the Central Administration Monitoring options. Let's consider each of these settings.

Event Throttling

Event throttling enables administrators to control the types of events that SharePoint Server logs based on the level of severity. The administration of throttling is divided into destination and category. Destination log entries can be reported in two places. The first is the standard Windows Event Log, which I have already discussed. Administrators can use the Windows Event Viewer application to review entries. The second is the ULS or "Trace Log," a text-based log format that is specific to SharePoint Server and is stored on the file system.

The event throttling dial can be applied to specific categories that map directly to SharePoint Server functionality. This enables the administrator to increase the logging detail for SharePoint components individually, thereby managing the size of the logs and the amount of information to review. The default settings for all categories are as follows:

- Event Log: Information

- Trace Log: Medium Level

During normal operation, these settings are an appropriate balance of detail and performance. During substantial reconfiguration of SharePoint Server, during the installation of custom solutions, or when SharePoint Server is experiencing issues, the throttling dial should be turned down. This ensures as much information is available as possible for troubleshooting. Finally, after completing any troubleshooting, logging can be returned to the default by selecting the "Reset to default" option in the throttling drop-downs. Settings that are not currently configured with the default option will appear in a bold font.

Event Log Flood Protection

Event Log Flood Protection prevents the Event Log from being overwhelmed with many repetitive events. When it is enabled (default), it will start trimming events after the same event is logged five times within two minutes. At this point, it suppresses additional entries. After an additional two minutes, it throws a summary event that describes the number of times that the event would have been repeated. An administrator can modify these thresholds.

Trace Log

The trace logs are the standard log files for SharePoint. They are tab-delimited text and open with any tool that can open text files, but as I mentioned, the ULS viewer is a great way to look at these. By default, trace logs are located in the LOGS directory of the SharePoint root (also called the 14 Hive) at `C:\Program Files\Common Files\Microsoft Shared\Web Server Extensions\14`.

Summary

> *mens sana in corpore sano ("A sound mind in a sound body")*

> —Juvenal, Satire X

You can see there are two ways to approach monitoring SharePoint: through the general Windows tools like Event Viewer in Server Manager or monitoring in SharePoint Central Administration. Which is better? I think of SharePoint as the mind: it contains the information generated by users and developers. The farm hardware, network, and software is the body: it sustains and holds the SharePoint application. If the body is sound, the mind will be, too. The SharePoint application is so dependent on the network infrastructure that if anything is wrong with SQL Server or Windows or the network, it will affect SharePoint. I tend to keep my monitoring focus on Windows in general as there is more that can go wrong there. If I can't identify the cause there, I look deeper into the SharePoint logs via the ULS viewer. The information in this chapter gives you the guidance and direction you need to do the same.

CHAPTER 8

DIY DR

Until now, this book has focused on disaster recovery and backup from the point of view of the business stakeholders and the infrastructure owners. A full farm backup will recover content databases, farm settings, solutions, and service applications. These solutions are only useful if the entire farm is lost but they don't address recovery from a user's perspective. Users sometimes only need to recover smaller parts of the farm as their focus is just on their content. SharePoint provides options for recovering the following elements of interest to users:

- List items
- Documents
- Lists
- Libraries
- Sites
- Site collections

The following low-level configuration and structuring elements can also be preserved:

- Lists of who has access to one library or site
- Site columns and content types
- Web Part pages

SharePoint puts more and more of the options for preserving content into the hands of the users themselves. This makes sense: they can preserve a site or list immediately without having to ask the IT department to do it for them. The focus of this book so far has been what the architects, farm owners, and SharePoint strategists can do to deliver a high availability and disaster recovery strategy. This chapter shows that the means to back up and restore content are increasingly becoming available to the user community. Knowing the information contained in this chapter means you can plan for training and processes to ensure that users can Do It Themselves. Specifically, with Service Pack 1 for SharePoint 2010, users can now restore deleted sites from the Recycle Bin. This is a sure sign that the trend is towards users owning recovery of data, not IT.

Even an enterprise architect occasionally needs a few small tools in their box for backing up and recovering these small parts of the farm. Knowing how to use the big tools to back up the entire farm is only part of the range of options you should have in the event an individual content owner requests a solution to maintain their own disaster recovery strategy. If some of the smaller parts of the farm are lost, you can recommend the options covered in this chapter to restore them. It shouldn't be necessary to restore a copy of a whole farm to get one list back.

Again, the purpose of this chapter is to show these Do It Yourself (DIY) options to put some of the tasks of maintaining backups of valuable content and settings in the hands of the users. I am using DIY in the sense that these are tools the users themselves can use without requiring farm administrator rights. Some require Site Collection Administrator rights, like saving a site as a template, but others, like recovering a file from a Recycle Bin, only require site membership. If you have focused most of your energy on looking at SharePoint from the 10,000-foot architecture level, you may have missed some of the small, handy options available to your users, so I have focused this chapter on detailing them for you.

One of the reasons SharePoint, and indeed Microsoft in general, is successful is that it puts the control in the hands of the users. Technology is complicated, but tools can use simple metaphors to make them more accessible. SharePoint allows users to back up and recover some of their own content; in this way, it not only saves resources on the infrastructure side, but it also saves the users' time because they can restore what they need more quickly.

This chapter will focus on the following recovery options:

- The Recycle Bin

- Versioning in SharePoint

- Recovery of sites and site collections

- Office as a DR tool

- Templates

Let's start with the simplest scenario: accidental deletion of a document.

The Recycle Bin

Despite appearances, every SharePoint site doesn't fully delete a document or list item if you select that option. It actually hides the item from the List view and displays it instead in the Recycle Bin. It is not moved until it is really deleted. Until then, if you restore it from the Recycle Bin, it appears again in the list with all the same permissions, version history, and list item ID because it was not actually deleted at all. That happens later depending on the settings for the site.

Recycle Bin Settings

The settings for the Recycle Bin are set by the Farm Administrator and these determine if there is a Recycle Bin and how it functions. First I'll recap some terminology. Web applications in logical terms are the settings for the web site SharePoint resides in. The settings include the type of authentication used and general settings that apply to all the site collections within it, such as the regional time zone. Site collections consist of a root site based on a specific template and all the subsites under it. These also share some settings, like groups and content types. In code, the subsites are referred to as *webs*, while the site collection is referred to as *the site*.

You turn on and configure Recycle Bins at the web application level. By default, Recycle Bins are turned on in all the site collections in a web application. Here are the steps to configure Recycle Bin settings for a web application:

1. Verify that the user account performing this procedure is a member of the Farm Administrators SharePoint group.

2. On the SharePoint Central Administration web site, click Application Management.

3. On the Application Management page, click Manage Web Applications.

4. Click the web application for which you want to configure Recycle Bin settings. The ribbon becomes active.

5. On the ribbon, click the General Settings drop-down menu, and then click General Settings (Figure 8-1).

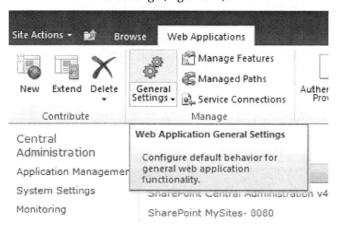

Figure 8-1. Select the web application and the General Setting option appears.

6. On the Web Application General Settings page, in the Recycle Bin section, you can configure certain settings (Figure 8-2).

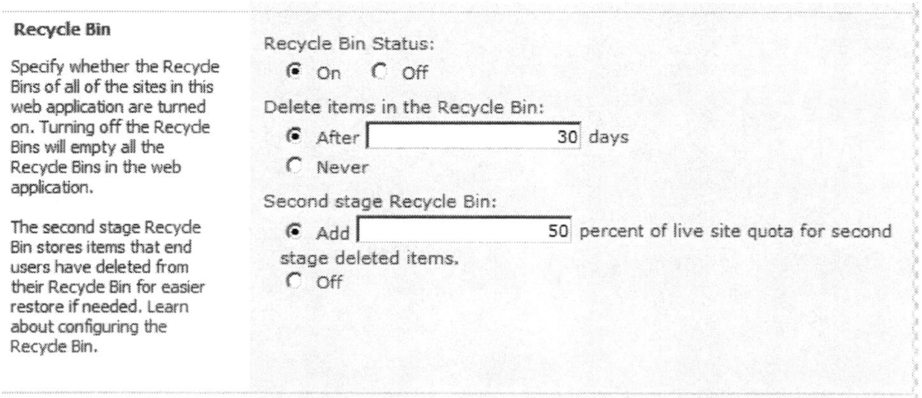

Recycle Bin

Specify whether the Recycle Bins of all of the sites in this web application are turned on. Turning off the Recycle Bins will empty all the Recycle Bins in the web application.

The second stage Recycle Bin stores items that end users have deleted from their Recycle Bin for easier restore if needed. Learn about configuring the Recycle Bin.

Recycle Bin Status:
- ⦿ On   ◯ Off

Delete items in the Recycle Bin:
- ⦿ After [30] days
- ◯ Never

Second stage Recycle Bin:
- ⦿ Add [50] percent of live site quota for second stage deleted items.
- ◯ Off

Figure 8-2. Options for the Recycle Bin

The options refer to the first and second stage Recycle Bin. Each site in the site collection has a Recycle Bin, but if an item is deleted from there, it is then shown in the second stage Recycle Bin. Think if this as the large bin behind the building. The document hasn't been taken away yet, but it's no longer in the bin under your desk. This bin is only accessible to site collection administrators, and most users are not aware of it. I once had a situation where a pompous manager e-mailed all the staff in his department trying to find out who had deleted an important document. The funny thing was, after he realized it was him, he tried to cover his tracks by deleting it from the Recycle Bin. When I restored it from the second stage (Site Collection) Recycle Bin, I made sure some of his staff knew what he'd done because I knew he wasn't going to tell them!

Accessing the Second Stage Recycle Bin

Because the second stage Recycle Bin can use a large portion of your site quota (the default is 50 percent; see Figure 8-2) you should know how and where to manage it. This is not something you can rely on your site collection administrators to know about unless they have had thorough training. From a farm capacity management perspective, you can keep the site Recycle Bin only and turn off the second stage Recycle Bin if you wish. You may do this to allow users to maintain their site quota without needing site collection administrator rights. If they empty their site Recycle Bins, they can reclaim space from their quota immediately without needing the content to then be deleted from the site collection Recycle Bin. As a high level farm owner, you may not be aware of how to access the site collection Recycle Bin, so here are the steps:

1. First go to site settings logged in as a site collection administrator or higher (see Figure 8-3).

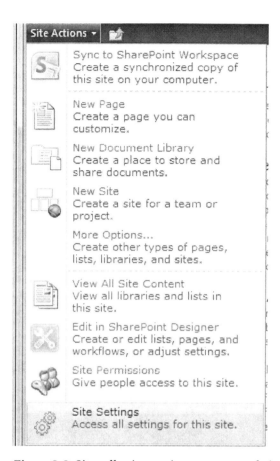

Figure 8-3. Site collection settings are accessed via Site Settings.

2. Then click the Recycle Bin link under Site Collection Administration (Figure 8-4). This section will not be there if you are not logged in with site collection administrator rights, even though you can access the page with site administrator rights.

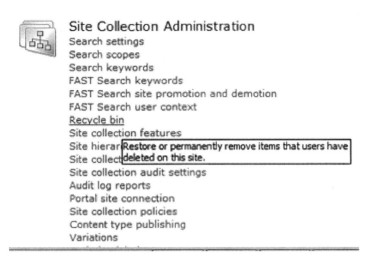

Figure 8-4. *How to access the second stage Recycle Bin settings*

3.   You can now find out a few things about the deleted items, such as the original location, who deleted it, and at what time (Figure 8-5).

Figure 8-5. *Deletion history*

4.   You can filter the bin by these columns. You can also only view items that were explicitly deleted from the site Recycle Bins, also known as the first stage Recycle Bins (Figure 8-6). By default you see everything in the first stage Recycle Bins also.

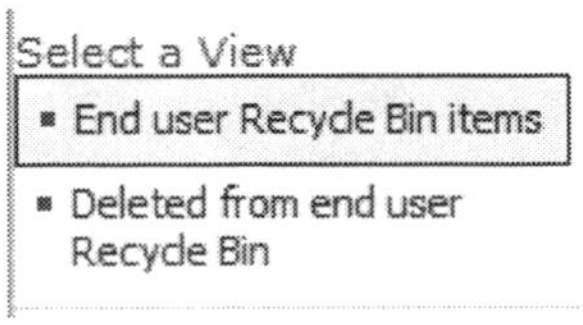

Select a View

- ▪ End user Recycle Bin items

- ▪ Deleted from end user Recycle Bin

Figure 8-6. *View options*

Note the default 30 days applies to the total time after the item was first deleted and not the time spent in either Recycle Bin stage.

When a second-stage Recycle Bin is enabled for a web application, Microsoft recommends that you designate how much disk space is available to the second-stage Recycle Bin as a percentage of the quota allotted to the web application (Figure 8-3). Items stored in the second-stage Recycle Bin don't count toward the site quota; however, the size that is specified for the second-stage Recycle Bin increases the total size of the site and the content database that hosts it. If no site quota has been set, there is no limit on the size of the second-stage Recycle Bin. As a result, the user could be within her quota but actually using far more capacity in SQL Server.

For example, if you have allotted 100MB of space for the web application, allotting a 50 percent quota for the second-stage Recycle Bin allows for 50MB for the second-stage Recycle Bin and 150MB for the web application as a whole. You can specify up to 100 percent for the second-stage Recycle Bin quota.

Exceptions

There are exceptions and reasons why content may not be in the Recycle Bin. The main point to note is that content deleted via the Datasheet view is not preserved in the Recycle Bin. The Datasheet view is an Excel-like interface for a list to allow fast editing of multiple rows and columns.

You should also note that the Recycle Bin still enforces the item's security. The user who has deleted the content will be able to see the content in the Recycle Bin. Other users will not be able to see the items in the Recycle Bin if they don't have access to the location the item is in. Otherwise, the Recycle Bin would be a serious security hole. Every user who has access to the site, even viewer level, can open the Recycle Bin, but they will only be able to see content they otherwise have access to. This is because the item is still in its original location—just hidden from there and shown in the Recycle Bin. If you have deleted a top level item like a folder or a list, and you try to find a document available at an inner location, the item will not be viewable. By default, the Recycle Bin shows the top level content and doesn't have the capability to show the items in a tree structure or drill down mode. Also, if the item was deleted before the default 30-day limit or if it was pushed beyond the second stage Recycle Bin quota, it will not be in the bin.

Versioning as a Recovery Tool

Versioning is the functionality that keeps each previous iteration of a document as a separate file; you can open a copy of the file as it looked in the past without losing the current iteration. In the context of DIY DR, it means that if a user overwrites or deletes part of a document, she can recover it from the previous version of the document. This is often overlooked as a means of recovering lost content. But it must be configured by the site administrator, and the user must diligently create versions of the document—not just keep pressing Save. Setting the versioning for an individual library is done via the Library Settings page (Figure 8-7).

Library Tools
Site Actions
Browse
Documents
Library
spsfaq\Administrator
Standard View
Datasheet View
View Format
New Row
Datasheet
Create View
Current View:
All Documents
Current Page
Manage Views
E-mail a Link
RSS Feed
Share & Track
Sync to SharePoint Workspace
Connect to Office
Connect & Export
Form Web Parts
Edit Library
New Quick Step
Customize Library
Library Settings
Settings
Libraries
Site Pages
Shared Documents
Type
Name
Modified
New Microsoft Word Document
8/31/2011 4:08 PM
Add document
Library Settings
Go to the Library Settings page to manage settings such as permissions, columns, views and policy.

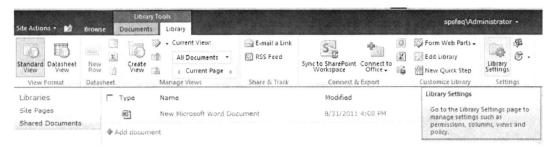

Figure 8-7. *Accessing library settings*

Figure 8-8 shows the available settings.

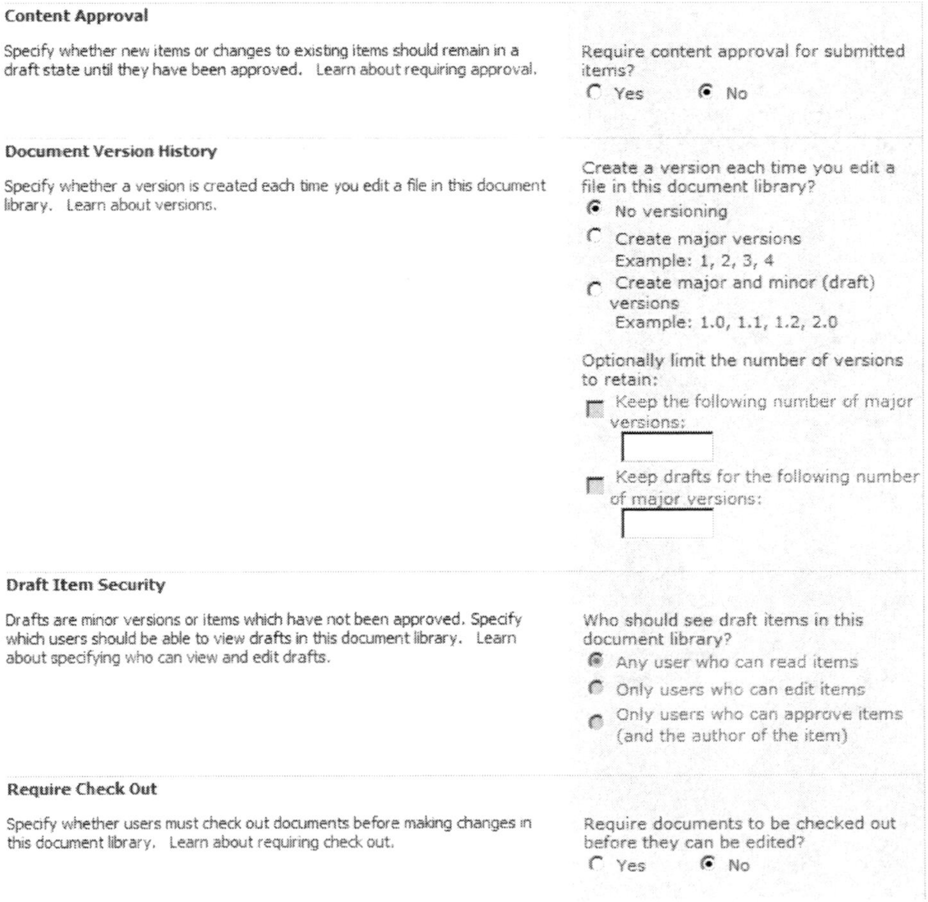

Content Approval
Specify whether new items or changes to existing items should remain in a draft state until they have been approved. Learn about requiring approval.
Require content approval for submitted items?
Yes
No
Document Version History
Specify whether a version is created each time you edit a file in this document library. Learn about versions.
Create a version each time you edit a file in this document library?
No versioning
Create major versions
Example: 1, 2, 3, 4
Create major and minor (draft) versions
Example: 1.0, 1.1, 1.2, 2.0
Optionally limit the number of versions to retain:
Keep the following number of major versions:
Keep drafts for the following number of major versions:
Draft Item Security
Drafts are minor versions or items which have not been approved. Specify which users should be able to view drafts in this document library. Learn about specifying who can view and edit drafts.
Who should see draft items in this document library?
Any user who can read items
Only users who can edit items
Only users who can approve items (and the author of the item)
Require Check Out
Specify whether users must check out documents before making changes in this document library. Learn about requiring check out.
Require documents to be checked out before they can be edited?
Yes
No

Figure 8-8. *Library settings*

It is wise to set a limit on the number of versions kept because each version takes up the same amount of space as the main file. This can really add up. I once had a situation where 400 versions of a 3MB Excel spreadsheet were using up all of a site collection's quota: 1,200MB is about 1.2GB.

Requiring checkout ensures users create a "hard" version of the document each time they want to edit it. If a user opens a file and starts to edit it, this is called a "soft" version. This is because a new version is not created until he explicitly checks it back in. It is checked out to him behind the scenes and locked, but there is no new version yet even though changes are saved. This option can slow down access to files, however, so it should only be enabled if the documents must have this level of control. User training should explain the value of versioning as a DIY DR option.

If you wanted to set this all across your sites, you would have to create a site template with these options set. What constitutes the best settings here will require consultation with your users. Best practices would be to ensure versioning is turned off if it's not needed. A good threshold is 10 versions. This is reasonable when there are 3-5 people collaborating on a document, as each of them will have around 2-3 versions of the document. When an 11th version is added, it becomes number 10 and the 1st is removed. There is no hard and fast rule, however. Training users to know about and adjust these settings themselves is the ideal solution here. They are not meant to be controlled centrally, which is why they are available at the Library level.

Recovering Sites and Site Collections

The philosophy behind SharePoint has always been to delegate decisions to users, like with versioning. Deleting a whole site collection and all its content is quite easy for the owner of that site collection to do. From a user point of view, after clicking the option to delete a site collection, the owner is presented with the message shown in Figure 8-9, which warns them of the ramifications. Even after they click Delete, another prompt appears to ensure they want to do this (see Figure 8-10). But occasionally mistakes are made.

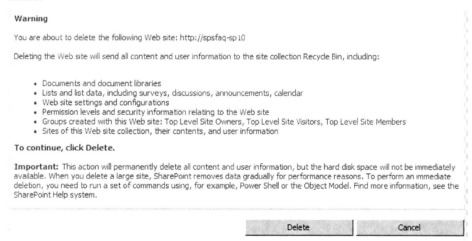

Warning

You are about to delete the following Web site: http://spsfaq-sp10

Deleting the Web site will send all content and user information to the site collection Recycle Bin, including:

- Documents and document libraries
- Lists and list data, including surveys, discussions, announcements, calendar
- Web site settings and configurations
- Permission levels and security information relating to the Web site
- Groups created with this Web site: Top Level Site Owners, Top Level Site Visitors, Top Level Site Members
- Sites of this Web site collection, their contents, and user information

To continue, click Delete.

Important: This action will permanently delete all content and user information, but the hard disk space will not be immediately available. When you delete a large site, SharePoint removes data gradually for performance reasons. To perform an immediate deletion, you need to run a set of commands using, for example, Power Shell or the Object Model. Find more information, see the SharePoint Help system.

| Delete | Cancel |

Figure 8-9. Deleting a site collection: first chance to turn back

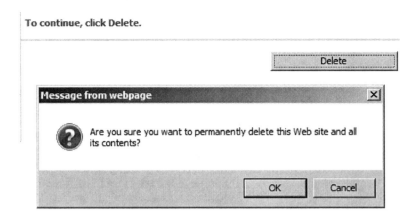

Figure 8-10. Deleting a site collection: the last chance dialog box

Previous to Service Pack 1 of SharePoint 2010, the only way to restore the site collection was for the site collection administrator to ask the farm administrator to take the backup of the content database and restore it to the night before, thus restoring the site collection—and many other site collections in the same content database. This was not a satisfactory solution as in most cases it lost more content than was deleted. Deleting subsites also gave similar dialogs, but if the site had to be restored, again the only option was to bring it back from a backup of the whole content database.

However, Service Pack 1 for SharePoint Server 2010 added the facility to place subsites in the second stage Recycle Bin (Figure 8-11). This is the clearest indication that backup and restoring have become more user-centric.

Figure 8-11. Restoring a site with SP1 installed

Recovery with PowerShell and Service Pack 1 for SharePoint 2010

For site collections to be restorable via PowerShell, you must have the service pack installed on your farm to add this functionality. It's a significant improvement on the previous situation as now a site collection administrator can recover a site, not just a farm administrator. The deleted site collections are stored in the SPDeletedSite object. The Get-SPDeletedSite cmdlet lists all the deleted site collections. The Get-SPDeletedSite returns an array if Get-SPDeletedSite is greater than one. Use the following command to get the count:

```
(Get-SPDeletedSite).Count
```

All you need to do now is bind this with the Restore-SPDeletedSite cmdlet.

```
Get-SPDeletedSite | where{$_.SiteId -eq "xxxxxxxx-xxxx-xxxx-xxxx-xxxxxxxxxxxx"} | Restore-
SPDeletedSite
```

Office as DIY DR Tool

It is worth mentioning, even though it's not strictly SharePoint, that Word (2010) also helps preserve your users' content by auto-saving and using something called the Backstage view. This is the default view when you click the File tab in Office. Documenting, training, and presenting this to users is the likeliest route for this information to get to them. I am presenting it here as another method for recovering lost content in the interest of completeness. It's part of your organization's disaster recovery processes in the sense that it's a way to recover data. In prior versions of Office, Word would periodically save your document in the background when you were editing it. This file was retained so the user could use it to recover their work if the application crashed. For Word, Excel, and PowerPoint, Office 2010 improves on this idea. In the Backstage view, Microsoft exposes the periodic auto-saved files from your current editing session and allows you to compare or restore them as the newest document (see Figure 8-12). Even if you don't save a file, these are kept for five days.

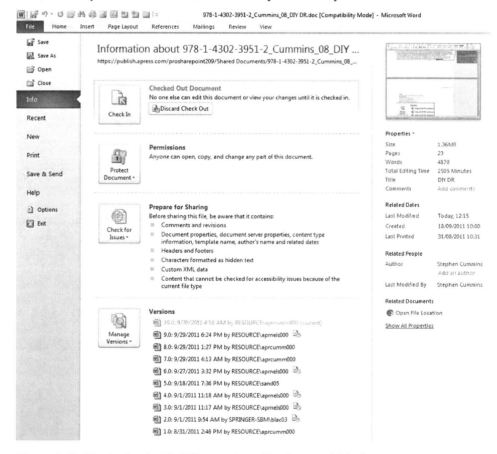

Figure 8-12. Versioning inside Office: a view of Backstage of this chapter

These unsaved versions are purged when you save and close your editing session. The settings for how documents are saved are found in File Word Options Save (Figure 8-13).

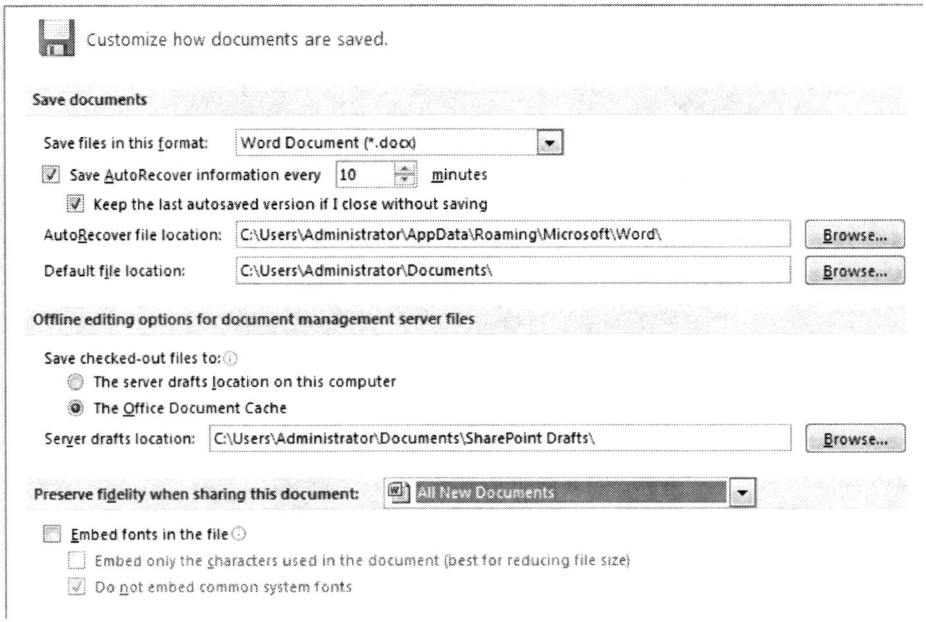

Figure 8-13. *The Save options in Word*

Even if you close an editing session without saving the file, Office will now keep the last auto-saved version. When you open the document again, the unsaved version will appear in the Versions section of the Backstage view's Info window (see Figure 8-14). Office also lets you access it directly from the Backstage view by clicking Manage Versions in the Info window and selecting Recover Unsaved Documents (see Figure 8-15). The Recover Unsaved Documents link also is available at the bottom of the Backstage view's Recent window.

■ **Note** When you click the Recover Unsaved Documents link, Office takes you to the default UnSavedFiles folder. However, your AutoRecover file location may be different. If you don't see the auto-saved files, check your Save options (Figure 8-13) and then navigate to the appropriate location.

Versions

🖼 Yesterday, 4:41 PM (when I closed without saving)

Figure 8-14. The Versions section after reopening a file that wasn't resaved after a Word autosave

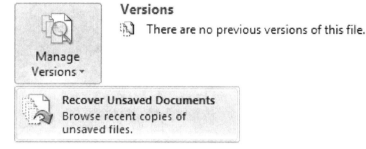

Figure 8-15. In Backstage view, select Info and then Manage Versions to see the link to recover unsaved documents.

Content Backup Using Templates

Another way in which SharePoint is putting content retention in the hands of users, albeit as an indirect benefit, is in the use of the SharePoint template process. Templates in SharePoint Server 2010 are intended to allow you to reuse content by making a copy of a list or site, including its content, and allowing you to make a new list or site in a new location with that same content. This functionality can also be used to make a quick backup of a list or site at any time by any user who has only site owner rights. So if a site owner desires an extra level of security, this can be achieved without the intervention of the farm-level administration staff. This can be useful if an instant snapshot is required.

It should be noted this method will not preserve the Created By and Created time, nor will it preserve the access rights on the site or list. It will, however, preserve the content and views, which would likely take more time to recreate. Another caveat: Microsoft has restricted the maximum size of list and site templates to 10MB (10,485,760 bytes). If you try to save site/list templates that are larger than 10MB in size, you will get a "The list is too large to save as a template. The size of a template cannot exceed 10485760 bytes." error. To resolve this issue, I have seen it suggested you can run this command in the command prompt:

```
stsadm -o setproperty -propertyname max-template-document-size -propertyvalue 524288000
```

However, I don't recommend you do this. It can lead to errors in the restore process of the site; sometimes the command completes successfully, but the limit stays in place. With these warnings in mind, templates are still a useful way to make a quick backup of content, so I will show you how to do it. If your site is too large to be preserved this way, using Central Administration is your only fallback—and one that is not available to the average user.

How to Make a List Template

First, browse to the list or library you wish to back up, then click the Library tab under Library tools (Figure 8-16).

Figure 8-16. *Accessing Library settings*

Second, click List or Library Settings, and then under Permissions and Management, click "Save list as template" (Figure 8-17).

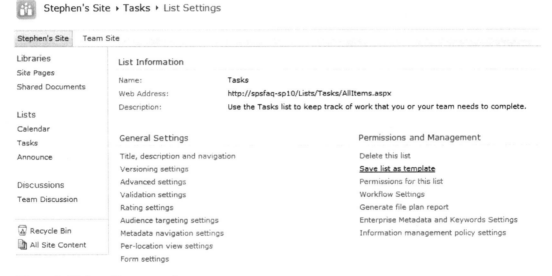

Figure 8-17. *Save list as template*

■ **Note** The procedure is the same for a list or library. For example, if you browse to a Document Library, the link to the Settings page is called "Library Settings." In the case of a list, it is called "List Settings." Following this idea, the links to save a template are called "Save document library as template" and "Save list as template," respectively.

Once you have clicked the "Save list as template" link, the form shown in Figure 8-18 opens.

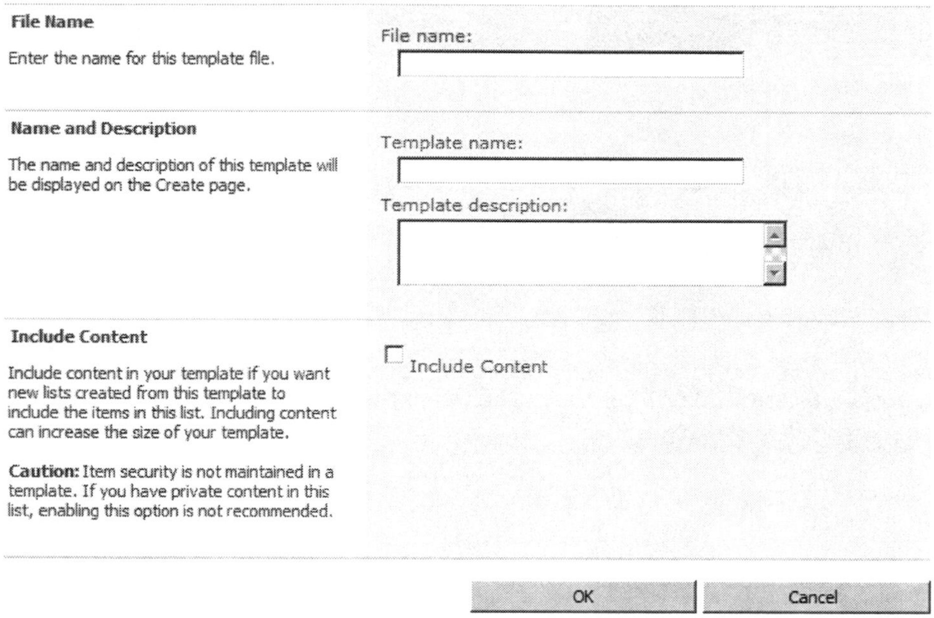

File Name

Enter the name for this template file.

File name:

Name and Description

The name and description of this template will be displayed on the Create page.

Template name:

Template description:

Include Content

Include content in your template if you want new lists created from this template to include the items in this list. Including content can increase the size of your template.

Caution: Item security is not maintained in a template. If you have private content in this list, enabling this option is not recommended.

☐ Include Content

OK   Cancel

Figure 8-18. Creating your template

When completing this form, make sure you check the box that says Include Content. Otherwise, you are only preserving the columns and views. After completing the form, (in my case, I simply called the template "test"), click OK; you should see the message in Figure 8-19. Then click the "list template gallery" link.

Operation Completed Successfully

The template has successfully been saved to the list template gallery. You can now create lists based on this template.

To manage templates in the gallery, go to the list template gallery.

To return to the list customization page, click **OK**.

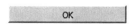

OK

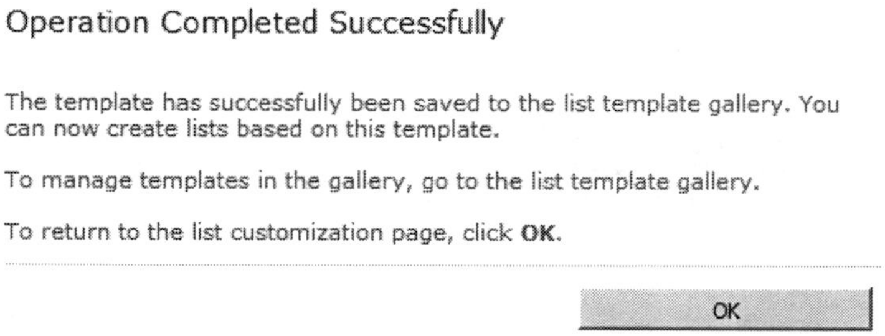

Figure 8-19. Click the list template gallery link

Once you click on the "list template gallery" link, you will be on a page like that in Figure 8-20. Selecting the list template you just created will change the ribbon to the one shown in Figure 8-20.

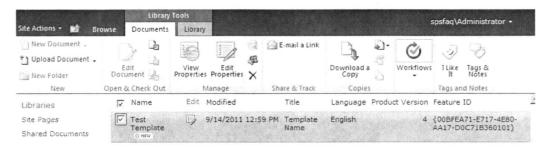

Figure 8-20. Select the template to change the ribbon

Click "Download a Copy" and copy the file (which has an .stp) extension to a location where you can access it easily. This file (see Figure 8-21) now contains all of the content from your list.

Figure 8-21. Your backup of the list

If you want to just find the template again, browse to Site Actions Site Settings Galleries List templates. With this .stp file, you have a backup of your list. You can now import that into any list template gallery and use it to recreate your list and its content. Just click Upload Document (see Figure 8-22) to add the template and use it in that site collection. I uploaded mine and called it "Book Template Test."

Figure 8-22. Upload a template to a Template Gallery

Now the most important step: you can now use this template to restore the list. You can even restore it alongside the existing one by giving it a different name, just to recover something from it. This would only be necessary if it was not in the Recycle Bin, like the example of something deleted via Datasheet view, or if you had to restore something that was older than the time limit on the primary or secondary Recycle Bins. This could be useful in the case of SharePoint Online.

To do this, go to Site Actions and select More Options (or New Document Library in the case of a Document Library), as shown in Figure 8-23.

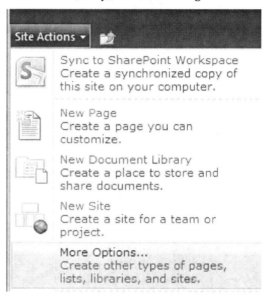

Figure 8-23. Create a new list or library to recreate your content

As you can see from Figure 8-24, your list maintains the same list type it was based on. Mine was based on the Announcement list, so it has the same icon and structure.

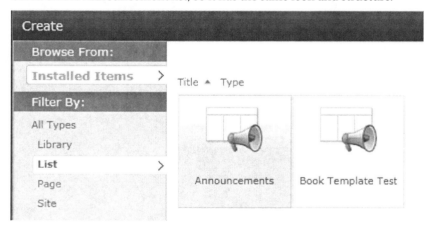

Figure 8-24. Book template test: the new list template including the content

Create your list and you will see you have all the content and views again.

How to Make a Site Template

The process of creating a site template is similar to that of creating a list template. First, click Site Actions Site Settings. Under the Site Actions heading click "Save site as template" (Figure 8-25).

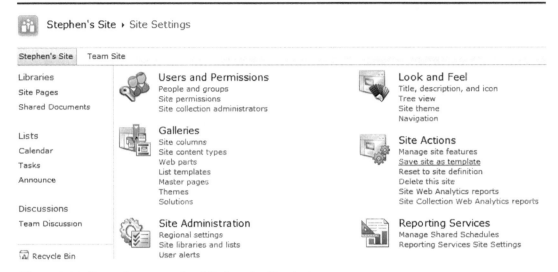

Figure 8-25. "Save site as template" link under Site Actions

Once you have clicked this link, the form in Figure 8-26 opens.

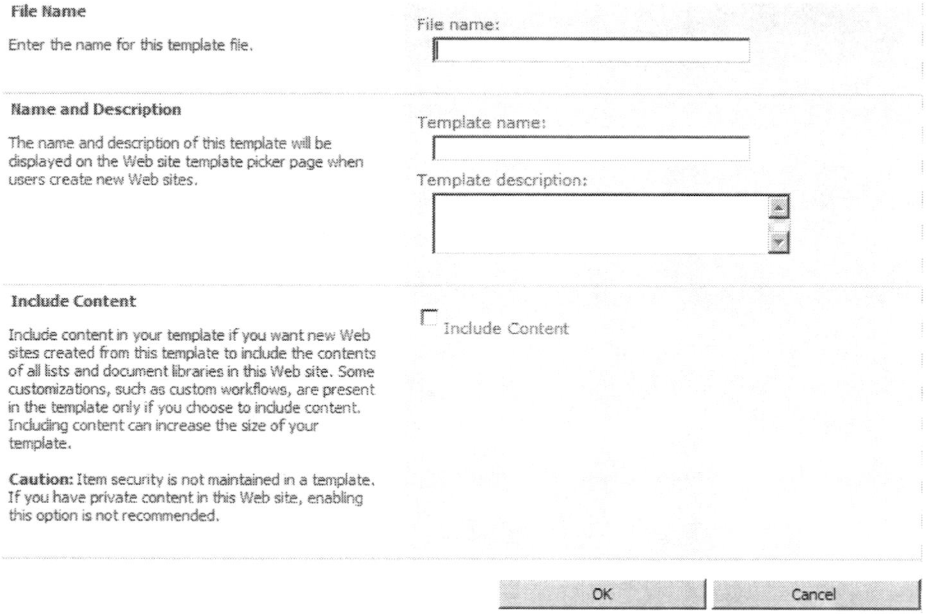

File Name

Enter the name for this template file.

File name:

Name and Description

The name and description of this template will be displayed on the Web site template picker page when users create new Web sites.

Template name:

Template description:

Include Content

Include content in your template if you want new Web sites created from this template to include the contents of all lists and document libraries in this Web site. Some customizations, such as custom workflows, are present in the template only if you choose to include content. Including content can increase the size of your template.

Caution: Item security is not maintained in a template. If you have private content in this Web site, enabling this option is not recommended.

☐ Include Content

[OK]   [Cancel]

Figure 8-26. Creating your template

When completing this form, make sure you check the box that says Include Content. Otherwise, you are only preserving the lists, libraries, and web part page layouts. Click OK and the message in Figure 8-27 should display. Then click the "solution gallery" link.

Operation Completed Successfully

The web site has successfully been saved to the solutions gallery. You can now create sites based on this solution.

To manage solutions in the gallery, go to the solution gallery.

To return to the site administration page, click **OK**.

[OK]

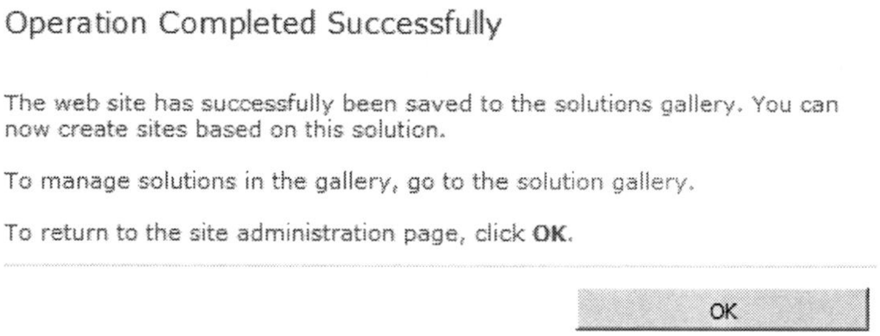

Figure 8-27. Click the "solution gallery" link

Once you click on the "solution gallery" link, you will be on a page like the one in Figure 8-28. Right-click the site template you just created and select "Save target as" to copy the file (which has an .wsp extension) to a location where you can access it easily.

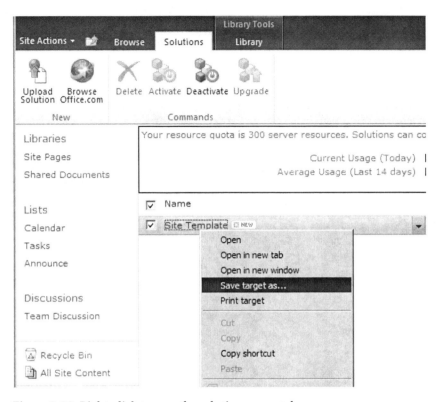

Figure 8-28. Right-click to save the solution separately

This file now contains all of the content from your site. With this .wsp file, you have a backup of your site. You can now import that into any solution gallery in any site collection and use it to recreate your site and its content. Just click Upload Solution to add the template and use it in that site collection (Figure 8-29).

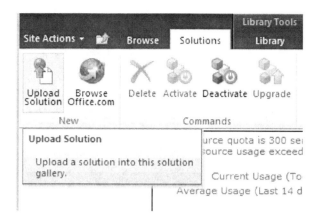

Figure 8-29. Upload a site template to a solution gallery

Now the most important step: you can now use this template to restore the site. You can even restore it alongside the existing one by giving it a different name, just to recover something from it. This would only be necessary if it was not in the Recycle Bin, like if you had to restore something that was older than the time limit on the primary or secondary Recycle Bins. This could be useful in the case of SharePoint Online.

If you want to find the template again, browse to Site Actions ▸ Site Settings ▸ Galleries ▸ Solutions. You can now use this template to restore the site if it is deleted. To do this, go to Site Actions ▸ and select New Site (Figure 8-30).

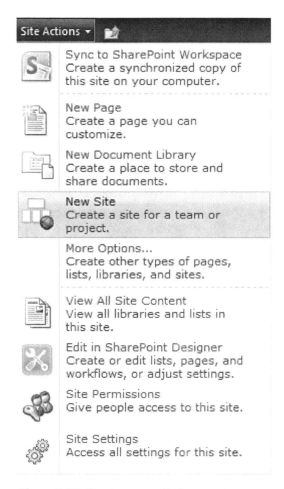

Figure 8-30. Create a new site to recreate your content

Create your site and you will see you have all the content and views again (see Figure 8-31).

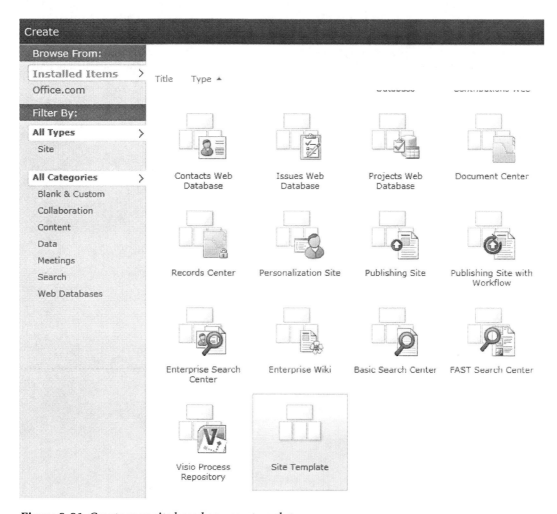

Figure 8-31. Create your site based on your template

In both cases, this is a way to recreate the site or list in another place, either in the same site collection or just in another site.

Summary

This chapter shows that the task of maintaining backups of valuable content need not be the exclusive domain of the IT staff. Giving users the responsibility for and means to back up their own content is an excellent idea from an organizational point of view as it is likely to save resources in both backup space and IT man-hours. IT usually has to back up everything that users produce because IT has no idea what's important and what isn't. If something goes wrong, the pressure is on IT to have preserved the right content and to be able to recover it. If users own these processes themselves, they will have a greater sense of control and ownership of the platform and a sense that they can create reassurances for themselves. This has the added benefit of freeing up resources in the IT department for other tasks. It not only save resources in the form of people: a quick backup of a site or list using these methods means that large amounts of unnecessary data doesn't need to be duplicated in multiple locations. This way, there is a duplicate but it's for a good reason. Users can think of it as their own personal lifeboat in case of disaster.

CHAPTER 9

Change Management and DR

"The one unchangeable certainty is that nothing is unchangeable or certain"

—John F. Kennedy

In this chapter I will describe two processes: one for managing non-development change in SharePoint and one for approving and rejecting development changes to your SharePoint environment. The processes for assessing which adjustments should be made to your SharePoint system are referred to as change management. The continuous process of managing the life of an application through governance, development, and maintenance is referred to as application lifecycle management. I will provide you with templates for both of these processes. I'll also describe some of the reasons why change is resisted by IT departments, why change is necessary, but also why too much change is dangerous in a way that can be more sudden and destructive than too little.

Things change. Organizations reorganize. People move to different roles or employers. Business requirements change to realign with the changing needs of customers. IT systems are patched and changed to grow with greater demand and usage from the business. Changing SharePoint is not simple. The SharePoint platform is complex and interdependent with other systems. As a result, changing it can have unpredictable results in SharePoint and in the interdependent systems. Trying to resist change by seeing it as merely a risk to the system, however, only leads to it being forced upon the system eventually by something beyond your control. It is fair to say there are risks inherent in change, such as the following:

- Unavailability

- Poorer performance

- Weaker security

- Non-adoption by users

- Greater cost

- Need for more training

There are potential gains, too, which are based on the fact that better technology should make your tasks and processes better. These gains include the following:

- Higher availability

- Faster performance

- Stronger security

- More adoption by users

- Lower costs

- A simplified user experience (UX) means less training

The focus in relation to change by those who own SharePoint should be proactive—a process of refinement and improvement. For this to be possible, you must first have processes in place to manage change in your SharePoint environment. If change can be done properly, it will be the life-blood of your system, increasing its value to the organization constantly. If change is not managed properly, it leads to system stagnation and lack of use, and eventually it becomes a cost with no benefit to your organization. In terms of availability, the biggest threat to your SharePoint farm is the system owners' inability to manage change. In a sense, change is the engine of SharePoint that needs constant fuel to keep the whole system moving forward and moving toward the organization's goals.

Entropy

"Any method involving the notion of entropy, the very existence of which depends on the second law of thermodynamics, will doubtless seem to many far-fetched, and may repel beginners as obscure and difficult of comprehension."

—Willard Gibbs, *Graphical Methods in the Thermodynamics of Fluids* (1873)

Like everything else in our universe, SharePoint is a system prone to entropy. I'm defining it as "the tendency for all matter and energy in the universe to evolve toward a state of inert uniformity." Too much entropy is the enemy of SharePoint: if entropy takes control, SharePoint loses energy and eventually ceases to be useful to the organization. Ultimately, SharePoint is subject to what are known as the laws of thermodynamics: the relationship between energy and motion, or in a sense, change.

The second law of thermodynamics states that in general the total entropy of any system will not decrease other than by increasing the entropy of some other system. Your IT owner is acting on this idea: if SharePoint isolated from the users, the entropy of SharePoint will tend not to decrease. If you keep the users from changing it, SharePoint will not change. But keeping SharePoint useful takes work; it can't simply be left unchanged to stay effective. Adding content doesn't really change the system. The structure and processes in the system have to be changed and become more efficient. Users and the IT owners must be constantly looking for ways to use SharePoint to make their tasks easier, faster, cheaper, or at least more pleasant.

Secondly, to keep something running, you have to keep adding energy. You can't make SharePoint "run itself" by one big shove at the beginning. This is an assumption in many businesses: put a large amount of effort into launching SharePoint and it will create its own momentum and run itself. It eventually runs out of momentum just by following the laws of entropy. The business then complains that it is SharePoint's fault when it gradually becomes more inert and useless. Entropy takes over.

It follows that a reduction in the increase of entropy in a specified process, such as a chemical reaction, means that it is more efficient. This is good news for us if we put this in a SharePoint context: if we can make changing SharePoint less work, we not only make it more efficient, we reduce the risk of entropy in the system, which will destroy it.

There is an unspoken assumption among infrastructure people that system stability and reliability are best maintained by keeping the business away from the technology. They are trying to reduce entropy. The users' needs are perceived as a threat to the integrity of the SharePoint farm. For it to continue to be stable, the IT department's role is to resist change; they think in the long run they are acting in the best interests of the users because the SharePoint farm is not being compromised by non-IT literates who don't understand it. This assumption is fundamentally wrong because it ignores the fact that by not allowing users to apply their energy to the system, it will inevitably slow and stop.

Application Lifecycle Management

As indicated, the continuous process of managing the life of an application through governance, development, and maintenance is referred to as application lifecycle management. An important element that informs an organization's approach to this process is its philosophy of application development and change management. In some cases, a formal, somewhat tightly controlled approach is preferred. In such an organization, custom development or packaged solutions are often the first course of action. Although understandable in many situations, applications like SharePoint offer organizations an alternative to this approach.

In my opinion, too many solution providers rely on writing code to meet user requirements because it fits these processes instead of looking at providing a solution first. Complex code-based solutions are more cost-effective and profitable for the developers and companies who write them. They also require years of paid assistance to support them, so it's in their best interest not to use out-of-the-box (OOB) functionality. Many times users shy away from that because they don't want the extra work of managing the solution. In this section one of the things I'll consider is the actual cost of developed solutions.

Later I will describe the processes within the business to manage change (RFCs, BIAs, and CABs) and change testing and review. First, however, let's look at several different types of development models and consider what makes the most sense for SharePoint changes. Of course, there will be different solutions depending on the scale of your SharePoint environment, the number of developers you have working on the same code, and the number of different pieces of code that have to be developed and deployed at the same time. However, some basic considerations are often overlooked or misunderstood, and they are important for flexible and manageable change in a SharePoint environment. They apply to many of the changes most organizations need.

Development Models

Bringing user requirements all the way to being used in production can be done in a number of ways. You will likely have heard of development project philosophies like "waterfall," "Scrum," and "lean". These provide models for application development; understanding them provides important context for the variation I think works most effectively in many SharePoint situations. I'll also describe that variation in this section.

Waterfall

Waterfall gathers requirements at the beginning and users don't see the solution until they are testing it at the end, close to deployment (see Figure 9-1). This model was developed over the past 20-30 years starting at the time when developers had to book time on mainframes to compile their code. It has not moved with the times, as more complex solutions can be developed more quickly now due to better programming object models. The model requires developers to plan, build, test, review, and deploy in one linear sequence. There is only one compilation of the code as part of deployment. If there are major mismatches between the solution and the requirements, it's too late to fix them.

Waterfall

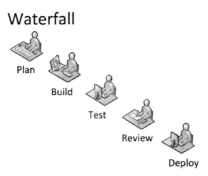

Figure 9-1. *Waterfall is linear, like an assembly line.*

Iterative Waterfall

The iterative waterfall model was developed in response to the limitations of the classical waterfall model. This model is somewhat better, but it still requires a lot of risky up-front development, some testing, and finally deployment (see Figure 9-2). This is how software like Office is created. Approximately every two years a new version is completed. From a user point of view, two years is a long time to wait for new functionality.

Iterative Waterfall

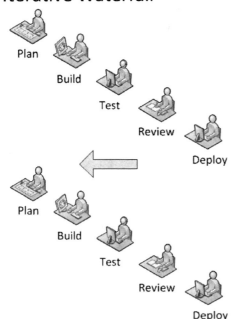

Figure 9-2. *The iterative waterfall process simply repeats the waterfall process.*

Scrum

Scrum has short phases where the solution is made usable and tested as quickly as possible, and features are gradually added until it is finally reviewed and deployed (see Figure 9-3), the benefit being that users can provide input sooner and the solution can evolve with them.

The reason Scrum evolved is that users generally don't know what they want until you show them something. For this reason, the hardest solution to write is a reporting solution not because the code is difficult, but because the business tends to only know that it would be a good idea to look more deeply at the data they are producing because they know there is information of value in there they are not seeing. The problem is they won't know what's valuable until they see it. A Scrum approach allows the solution to evolve and allows the business to learn what they could do potentially with the solution and refine their requirements accordingly.

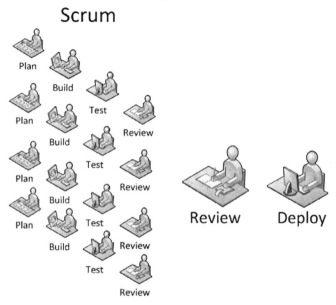

Figure 9-3. Multiple Scrums of independent features lead to one final deployment.

Lean

Lean takes the Scrum approach one step further: the product is constantly added to by separately creating independent features (see Figure 9-4). If a feature is added and users don't like it, it can be removed. This is similar to how Gmail was developed. Features were incrementally deployed, but it functioned from the start.

Lean

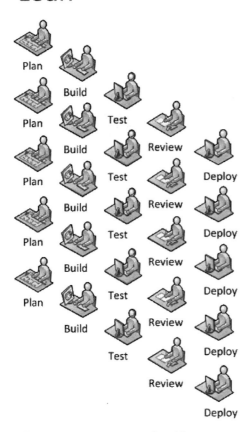

Figure 9-4. Lean constantly adds separate new features.

The main difference between waterfall, iterative waterfall, Scrum, and lean is how often the users are brought back in to assess the solution. That it doesn't meet their ever-changing needs is the greatest risk, not to mention the fact that people don't know what they want until they see it. As a result, the lean approach is now most common. The main benefit of all these approaches is they control the process of change in software, which reduces risk.

SharePoint is software in the sense that is has parts that are compiled and installed. Like all Microsoft software, it has already gone through some kind of build process. But while it has already been built, it is also a platform that is composed of a raft of features that allow people other than developers to change the relationship between them and their content. There has to be a process to manage these changes too, but it can't be something as old-fashioned and simplistic as the waterfall model. What approach is needed for deploying SharePoint?

SharePoint Variation: *Build*/Plan/Test/Review/Deploy

The plan/build/test/review/deploy model doesn't fit comfortably with SharePoint because it is an application that already has so many functions built in for creating solutions. Unfortunately, these are rarely known about by users, so developers are employed to step in and write code that really isn't needed, but has the added advantage from the businesses point of view of adding security because the changes can be put through rigorous change management processes.

The better solution with SharePoint is to remove the build step, which already is part of the process Microsoft uses to create SharePoint. Microsoft goes through the entire process before you ever install it, which simplifies the change process for you. Because most of the functionality an organization needs from SharePoint has already been created, the change process becomes more one of implementation than development. However, changes should still be researched and planned carefully. They should be tested in a non-production site or farm, reviewed by users, and only then deployed to production (Figure 9-5). For example, say you have a live InfoPath form tied to a workflow for approval and the users want new functionality added to the form that fills in the values of two fields based on the contents of another. Achieving this can be planned with some research, then built into a copy of the InfoPath template deployed to a test SharePoint site. Once the change is tested and reviewed by the business, it can be deployed into production with confidence it won't destroy existing live data and will function correctly. It is a mixture of waterfall and lean. Let's call it a lean waterfall!

SharePoint

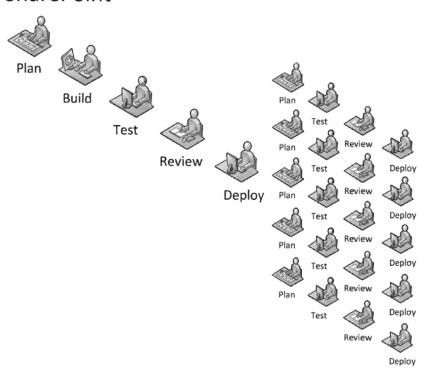

Figure 9-5. Microsoft builds, but owners of SharePoint should still plan, test, review, and deploy.

Cost of Change

There is one simple reason why leaving development to Microsoft (most of the time) makes sense: cost. SharePoint probably had thousands of developers working on it over years at a cost of millions of dollars. This level of expense is not something most companies want to take on. That is why your approach to changing SharePoint should be different.

Sometimes organizations have change requirements that are only possible to make at a disproportionate cost. The most common example in my experience is where the business contracts a developer to meet their requirements rather than requesting the change through the owners of the infrastructure. The developer listens to the users requirements and fulfils them using a combination of AJAX, C#, and custom controls so that the work is done in a matter of weeks. The business is happy and the developer goes on his way. Months, weeks, or even days later, the users decide they want to make a small change to the pages the developer created. They think it is a small thing so they ask their internal IT department. This is the first time IT has heard of these changes. They don't even know how the business got the access rights to make them; maybe from someone in the IT department who didn't think it would cause any harm since the developer knew what he was doing. Regardless, now IT is expected to own this solution, and they have no documentation as what was done, how, or why. They spend time untangling the developer's code and eventually make the change. They realize the developer could have simply used an OOB Web Part to do what they did but likely knew very little about the application itself, only how to develop on the platform, so he wrote something that is actually very expensive to maintain.

The users now blame IT for the fact that every small change takes hours or days. They also resent the fact that even the smallest change has to be made by someone in IT. Eventually, the solution succumbs to entropy and is no longer used. It cost a lot to create and a lot to maintain, but it never stayed current with the business' needs.

What the business didn't do was consider the cost of ownership of the solution. They only thought of the initial cost of hiring the developer for a few weeks. Had they taken the time to learn what SharePoint can do OOB, they could have created something they could manage themselves. The initial cost to learn the skills might have been higher than paying a developer, but the ongoing costs would have been lower. This is like my example of a thermodynamic system that gets more efficient. IT could have provided guidance and support to the business at a lower cost to them, too. The conclusion: change can be costly, but in the long run, the returns can be higher if the energy expended at the start is expended wisely. Change must be managed in a collaborative way within the business for everyone's benefit.

Solution/Problem

Solution packages have made deploying and activating code in SharePoint much more streamlined and automated. As a result, less is likely to go wrong. However, users and developers tend to use them as a substitute for the more controlled plan/build/test/review/deploy process. Solutions only aid with deployment. Furthermore, they don't automatically provide for a process of incremental updating. The important questions are rarely asked. What if we want to change this later on? What will happen? How will we change the existing live system as seamlessly as possible? Solutions can cause problems. They are also subject to entropy, but now they have added greater complexity and risk into your environment. Users are dependent on the solution as it is, but it's slowly getting less beneficial because it isn't evolving with their needs.

For example, I was recently asked to help the owners of a training page by making some small changes to their SharePoint site. They required a link to a new forum they wanted created but they also wanted to add a column to a Web Part on the home page. I quickly added the forum and the link, but the

Web Part had been created using AJAX rather than using the OOB Web Parts or even SharePoint Designer. There was no documentation or comments in the code, and the developer was unreachable. The only solution was to hire another developer for a week to come in and make a change that should have been a few minutes work. The solution looked great, but the cost of owning it and changing it was too high to be practical. So the question should always be asked, What will it take to change this code later on?

Development Developments

Virtualization makes creating an environment for writing code against a development SharePoint instance much simpler now than even a few years ago. This means organizations can have multiple development, test, and UAT environments much more cheaply.

A standard development cycle goes like this:

1. Users report a bug or request a change.

2. Developers can run multiple builds in their development environments in parallel before deploying them to a collective test environment.

3. Some of these builds are deployed to a UAT environment that users can access and report if the bug is fixed or the new functionality meets their requirements.

4. Changes to production can now be put through the RFC/CAB process before they are made.

5. Production changes may be tested in a staging/preproduction environment.

SharePoint as a platform should make this kind of complex change management unnecessary. An ideal situation is where all evolution in the SharePoint environment is made at the browser or application level. I have seen many SharePoint environments where all development is banned, so users and the business are forced to use SharePoint to its maximum potential. Ultimately, I think this is in the best interest of the business, but sometimes the option to make something complex and costly is seen as better than something simple and cheap just because the problem is not fully understood.

Virtualization does make having multiple environments cheaper, but where does it end? You can end up with multiple virtual farms all running different builds of different developed solutions. One dev/test/prod environment is only fine if you only have one change being made at a time. If you have 50, do you really want to have 50 virtual SharePoint farms? The best way to keep SharePoint vital and changing is for the users themselves to instigate and make changes. This may require effort on their part to learn SharePoint, but it's a process that will yield more benefit to them directly than engaging external developers or trainers to whom they can delegate the responsibility.

Evolution

Everything in our universe follows the laws of thermodynamics. (Note I say "our" universe because for all we know there are other universes with different laws.) But is change always good? Too much change in a SharePoint system can lead to a breakdown of the system by accelerating the entropy. That is what IT infrastructure owners are resisting. Changing SharePoint without testing and doing a proper business impact assessment of the change and without review by the IT staff and the business can lead to rapid failure of the system. Think of too much change as being like the pressure the captain of the Titanic was under by the passengers and the owners of the ship to get to New York in record time. By doing so, he would increase the publicity for the ship, increase the number of passengers, and ultimately increase the success of the whole operation. However, the big chunks of entropic ice floating down from higher and colder latitudes put a sudden stop to that plan. Entropy is not merely the risk to SharePoint of gradual inertia, it's also the risk of sudden, catastrophic change caused by moving too fast.

The solution is to evolve the SharePoint platform in a gradual and tested way. This is how evolution works. Multiple variations occur in the environment and the fittest survive and continue while the unfit die off. Survival means your successful genes are passed on to your offspring and the cycle starts again. The environment inevitably changes and other species (indeed other members of your species) compete for the finite resources, but because there are multiple generations, change is always accommodated because the species as a whole can evolve to suit the change.

Who Controls Change in SharePoint?

Determining who should have what rights to change what is a balancing act between the needs of the owners to maintain the integrity, security, and manageability of the system and the needs of the business. This is a role that has to be taken by strong leaders who see the needs of the business and IT as a whole as opposed to different sides. Sometimes the solution to why a user or group is receiving an access denied error would take longer to find than just giving the user or group higher privileges. This solves the immediate business need, but in the longer term, the granting of excessive rights can lead to security or stability problems. From the business point of view, security is only used to control access to content, but from an infrastructure point of view, it's to prevent users from making changes to the system that have negative repercussions—ones that IT must ultimately fix.

It's also true that some organizations have overly strict policies. These just lead to users finding ways to break or sneak around the rules. There has to be communication between IT and the business. It is like any relationship: both sides have to see they are part of the same organization and have to act as the same team, not opposing teams. In my experience, this comes down to great managers, people who listen to both sides and make decisions in everyone's best interest when others can't do this for themselves. It's true to say that leadership is not something you can formulate in a book. It is a process of synthesis more art than science. But the benefits are clear to see: businesses that get the best from technology.

Change Categories

Not all changes are equal. From a technical standpoint, to understand the scope of a change you have to be able to understand which category it belongs in. There is also the business impact of a change, which can have nothing to do with the technical impact. A change may be technically very simple to make but can have a very large business impact. An example would be unplugging the cooling system of a server room. But if a business person has to make a decision about a change, they have to have some basic understanding of the technical level. SharePoint changes can be placed into three categories:

- Configuration
- Design
- Development

The category a change belongs in depends on the tool used to make the change and the rights required to make those changes. Changes are fundamentally assessed by their potential impact on the integrity of the overall system. The lower the impact, the lower the rights required to make them and the less restricted the tool required to make the change. The three tools required to make changes in each category are

- SharePoint

- SharePoint Designer

- Visual Studio

When assessing a change you must understand the scope of the change and its potential impact on the integrity of your SharePoint environment. The larger the impact of the change, the higher the rights required to make it. Granting these rights to people who don't know the impact of their changes is poor governance. The principle of least privilege should always be followed: never give users more rights than they know how to use. These categories help you classify the change's severity level and who should be trusted to make the change.

Configuration

Changes that require only the browser and the pages of the SharePoint sites are configuration changes. These can be subdivided depending on the level of access required to reach the pages, and these depend on the scope of the changes to the farm as a whole.

- Farm

- Site collection

- Site

- Page

- List/Library

Configuration changes are made directly into your production environment and they are not automated. Changes can be first made in a development or testing environment but they then have to be manually redone in production. The changes generally can't be replicated or migrated in one batch into production unless you are able to backup and restore from development or test to production. This would only be possible if there has been no change in production content. Making manual changes, no matter how well documented, adds the risk that the steps made in development or testing will not be replicated accurately. The person making these changes must fully understand them; otherwise there is room for misinterpretation.

Farm

Membership in the Farm Administrators group is granted in SharePoint Central Administration (see Figure 9-6). This is a site for managing the SharePoint farm as a whole. Changes made here impact the entire farm. For example, you can add a new Crawler server, or change when Search crawls content. To make changes here, you need to understand the impact not just on users but also on SQL Server, the network, Windows Server, and SharePoint itself. In other words, a change here is high risk and should be managed carefully.

Figure 9-6. Central Administration for a SharePoint farm

Site Collection

Changes at the site collection level impact that parent site and all the sites below it. For example, if you deleted an existing site template from the gallery, it would no longer be available to any site in the site collection. Users with site collection owner rights should take time to thoroughly understand the impact of changing any of the many somewhat obscure settings on the Site Collection Settings page (see Figure 9-7). Until they do understand, they have to listen to IT infrastructure's point of view, which is always to preserve the system. This may initially be at odds with the needs of the business, but as the site collection owner's knowledge grows, they will act in the interests of the organization as a whole.

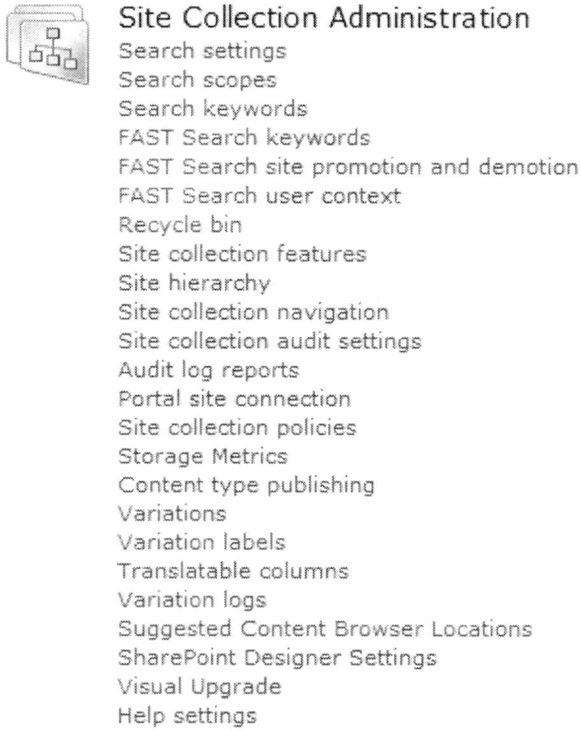

Site Collection Administration

Search settings
Search scopes
Search keywords
FAST Search keywords
FAST Search site promotion and demotion
FAST Search user context
Recycle bin
Site collection features
Site hierarchy
Site collection navigation
Site collection audit settings
Audit log reports
Portal site connection
Site collection policies
Storage Metrics
Content type publishing
Variations
Variation labels
Translatable columns
Variation logs
Suggested Content Browser Locations
SharePoint Designer Settings
Visual Upgrade
Help settings

Figure 9-7. Site Collection Administration options

Site

Changes at the site level impact that site and all the pages on it. For example, if you changed the site theme, that change would be seen on the pages of all the lists and libraries on the site. Users with site owner rights should thoroughly understand the impact of changing any of the many settings on the Site Settings page (see Figure 9-8). Learning about these settings is a process of experiment and discovery. You can also find many online and written resources. No one source is complete, however. The following is my process:

- How can I achieve this business need?

- From my research of written and online sources, how have others met this need?

- Can I test potential solutions in a sandboxed, non-production site?

- Can I show it to users for their feedback?

Applying a process like this may not achieve a perfect result every time, but it is better than a short-sighted jab at the first seeming solution.

Users and Permissions
People and groups
Site permissions
Site collection administrators

Galleries
Site columns
Site content types
Web parts
List templates
Master pages
Themes
Solutions

Site Administration
Regional settings
Site libraries and lists
User alerts
RSS
Search and offline availability
Sites and workspaces
Workflows
Workflow settings
Related Links scope settings
Term store management
Content and structure
Searchable columns
Content and structure logs

Look and Feel
Title, description, and icon
Tree view
Site theme
Navigation

Site Actions
Manage site features
Save site as template
Reset to site definition
Delete this site
Site Web Analytics reports
Site Collection Web Analytics reports

Reporting Services
Manage Shared Schedules
Reporting Services Site Settings

Figure 9-8. Site Administration options

Page

The Web Part framework was conceived as a way to change page properties simply through a browser, such as the properties to view a Shared Document Library (see Figure 9-9). Changes at the page level impact that page. For example, if you move a Web Part to the bottom of the page, all users who can access that page will see the change. It is also possible to specify that a change be only seen by you; this is a personal view of the page. As with the other changes, users with page edit rights should thoroughly understand the impact of their changes. Pages usually inherit their administrator as the administrator of the site; individual pages rarely have a different person as their owner. Users with specialized skills can even use content editor Web Parts to make very interactive changes to the page using technologies like AJAX and web services, but their impact is still only page level if they fail.

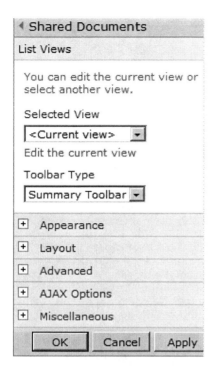

Figure 9-9. Changing a Web Part page

List/Library

Users can be given the rights to add content to lists/libraries, create or modify views within the list, or add/delete/modify columns to the list. Even these small changes can have a major impact on other users because if a column is deleted, it's not stored in the Recycle Bin. As another example, metadata navigation settings make it possible to browse the content of libraries using the metadata as if they were folders (see Figure 9-10). This may confuse users unless it serves a prior need to make content easier to find. Just because a feature is available doesn't mean you should enable it.

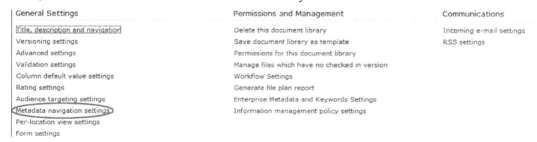

Figure 9-10. List settings

Importance of Managed Change

Just making configuration and structural changes through the SharePoint UI straight into production by users, site, or farm administrators introduces a complication: it breaks the cycle that is part of all these approaches, that of plan/build/test/review/deploy. With SharePoint, via the web browser only, you can make very impactful changes to your SharePoint environment and users. The higher the credentials the user has, the more impactful the change. Sometimes a change can have unforeseen consequences because the user is unaware of exactly who is dependent on what they have ownership of.

For example, I once had to troubleshoot a situation where 15 levels of sites in a site collection suddenly had SharePoint groups disappear overnight. As a result, teams all over the organization couldn't access SharePoint, and there were hundreds of calls to support from aggrieved users who thought they had been personally locked out. Before I got there, Active Directory and SQL Server were checked, a Microsoft support call was opened, and SharePoint thoroughly checked for errors. Then foul play was suspected: had hackers deleted the groups? Finally the branch manager came in; I immediately suspected him because he had a history of doing little DIY SharePoint projects in the evening.

Previously, he'd tried to create a Web Part with SharePoint Designer and made the portal's home page inaccessible. I spoke to him and he insisted he'd done nothing that could have caused this issue. Eventually, he remembered removing some user groups from "his site" that shouldn't have been there. But he'd not done this on any other site. Therefore, there was a bug in SharePoint, etc., etc. It turned out that he had navigated from his site to the Site Collection Settings pages without realizing it. Because permission inheritance was turned on, he had not only removed the access of these groups to "his" site, he had deleted them completely from the whole site collection, thus removing the access rights of all the users in those groups across the whole 15 levels of sites in the organization!

To this day, that manager still has those rights; unfortunately, he insists he needs them, but also insists he doesn't need to be trained to understand them. But the point of this example is that a change management process is dependent on good governance, which is dependent on users not having more rights than they understand how to use. It also requires that users who have rights take responsibility for using them.

Design

Design-level changes require SharePoint Designer (see Figure 9-11). SharePoint Designer allows you to make changes that impact the structure and visual presentation of a site, so although they can be made with Designer rights, they really should only be made with the approval of the site owner as they can impact all the content and users. For example, SharePoint Designer allows you to change page layout templates for a site. This change would impact every publishing page on the portal using that page layout.

Like configuration changes, SharePoint Designer makes changes directly onto the production environment. Like configuration changes, they can be made in a development or testing environment but the changes have to be redone in production. In fact, the changes generally can't be replicated or migrated in one batch into production. This adds the risk that the steps made in development or testing will not be replicated accurately. As before, the person making the changes must fully understand them to avoid misinterpretation.

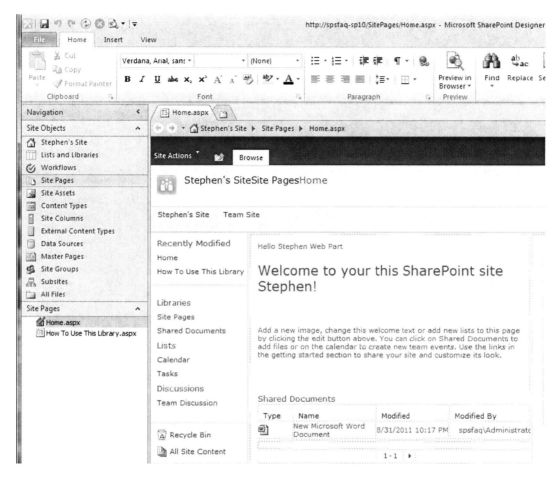

Figure 9-11. SharePoint Designer

Development

While I have indicated that SharePoint should be seen as a complete application that is mainly configured rather that developed, SharePoint also has a rich environment for extending it and developing on it. This is not something always to be avoided—it should just be taken as something where the cost of ownership is understood and accepted. Development on SharePoint can automate configuration by adding content types, site definitions, Web Parts, and workflows, which can't be done as well, or at all, through the web UI.

Development-level changes can be made directly onto the server, but it should be policy that only changes packaged as features or solutions should be deployed. A SharePoint solution is a deployable package that can contain features and assemblies. The solution package is a .cab-based file with a .wsp extension. The Visual Studio 2010 SharePoint project templates create .wsp package files for you as part of your development project. A solution might contain a number of SharePoint features, and these features provide functionality such as Web Parts, list definitions, modules, and event receivers. Features and solutions require PowerShell to deploy.

Like configuration and design changes, PowerShell will deploy the features or solutions directly onto the production environment. Like configuration changes, they can be made in a development or testing environment first and then redeployed in production. Because they are packaged, there are no complex steps to deployment. As before, the person making the changes must fully understand them to avoid misinterpretation.

Testing in Production

Knowing what can be done in production without risk comes with experience. But if you are not sure of the consequences of a change, how can you mitigate the risk? The principle that should always be followed when you are making any change in SharePoint is this: can I roll this change back if it doesn't work as predicted? If the answer is no, take the plan/test/review/deploy approach. Remember that the goal is never to lose content it has taken a lot of time and effort to produce. For example, if you want to change an InfoPath form library template, you must understand that when you change it, all the forms already created are linked to that template and thus could be affected. Make a copy of the template, publish it to another site, copy in some test forms, and make your changes there first. You can never make a change and know exactly what the results will be, but the bigger the potential impact, the more important a test replica is.

Change Management

No change management process is exactly the same, but they will all have some essential elements. When you construct your change management plan, you can incorporate these elements. They all help contribute to making change constructive and not destructive. They allow your SharePoint system to evolve just quickly enough not to succumb to entropy. I've illustrated these elements in a process flowchart in Figure 9-12. Here are the pieces:

1. Some kind of form to capture the details required for the change request.

2. Someone to review the initial request and ensure it has all the appropriate details correctly provided.

3. An assessment of the business impact of the change.

4. A Change Advisory Board (CAB) will approve/reject the request.

5. The change must be tested and scheduled.

6. The change is reviewed and marked complete or withdrawn.

7. All comments, approvals, and supporting documentation for the change request are stored for later reuse.

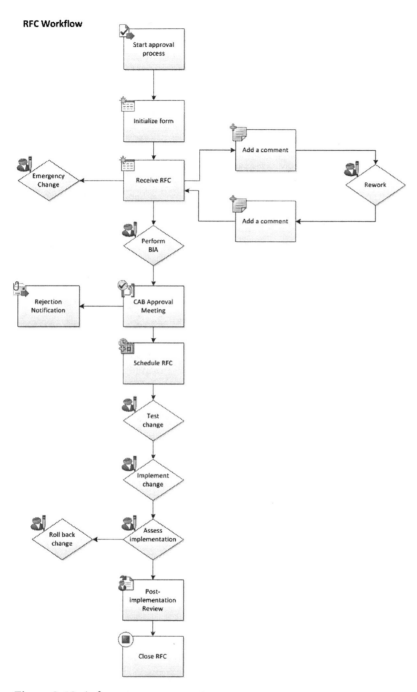

Figure 9-12. A change management process

Impact Assessment

Executing these steps correctly is your most proactive method to achieve high availability. The core of this process is the change impact assessment. Anyone familiar with the Information Technology Infrastructure Library (ITIL) has heard of an impact assessment. A change impact assessment is a systematic approach that seeks to discover possible risks associated with a Request for Change (RFC).

Most failed changes are simply the result of not taking into account current activities and a failure to communicate anticipated activities. This includes any situation that proposes to alter system configurations, operating practices, policies, or procedures, and any new or different activities to be performed.

For change impact assessment, or simply an impact assessment, to be effective the system owners have to explore all of the differences between normal operations and any conditions that introduce risks or may contribute to a failed change. Used effectively, impact assessment can proactively manage risk. It is a simple idea that can be implemented quickly using a word processor or spreadsheet. You can even use a SharePoint list. It requires no complex software. It does require careful adherence to a formal procedure, however, and teamwork.

Impact assessment is a fairly mature and formal activity in most organizations outside of IT. In particular, military branches around the world have deep experience in planning changes. Yet in many organizations most IT impact assessments consists of e-mailing around an RFC and waiting for someone to comment about it, or worse, one developer with too many rights working in isolation on "one little change." Another popular method for impact assessment is a meeting, usually a day or two before the change is to occur, where department heads talk about the work upcoming.

It's clear that existing impact assessments don't work. Every year all the big think tanks report that IT is its own worst enemy. Gartner and others have documented that about 80% of all incidents occur because of failed change management activities. It doesn't have to be this way. Change impact assessment is well known outside of IT, and there are models for performing impact assessment.

The main change request process (shown in Figure 9-12) also calls a subprocess called "perform impact assessment" (see Figure 9-13). The subprocess contains tasks for risk management, effort estimation, and testing recommendations which can executed in parallel. Once completed, information is passed back into the main process.

RFC Workflow

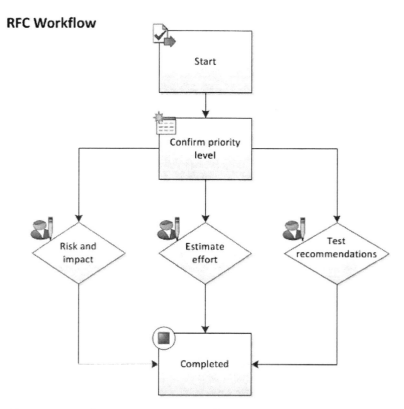

Figure 9-13. A change management subprocess: a business or change impact assessment

While effective and easily implemented, impact assessment is not a panacea and doesn't totally replace existing change procedures. Instead, it's simply part of the change management process. The procedure for performing an impact assessment consists of the following steps and I have detailed how they should be used in the following example, Sheep Watch. I will also show how this subprocess fits into the overall change management process.

Applied Scenario: Sheep Watch Impact Assessment

Figure 9-13 shows the steps of the process as well as steps off to the side that denote side processes. To describe the change management process, I will use the example of a Web Part being added to the home page of our fictional university in Newbridge, Co. Kildare, Ireland. This Web Part was mandated by senior management. Its purpose is to display a map of the roads approaching the campus to warn staff where sheep are blocking traffic. Staff can add updates based on their observations from the windows of the building on the campus. The goal is to reduce traffic bottlenecks around the campus during the day and when staff members are driving home.

The Web Part is called Sheep Watch. The developer who created it in IT on her own development environment submits the Request For Change (RFC) to have it added to the production portal home page. This RFC is a list item on a SharePoint site (see Figure 9-14).

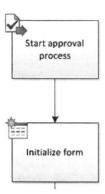

Figure 9-14. Initial submission

The Change Coordinator receives an e-mail alert when the RFC is added. She reviews it and notices the developer has not said whether the Web Part will be deployed as a solution. She adds a comment to that effect and the developer reviews it and adds her own comment to confirm it is indeed packaged as a solution (Figure 9-15). It is the University's policy to only deploy code in this way, so this had to be confirmed.

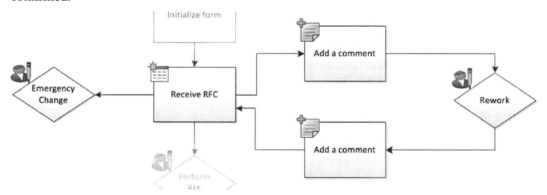

Figure 9-15. Review by Change Coordinator

The Change Coordinator decides this is not an emergency change and approves it for movement to the next phase. An "emergency" is any service interruption that is classed as high impact, either because of the number of users affected or because systems or services that are critical to the organisation are involved, and so it must be responded to immediately. It should not be the result of poor planning! Every Wednesday, representatives from the IT department including the SharePoint Administrator, the SQL Server Administrator, and the Network Administrator meet. Their task to perform the next step in the process: the business impact assessment, or BIA (Figure 9-16). To do this they perform the following tasks:

1. Define the extent of the change proposed.

2. Determine key differences in the changed state (proposed) from the original state.

3. Focus on the possible effects of the key differences from step 2.

4. Sort and prioritize the possible effects (step 3) from the key differences (step 2).

5. Make a decision using the results.

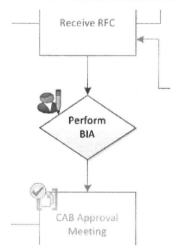

Figure 9-16. *The Business Impact Assessment*

Define the Extent of the Change Proposed

In the RFC, the developer writes that the Web Part is installed as a solution in the root site collection of the portal. It installs a Web Part that should then be added to the portal home page. It also creates a list to store the sheep reports and photos submitted by users. She describes the functionality of the Web Part as a dynamic map that displays the locations and sizes of the herds of sheep as submitted by users. She estimates that there will be 10-20 reports submitted per month and the capacity required to store the list and photos will grow to 500MB in 12 months. She anticipates the Web Part will not delay the loading of the home page much.

Determine Key Differences Between the Proposed State and the Original State

The IT team discusses that the main difference will be the increased capacity to store the images, the performance effect on the home page, and the downtime to install the Web Part.

Focus on the Possible Effects of the Key Differences

They factor 500MB into their capacity planning for the year and decide it can be accommodated. One of the team has spoken to the developer and seen the Web Part and says it looks like it won't slow the portal down much. The performance goal is to have the home page load in 2 seconds, and it loads really fast on the developer's laptop. The solution can be installed outside of work hours to minimize the impact on users.

Sort and Prioritize the Possible Effects from the Key Differences

The team determines the key risk is that the capacity required for the list could grow faster than expected. However, since only current images have to be preserved, it is determined that older images can be deleted if the list grows too quickly. Risk and effort estimation are determined to be low, and testing recommendations are that the Web Part be installed on the test system first to verify that the install works.

Make a Decision Using the Results

There is a SQL Server update scheduled for the coming Saturday and they decide to install the Web Part at the same time, subject to approval at the CAB approval meeting scheduled for that Friday.

Change Advisory Board (CAB) Meetings

A Change Manager should always act as the Chair of any CAB meetings either virtual or face-to-face. CAB meetings should be called by the Change Manager at appropriate times to ensure the prompt and efficient handling of all changes. During high levels of change, this could potentially be daily, but usually they are every Friday. For complex, high risk, or high impact changes, or when major projects are due to deliver products, a formal CAB meeting would be necessary. The meetings can then be used to provide a formal review and authorization of changes, a review of outstanding changes, and to discuss any impending major changes. Where face-to-face meetings are appropriate, they should have a standard agenda.

Relevant change information should be circulated in advance to allow CAB members to conduct impact and resource assessments prior to the CAB meeting. The CAB called by the Change Manager should consist of attendees who are relevant to RFCs being considered. This could potentially include attendees for other groups and parts of the business outside IT. Authorization at the CAB for each change must be given by appropriate representatives from all areas the change will affect. In the case of our example, representatives from the users who own the SharePoint content and the management team who requested the Sheep Watch web part should be present.

A Standard CAB Agenda

A standard Change Advisory Board meeting should be structured and well chaired to make it as efficient as possible. It could include the following as appropriate:

- A review of all failed changes

- A review of all backed out changes

- A list of RFCs to be assessed by CAB members

- A review of all implemented changes

- The change management process, including any amendments made to the process as well as proposed changes to the process (as appropriate)

- Change management successes for the period under discussion, such as a review of the business benefits seen as a result of the change management process (as appropriate)

CAB Considerations for Each Change (Prior to Authorization)

These considerations will include the information prepared at the BIA stage, but presented in a clearer and more concise way. The members of the CAB may not be very technical, so the technical aspects of the assessment of the change should be made in a clear non-jargon way.

- Risk/impact assessment (on the business)

- Effect upon the infrastructure and customer service, as defined in the SLA, and upon the capacity and performance, reliability and resilience, contingency plans, and security

- Impact on other services that run on the same infrastructure (or on software development projects)

- Resource assessment—the IT, business, and other resources required to implement the change, covering the likely costs, the number and availability of people required, the elapsed time, and any new infrastructure elements required

- The impact on non-IT infrastructures within the organization

- Effect/risk/impact of not implementing the change

- Other changes being implemented on the schedule of change

- Technical capability and technical approval

- Financial approval (if required)

- Third party/supplier involvement in the implementation of the change

- Business approval (if required)

- Review/assessment of the change priority

CAB Comments/Issues

All CAB comments on each change and any issues that have been discussed must be documented by the Change Manager within the CAB meeting minutes. These will not be things that directly affect the process but are just a record of individual points of view if there are differences of perspective. The issues may not lead to a rejection, but they will be noted and incorporated into the testing or the change itself.

CAB Recommendations/Decisions

All CAB recommendations and decision that have been discussed must be documented by the Change Manager within the CAB meetings minutes. Some decisions and ultimately approval may have to go beyond the CAB. This would be unusual, but if the decision is escalated, it is still recorded and implemented through the CAB.

CAB Authorisation/Approval

Once all aspects of the change have been considered (as per the CAB considerations outlined previously) the CAB will then give authorization for the change to be scheduled and moved into the change build stage of the process (Figure 9-17).

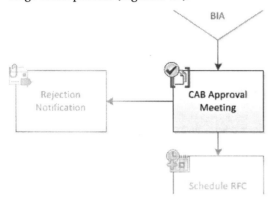

Figure 9-17. Outcome of CAB

If a change has been authorised by the CAB, the RFC can then be scheduled to happen. If the CAB can't make a final decision on the authorization of a change, then the change escalation needs to be initiated by the Change Manager to ensure that authorisation is given at a higher level. This could be the head of the University in our example, but this will rarely be the case. The escalation of change authorisation is documented in the request for change—the Change Manager will detail to whom the change was escalated and the final decision that was made, either authorized or rejected.

Rejection of a Change by the Change Advisory Board

If the CAB rejects the change, the Change Manager must document in full the reasons for the rejection and ensure that the decision is communicated to the person who requested the change. In our example, the Sheep Watch Web Part was approved. If it is rejected completely, the proposer can begin the process again with an improved version of the solution.

Schedule RFC

After the CAB meeting, the approval is communicated to the infrastructure owners. This communication could be in the form of an e-mail, document, or spreadsheet. Before testing of the change beings, the best time to make the change can be set (Figure 9-18). This will be a time that fits in with other scheduled changes in a way that prevents them impacting each other. It will also be a time that doesn't impact other processes such as backups. Finally, it will be at a time that has minimal impact on users while still meeting their needs. For example, a change to the payroll system might be best done a few days before the end of the month to ensure it is fully properly deployed before the payroll is done.

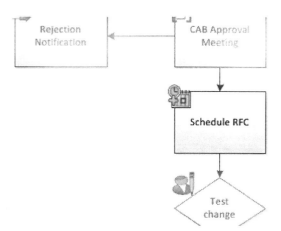

Figure 9-18. Schedule the change

Test Change

Testing (see Figure 9-19) has to be done as close an approximation of live as possible. With the advent of virtualization, it's easier to have replica builds of farms that can be rolled back. Even without virtualization, a staging or preproduction environment can be used to perform a test. This environment should be as close to a copy of production as possible. The more differences, the more risk that the test could miss a problem with the change. The test process should therefore include testing the rollback process for the change; now is the time to do this, not after an unexpected event in the live environment. Define at this point the criteria for the successful deployment of the change. Has its impact on resources been within planned parameters? Does it function as expected? Is it producing any errors in the system logs or within the application?

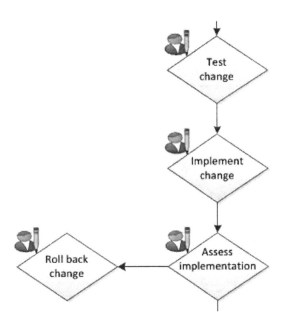

Figure 9-19. Test the change, implement the change, assess the implementation, and maybe roll back the change.

Implement and Assess, Perhaps Roll Back

In some ways the process of implementing and assessing the change is the same as testing it. The deployment process and the checks to ensure it went smoothly will be the same: has its impact on resources been within planned parameters, does it function as expected, is it producing any errors in the system logs or within the application? If it has met these criteria, it's a success; if not, it has to be rolled back. This is a process you should have tested, too (see Figure 9-19). Sometimes a change doesn't go completely to plan but may be left in production. This is unusual, though. Usually the previous state is restored, and the change request process starts again.

Review and Close

At this point, any lessons learned during the deployment should be noted as part of the process of formally closing the RFC. Its criteria for success should have been met, and if not, this information should be noted and communicated to the appropriate party. For example, if the code is using more resources can planned, it can be reverted to the developers for a fix or to Infrastructure to add more resources. In either case, the process is complete (see Figure 9-20).

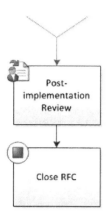

Figure 9-20. Review and close

Summary

Change management is a collaborative process where the impact of change has to be assessed from a business and a technical perspective. Change is the life-blood of SharePoint; without it the system succumbs to entropy, becomes less and less relevant to user needs, and becomes a burden rather than a boon to the business. SharePoint does require change management. The best approach is one where building the software is Microsoft's task, but planning, testing, reviewing, and deploying configuration changes are done by the users.

The exception is custom code, and because of its potential impact on the platform it must have a more stringent change management process. Solution packages make deployment more automated, but they are not a substitute for full application lifecycle management. By policy, custom development should be the exception, not the rule, because SharePoint at its best is a user-driven tool. Custom code puts the platform at greater risk and it takes the control out of the hands of the users and infrastructure owners.

SharePoint is successful because changing it is not something that relies on arcane, hard-won specialist knowledge. It can be done by learning which changes can just be made and which require planning and testing before deployment. If a change can't be immediately undone with no impact on the system or users, it needs planning and testing.

If changes can be kept within the scope of what users can do, change can be faster without resorting to a complex RFC/CAB process. Without change, SharePoint dies, but it doesn't have to stay static either: managed change, or the "lean waterfall" is the solution. With it, SharePoint can grow in a way that ensures its continued benefit to the organization.

CHAPTER 10

DR and the Cloud

Cloud computing has finally matured enough that the time has come to properly understand what benefit it could provide to SharePoint owners. The SharePoint owner in your organization will still ultimately have responsibility for users' content despite the fact that the infrastructure is owned by an external third party. There will also be the responsibility for credential federation and single sign-on. SharePoint in the cloud is available on dedicated hardware as well as in multi-tenancy environments. In either case, the administrator has to adapt or replace existing plans and procedures for HA and DR. These concepts have to be thought about differently now because some aspects of the HA and DR are in the hands of a third party and a whole new raft of servers will have to be managed if you want single sign-on.

The cloud in relation to SharePoint mainly means SharePoint Online as part of Office 365 hosted by Microsoft, but it can also mean services provided by other cloud hosting companies, such as Rackspace or Amazon, who will provide you with physical or virtual off-premises hosting services. The focus here will be on SharePoint Online as it will be the most common option taken. There is also the option of a hybrid solution where some of your content is in the cloud and some is on-site. This is currently the most common situation as organizations gradually transition to cloud-based services. But in this case it is as a result of a phased migration rather than a plan to keep the valuable, mission critical, or sensitive content more securely on-site while less valuable, mission critical, or sensitive information is hosted more cheaply off-site.

In this chapter I will look at

- How SharePoint has gradually become a more "cloud ready" application.

- Cloud options: private, public, and hybrid cloud architectures.

- The steps for adding resilience and redundancy in cloud scenarios.

By the end of this chapter you will see that single sign-on and active directory synchronization still mean you will be planning, installing, and configuring new servers on your domain. You will also still be planning, installing, and configuring software on your users' client machine. You will also still be patching and updating these components. You can't simply accept the marketing promises. I'll begin by showing how SharePoint has been rising into the clouds for years and how it's almost there now.

SharePoint Time Machine

Let's look at SharePoint in the past to see how it has evolved to where it is now. SharePoint had modest beginnings in 2001 at a time when the Internet was finally being noticed by the business community as something that could enhance communication and sharing within their organizations, similar to the way academic institutions around the world used it for years. At first, the rush was simply to build web sites that were no more than elaborate business cards for the organizations that commissioned them.

There were very few real web applications. There was no concept of Infrastructure as a Service or Software as a Service (IaaS or SaaS).

Then companies like Amazon started to make real money online. Amazon was also one of the first companies to see the potential of cloud hosting and is now a major player in this area as a result. Amazon invested in becoming more than just a retailer by leveraging its knowledge of creating huge infrastructures in online retail to creating a cloud platform.

Microsoft also saw the importance of the Internet and how it would replace the PC as the location of applications just as the PC had replaced the mainframe. Microsoft was busy looking for ways to create distributed applications over the Internet. The Windows Azure platform is the culmination of this work, but I don't think Microsoft even realized how successful browser-based applications like SharePoint could be. SharePoint was the fastest Microsoft product to reach $1 billion in revenue at a time when Microsoft was being perceived as becoming less relevant in the online world. Companies like Google and Facebook now have the challenge to find a way to diversify like Amazon did. Otherwise they will simply be surpassed by younger, leaner competitors eventually. Both companies still only have a limited source of revenue and have not diversified successfully. In business, the ability to adapt and change beyond your origins is crucial. By contrast, Apple, which began at the same time as Microsoft, will become a bigger player in the cloud arena, and Amazon will also become even more important in this arena because of its ability to adapt to new opportunities. Google and Facebook still only make money from advertising. If people stop using them, they will quickly die off.

When I chose to specialize in SharePoint in 2001, it was because I saw it as the best way to successfully monetize my Internet skills. I had already worked in the Internet area for four years but saw that creating web sites was no longer a viable business direction. There were too many small competitors doing web sites for free or big companies who had many more resources. I wanted to remain an independent consultant with valuable skills and I saw that SharePoint had the potential to allow me to make a living doing so. It has taken 10 years for SharePoint to reach the point where it can be called a true Internet application. It still has to bridge a few more gaps to achieve its full potential, however, and I'll talk a bit more about where it is going later in this chapter.

SharePoint Past

When SharePoint came about, it was behind the curve compared to more mature collaboration offerings like Lotus Notes, which combined workspaces and e-mail well. Lotus Notes was and still is a more centralized system and that is why I think it was surpassed by SharePoint. SharePoint also had the advantage of integrating better with Windows and Office. It held the promise of being a full web application but was still wrapped in the vestiges of a compiled application. You still purchased it on a CD and someone with server administrator privileges installed it on a server. You patched that server yourself also. Users did access the application via a web browser (Figure 10-1), so in that sense it was a web application. But the limitations of how it was implemented soon became clear. Users could only authenticate and access it if they had a Windows account. They also needed to be logged in at a computer on the network. They were tethered to that Windows account. They could access SharePoint from outside the office but only by extending the network securely using encryption technology like VPN. Otherwise, it was possible to give a SharePoint server an external IP address, a fully qualified domain name (FQDN), and make it available through anonymous or basic authentication, but this was very insecure and no business wanted to do it.

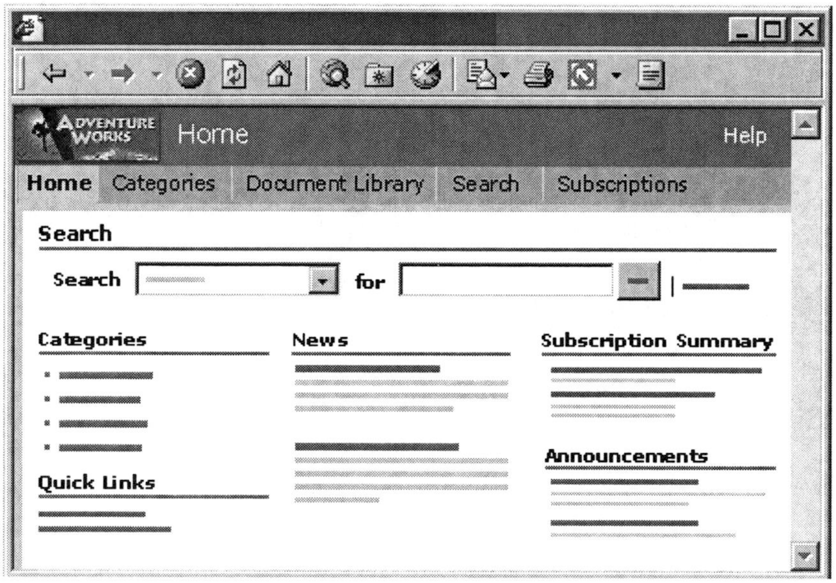

Figure 10-1. The SharePoint 2001 user interface

Sharing Content

Data in SharePoint could not be easily shared outside and data outside could not easily be shared in SharePoint. It looked like a web application but acted like a typical Windows application: once you put content in there, you couldn't access it from other applications and you couldn't draw in content from other locations easily. Options like Really Simple Syndication (RSS) were a way for other companies to share their content, but you had to write the Web Part and the XSL to read the RSS feed (an XML file) yourself. SharePoint did not become RSS-enabled until 2007 (Figure 10-2), even though RSS had been available since the mid-90s. Now you could view SharePoint list data in other applications and vice versa, but it was still very basic and weak, and it hampered by not having a simple and secure authentication mechanism.

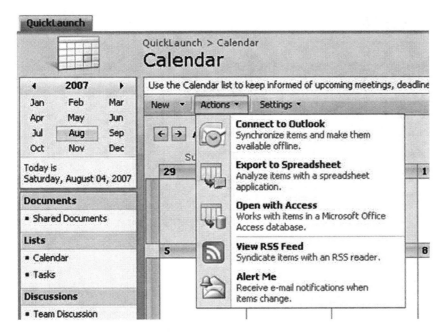

Figure 10-2. RSS in SharePoint 2007

Gradually, things changed, but I still think there is a long way to go. Sharing data between applications (between SAP and SharePoint, for example) means building more infrastructure and learning arcane knowledge like SPNego, BSPs, and WebDynPro. Web services and Business Connectivity Services (BCS) have helped with data sharing, but it is still a very technical domain.

Design and Development

You saw SharePoint was clearly just another Windows application that happened to use web pages when you tried to extend it with new functionality. New code had to be installed manually directly onto the servers. It was very difficult to install, uninstall, proactively upgrade, or retract. Developing for SharePoint 2001 meant writing WebDAV and some XML/XSL, HTML, and JavaScript. ASP pages existed but could only be shown in iFrames in SharePoint 2001. Gradually, the .NET Framework and the SharePoint development platform became more like one platform. In 2007, ASP.NET Web Parts were not the same as SharePoint Web Parts. Development with Visual Studio in 2005 required adding third party add-ons to automate packaging and deploying code to your SharePoint farm. Finally, because solutions and features are more mature today, you can deploy code to SharePoint, retract, and update it more easily.

The front end looked like a web site so it appeared that if you knew Internet scripting languages like HTML or JavaScript you could easily customize it. The reality was that important parts like the navigation controls were locked black boxes or implemented in non-compliant messy ways. Gradually, with themes and more support for cross-platform web design technology like CSS, AJAX, and REST, SharePoint now gives designers more free reign over the look of the interface.

Authentication

Verifying who users are (authentication) and what they are allowed to do (authorization) has always been something people using the Internet needed, and it has only grown more complex as the business world gets smaller and more connected. Even within a single large global organization it is a challenge to maintain one unique identifier for a member of staff across multiple domains within Windows. It becomes exponentially more complex when you want to share those credentials with other systems like SAP. Moving users to the cloud abstracts that complexity by creating a new platform for managing access, but there is still the issue of synchronising those credentials with the existing ones in Windows. This can lead to greater complexity and insecurity when keeping your network connected to the cloud. I'll discuss this more later.

SharePoint Present

With subsequent versions in 2003 and 2007, SharePoint gradually evolved and improved. The current version of SharePoint (2010) has become more like a real Internet application. It can be used to host a web site with anonymous pages, it supports multiple authentication methods such as Forms-based authentications, and it can share and access information more easily with web services and BCS. More external companies provide multi-tenancy so that they can offer SharePoint to multiple customers on the same servers off-premises cheaply with minimum setup planning. It can bring in data from other systems more easily using BCS and SharePoint Designer 2010 (see Figure 10-3).

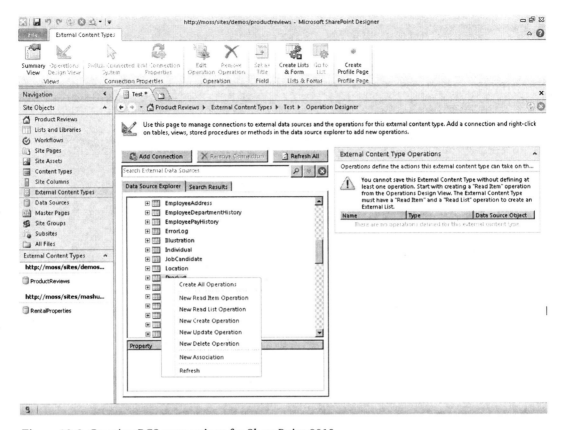

Figure 10-3. Creating BCS connections for SharePoint 2010

Finally, Business Productivity Online Services (BPOS) and now Office 365 including SharePoint Online became available. SharePoint has actually escaped the shackles of its network application ancestry and fulfilled its promise to become a real web application. SharePoint Online means your SharePoint content is hosted on infrastructure you don't own or have responsibility for patching, backing up, or managing in general. You can provision new user accounts immediately to anyone, even people outside your network, and then simply pay a monthly fee for the account license. SharePoint grew in 2001 from being a simple implementation of Exchange and IIS on one or two servers to a large complex conglomeration of many servers running many service applications. The availability of SharePoint Online is timely because SharePoint 2010 for the Enterprise has become a very complex environment and being able to move the burden of managing that off-site will be a great option for many organizations. SharePoint is now in the cloud at last.

Getting used to SharePoint Online will take some adjustment for many of us owners of SharePoint farms. If we want to find out when updates are going to be made to the system, we have to wait for the information to be posted by Microsoft, most likely at http://community.office365.com/en-us/b/office_365_technical_blog/default.aspx. The frequency of these updates is not predictable but will likely be every six to nine months.

When hosting your own infrastructure off-premises with Microsoft you will have more control. For example, you will be able to host a different version of SharePoint than the latest. The change management processes you use in your organization for deploying to SharePoint will be mainly the same, but you will likely maintain an online test environment for your features and solutions rather than on-premises so that the test environment resembles production as closely as possible. Since SharePoint Online is still relatively new (at the time of writing in Fall 2011) the main source of guidance for moving to SharePoint Online is still Microsoft when writing your high-level design document. That being said, there are more and more excellent consultancies with skills and experience to offer in this area.

SharePoint Future

There is still room for improvement in relation to SharePoint and the cloud. The main areas are in interoperability with other systems to share data and in making the sharing of credentials more seamless. More organizations moving to the cloud will gradually facilitate this as they will be on a shared platform. So eventually it will be possible, for example, to create SharePoint sites that two different organizations can access using their own credentials. Eventually, with technologies like SharePoint, dreams like having one virtual medical record you can share immediately with any doctor in the world will become more possible. The browser itself is a barrier to the spread of SharePoint to different platforms such as Smartphones and tablets. The reliance on a WIMP (Windows, Icons, Menus Pointing Device) interface to interact with SharePoint means heavy customization is needed to make SharePoint work with touch screens. Microsoft is reacting to this need; by Windows 8 this situation will have improved.

The data center walls will replace the server towers as the barriers to integration, but eventually these will dissolve, too. In the meantime, building the most available and disaster-recoverable SharePoint architecture that includes a cloud element still requires careful planning, but there are many more possibilities than 10 years ago when SharePoint started.

Cloud Benefits

First, let's look at the rationale of deploying SharePoint in to the cloud rather than on-premises. In this section, I'll talk about capacity- and agility-related benefits of the cloud. There are, of course, many benefits to cloud hosting that are not directly related to HA, and I won't talk about all of them here. However, do keep in mind that there are a number of indirect HA benefits. For example, low cost of ownership means SharePoint is less likely to be a budget-cut victim, thereby making low cost a resilience benefit.

Load Variation

Great minds think alike, but fools seldom differ.

—English proverb

Every business that has an open door to the public or even to its own staff has to have a process to deal with the problem of load variation. Your SharePoint servers have to be available when no one is using them or when suddenly hundreds or thousands of people decide to use the system for the same thing at the same time. This section shows how the cloud has made addressing this variability more possible.

Cloud Bursting

Load variation is also known as bursting. Take the example of a coffee shop in a train station. The staff at the registers sits idle until a train comes in, then 300 people have to queue for 10 minutes to get their morning caffeine fix. Then those people leave and the staff is idle again until the next train arrives. The same thing happens with servers: the load can be very high first thing in the morning and again just after lunch. The rest of the day it is quiet. Another example I saw recently was a company who made it possible for staff to request a new Smartphone via an InfoPath form on the SharePoint intranet. Once the e-mail went out linking to this form, the load on the server increased 500%, performance crawled, and the staff was frustrated.

The problem with this peaking of load from a SharePoint point of view is the same as the train station coffee shop. It takes time and money to procure and retain servers (both of coffee and SharePoint pages). It is a waste of resources if they are idle 90% of the time. For the coffee shop owner, the ideal situation would be able to hire 20 servers for the morning rush, pay them for 2 hours, then send 19 of them home at 9:30 a.m. But people don't want to work like that, unless they are paid for the whole day, and no employer wants to do that.

The cloud, however, can support spinning up a set of new servers and then turning them off again after they're no longer needed. Additionally, most providers only charge you for the time the servers are running. They don't charge you for the procurement process or storing the servers when they are not in use because they are invariably virtual and the resources can be reallocated to another customer relatively instantly.

Managing the Unpredictable

The example I gave of a company offering staff a Smartphone was one of predictable bursting, like knowing the 8:50 train will be full every business day. A benefit of the cloud in the case of the Smartphone offer is you would be able to spin up new infrastructure to support the influx of load for just the first week. Most cloud providers also make real monitoring simple, so as the demand falls, you can offload the additional resources and thus only pay for it as long as it is need. The availability benefit here is clear and one not to be underestimated.

However, bursting is oftentimes unpredictable, and it's with unpredictable bursting that cloud computing really makes its availability, reliability, and resilience clear. Cloud providers all allow you to specify events when the system will automatically scale out to handle the demand. For example, you could specify an event where if the CPU loads of the front-end web servers are all averaging over 50%, the cloud provider will automatically add a new front-end server into the farm to help with the increasing load. This works 24 hours a day, every day of the week, anywhere in the world. Many businesses don't have adequate coverage outside standard business hours in one country, but the Internet is global and 24 hours a day, every day of the year, irrespective of national or religious holidays. Whenever the spike happens, the farm will automatically scale out to handle the new unexpected load and then scale back again after the levels die off.

Dynamic Resource Allocation

SharePoint can be a victim of its own success. There is usually a pent-up demand of a collaborative solution like SharePoint in a business, and once IT can meet the business demands and match their requirements, it will grow fast. This growth comes as a surprise to some organizations; they roll out a pilot environment and see teams leap on it, demanding access. Storage is rapidly filled to capacity because no allowance was made for real production usage and so no capacity planning was done. Users are given sites without any guidance; some see it as a substitute for dwindling network capacity and thus dump content into this new storage space. SharePoint in the cloud has a significant advantage over a slow-moving internal procurement department. A cloud provider can allocate more virtual resources and spin up new virtual servers to accommodate the load because their capacity should be and usually is far greater than any one company can generate. This is not to say Microsoft, Amazon, or Rackspace don't oversubscribe their capacity; they inevitably do, but they are not in the business of wasting money either. Over subscription is not the same as over capacity. It is fair to say that your problem of procuring enough hardware to cope with demand hasn't gone away; you have just transferred it to your cloud provider. There is no such thing as infinite capacity, but a cloud provider can dynamically re-allocate resources and so offer more than they actually have.

Meeting Demand

Let's use the example of the coffee shop owner in the train station. Imagine he also owns the shoe repair and dry-cleaning services in the station. Once the coffee rush is over, he can re-allocate his staff to fix the pile of shoes and clean the pile of clothes that have arrived at the other two businesses in the station. Customers of coffee don't need to know he's using the person who serves their coffee with a smile every morning to clean someone else's suit. Cloud providers can promise people resources to meet any demand so long as everyone doesn't demand resources at the same time.

Agility

You can have your users using SharePoint Online in a fraction of the time it takes to plan, requisition, install, and configure a SharePoint farm on your network. Of course, if you want to add branding, the sync with your Active Directory accounts will add time, but the basic idea is that you can get everyone in your organization onto SharePoint Online in the time it takes to sign up and create their accounts. This is very compelling for any organization. Users generally ask for something when they need it, not weeks or months in advance of when they will need it. This is simply because they don't know what they'll need when; they are invariably reacting to a change in the market such as the demands of customers. The organization that reacts fastest, especially if it means responding to the needs of the customer before a competitor can, will be the one to succeed in the long run.

SharePoint Online also has a much more reasonable cost of entry for small businesses. Building redundant servers as well as development, staging, and production farms is too costly for the majority of organizations. I have described all of the requirements in previous chapters. Using the cloud means the responsibilities for these things are mainly passed to your cloud provider. To recap, just to achieve most RTO and RPOs you'd need the following:

- Well-documented disaster planning and a process to activate it.

- Multiple load balanced and redundant front-end web servers.

- Redundancy for the servers running your service application instances.

- Redundancy of network components: switches, NICs, reverse proxies, and load balancers, to name a few.

- Database server-level redundancy using clustering, mirroring, and/or log shipping.

- Storage redundancy such as SAN replication and disk striping with RAID.

- Datacenter redundancy, meaning all the above in a second failover datacenter.

- A well-tested and documented backup process.

Most cloud providers include all of this even if you have only created a SharePoint site for one user for one month. It makes it very tempting to not have to consider all the information this book makes you consider.

What if your organization does buy all this hardware and makes all this effort and it still doesn't meet the users' needs or their needs have changed by the time the servers are ready? And what if the farm is set up and deployed incorrectly and so is a waste of money? Using cloud providers like SharePoint Online makes the cost of trying SharePoint smaller and thus the potential loss far less. With cloud providers in general, you pay monthly for what you use; if you decide to finish with the service, you only have to pay for what you have used up to that day (or month, at worst).

Cloud Architectures

You can't classify your cloud architecture simply by where the services you offer are hosted (on-premises or off-premises) because it's possible to have an on- or off-premises cloud and a combination of the two. When contemplating which option is better, the distinctions come down to cost and control. The differences are as true of SharePoint in the cloud as they are of all out-of-the-box (OOB) solutions vs. fully customised solutions: for greater cost you gain greater control, but it takes much more work and time to complete. Think of the example shown Figure 10-4: if you have a suit designed by a tailor to fit you, it will be exactly what you want but will take much more of your time and money to get. The risk is that the suit will be out of fashion or you will have put on weight by the time it is finished. If you buy a suit off the peg, it is cheap and fast and it will meet your basic requirements. If you don't like it, you can just throw it away and buy another with little lost. There is always a perfect balance between your available resources and requirements. The more unique your requirements, the higher the cost. This is as true of SharePoint as it is of suits. If you are now on-premises only and want to change, you have to factor in the level of cost and control your organization needs.

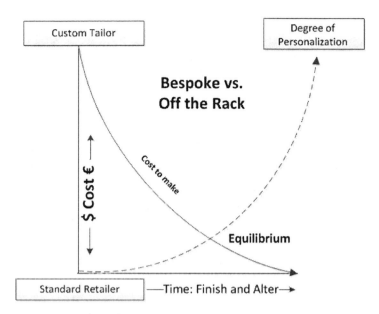

Figure 10-4. Bespoke means cost.

Public Cloud

With a public cloud, your whole SharePoint deployment is hosted externally to your organization. This model has all the benefits described previously. The disadvantages from the point of view of hardware and software are the lack of direct control over the infrastructure, which limits your control in the event of an outage, and the degree to which you can customise the application. SharePoint Online Standard and Dedicated editions are the best examples of SharePoint in a public cloud. SharePoint Online Standard means your sites share the same hardware as other clients; this is also referred to as multi-tenancy. With the Dedicated edition, you have your own hardware, which may be necessary from a security or compliance standpoint. It also gives a greater sense of control over the farm to the business and administrators. Dedicated plans also have better RTOs and RPOs in the SLAs from Microsoft. These will change, so here's the link to the current page that provides this information and the link for SharePoint Online Standard.

- "Microsoft Office 365 Service Descriptions and Service Level Agreements for Dedicated Subscription Plans" at http://tinyurl.com/3q96wet.

- "Microsoft SharePoint Online Standard Service Description" at http://tinyurl.com/3oaby5y.

In summary, the RPO for Dedicated SharePoint Online is 4 hours or less and the RTO is 2 hours or less (the 4 hours don't include scheduled outage time). With Standard, it is 12 hours RPO and RTO is 24 hours. That's a large difference.

Private Cloud

A private cloud is where a large company's IT team acts like a public cloud provider and sells services to the divisions, departments, and teams within the organization. It makes tracking the cost and earnings of the IT department easier. IT acts more like an independent business by reducing costs and maximizing profitability. They are, in a sense, competing with external public clouds because the business could choose not to buy from them and go outside. Even if they can't, they can compare prices. There are economies of scale associated with cloud computing: only very large enterprises can afford the upfront cost of setting up and maintaining a private cloud, but it can create a leaner and more efficient IT department and make the business appreciate the costs involved in providing IT services. This means less waste and ultimately more savings for the company. A private cloud can also have different policies and rules that reflect specific needs. It's like making your own suit: it's better suited to you than one from off the rack, but it's expensive in terms of time and effort to create and maintain.

Just because all your SharePoint servers are virtualized doesn't mean you have a private cloud. Virtual infrastructure requires just as much administration as physical infrastructure. Clouds are more automated. This automation is what makes the cloud available, scalable, and even self-managing. In addition to this infrastructure automation, clouds are designed to host multiple tenants that are separate from one another logically if not physically. SharePoint 2010 has built-in features that help maintain hundreds or thousands of these. Being built on separate tenancies is very important to the cloud concept. It means that SharePoint can support sandboxed groups of users whereby one group can't see the data of another; these groups can be business units, divisions, offices, teams departments, etc. It also means if one group creates a performance issue, it will not negatively impact the performance or availability of potentially thousands of other groups. This ability to separate and automate is what makes SharePoint 2010 cloud-capable, unlike the previous versions.

Hybrid: the Archaeopteryx

Microsoft uses the term "hybrid" to describe a mixture of a public and private cloud. I think the hybrid model is less a mix of two models and more a truly transition model, like the Archaeopteryx, which was a transition between dinosaurs and birds. The hybrid model is for an organization gradually transition to the cloud while slowly scaling down the on-premises architecture.

Technology has become smaller, cheaper, and more mobile. It has also become virtual. On-premises server farms are like dinosaurs: they require too many resources to live. The smaller, fitter creatures will survive. The Archaeopteryx got off the ground and up into the clouds. It and creatures like it evolved into the 10,000 or so bird species that exist today. This is the transition SharePoint is making now, too.

Migration

It is a common requirement of the business to migrate content from one location to the other. In my opinion, it's more important to migrate processes to the utility of the public cloud than to migrate data. Focusing on the content generated in the past is usually a reflex defense mechanism, a generally unconscious fear of change. There is generally no need to migrate 95% of old content to the new platform. That doesn't mean it should be deleted. The on-premises architecture can be slowly marked as read-only so it will not continue to grow. Some can be archived and eventually most can be deleted. There is more information on migration best practices in Chapter 11.

A reality I constantly meet when consulting for organizations is that users don't readily accept that the majority of the content they generate is only useful during the initial collaboration phase. Much of it is a by-product of a larger effort such as documenting a decision or process. These records can be transitioned to the cloud, but this is best done by the business itself, not IT or via a third party tool. Either way, transitioning such content is slower and more expensive than the benefits.

Users have to own their own content. If they really must preserve something, it can be easily moved from one environment to the other either by them gradually or perhaps with a tool. The real work in migration is

- Planning and coordinating the migration.

- Identifying who owns what content.

- Choosing what content to preserve.

- Defining what metadata to apply to it.

- Deciding what structure to put it in: sites, lists, and libraries.

- Deciding what security to apply to the content.

A tool can only apply what users have chosen. The majority of content no longer has an owner, has no metadata, and is unstructured, so it is impossible to know its future value to the business.

Evolution, like collaboration with SharePoint, is a process, and user process can be quickly moved to a new platform. One of the strengths of SharePoint is rapid creation of new collaboration spaces, workflows, forms, and sites. This is where the potential benefits of the migration to the cloud lie. Moving large amounts of valueless data is a waste of resources: hardware, software, and the time and effort of IT and business people. This is a reality rarely understood, but the real opportunity is in migrating business processes.

Architecting for Disaster Recovery in the Cloud

In this section I will show how SharePoint in the cloud is possible. The key point is that the content, users, and code from different tenants can be isolated from one another. Tenants who opt for dedicated hardware are treated better than those who share space with others: Standard SharePoint Online only supports a 30-day Recycle Bin and 14-day DR backup to tape. Full backups are only done every 12 hours and stored for 14 days. Dedicated SharePoint Online gives you 30 days backed up to tape. This is a large difference. In either case, once that 14 or 30 days has elapsed, there is no way to retrieve lost data. If that is not enough, the SharePoint Online cloud is not for you. Still, there are always third party hosts like Amazon or Rackspace where you can arrange to back up on any schedule you want so long as you pay for the capacity. Let's look in more detail at how SharePoint Online does multi-tenancy.

Multi-Tenancy

To understand how you would view disaster recovery in a cloud scenario, public or private, you have to understand how multi-tenancy divisions content physically and logically in SharePoint 2010. The metaphor of tenancy is used because the system is logically similar to how apartment buildings are organized. A given tenant only has access to their own space within the overall structure. They are, however, in the same building and they do share common infrastructure such as hallways, stairs, and elevators (or lifts, as we call them my side of the Atlantic). Multi-tenancy capabilities in SharePoint 2010 follow a similar logic. The logical containers for tenants' content are site collections. Think of them as rooms. Tenants can have multiple rooms in the overall building.

In SharePoint 2007, tenants could only be logically separated by web applications, and there is a limit to how many of these you can have in a SharePoint farm. It's in the hundreds. Think of it as the maximum number of floors you can have in an apartment building. The same tenants can't be on the same floor. Now, however, SharePoint 2010 allows multiple tenants in the same web application or floor. Here are the reasons why this is possible.

Subscriptions

A site subscription sounds like something related to alerts, but it's a piece of site metadata in the form of a unique GUID that associates it with a specific tenant. Think of it as a way of knowing which room in the building is being used by whom. Site subscriptions are created via PowerShell. The owner of the cloud creates a new tenancy for a new tenant and can then associate site collections with that GUID.

Administration Sites

This subscription GUID means a tenant can manage their site collections through their own administration site called the Administration Center. The Tenant Administration Site (Figure 10-5) is used to perform global configuration or structure changes such as creating further site collections, managing user profiles, term store, and other service applications.

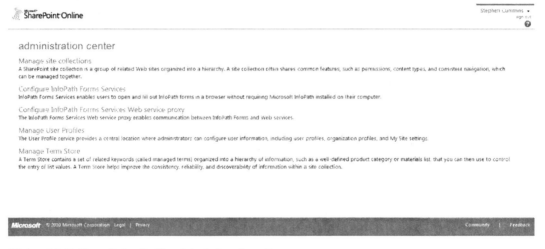

Figure 10-5. SharePoint Online Administraiton Center

Feature Packs

Feature packs are groups of features associated with one tenant. This is done the same way as site subscriptions: a GUID is associated with the feature to connect it to a tenant. This allows the cloud administrator or tenant to activate or deactivate features just for their site collections. It also creates the potential for an app store-like marketplace where cloud providers can sell or rent features to tenants. Tenants could also create stores in their own spaces. Features can be activated or deactivated through the web UI (Figure 10-6).

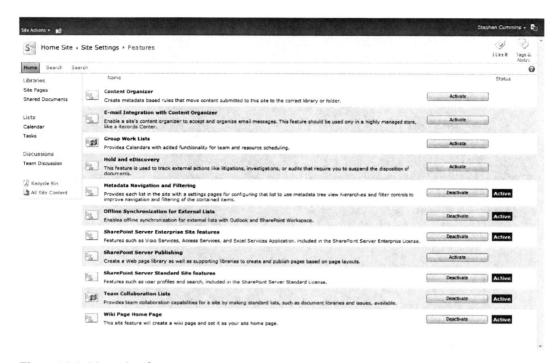

Figure 10-6. Managing features

Host Header Site Collections

Host header site collections also existed in SharePoint 20007, but they are still an essential method to sandbox tenant sites. Host header site collections enable the cloud administrator to assign multiple vanity domains to a given web application (Figure 10-7). This will allow you to give each tenant in the web application its own root level domain. For example, if the web application has a URL of `http://intranet.spsfaq.com`, a site collection at `http://intranet.spsfaq.com/sites/hr` can be accessible via `http://hr.share1point.com`.

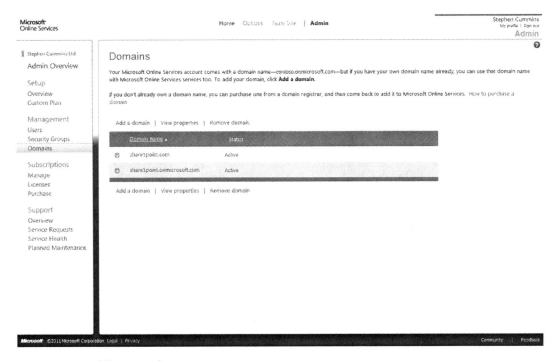

Figure 10-7. Adding your domains

Service Isolation

As mentioned in relation to tenant administration sites, service applications can be deployed in what is called partitioned mode. This means the service application is associated with a specific web application that contains tenants, and each tenant will see their own administrative interface to configure that service application. This is especially powerful with service applications such as user profiles and the term store. This would not have been possible in SharePoint 2007 because of the limited scope for dividing up Shared Service Providers.

Sandboxed Solutions

Sandboxed solutions mean two things that are essential to facilitate custom development in an environment where tenants are sharing the same resources. Previously, tenant's apartments seemed isolated, but if one tenant left their bath running and it overflowed, it would spill into multiple apartments below it and ruin them, too. SharePoint now runs custom code in its own memory space so that if the code demands too many resources or crashes, it only impacts on the tenant. SharePoint 2010 also allows tenants to allocate different portions of their apportioned resources to different solutions.

As you can see, multi-tenancy places the responsibility for much of the availability and resource management with your cloud provider, but certain parts can now be managed by the tenant and that applies to a public or private cloud. The greater complexity comes in planning single sign-on between your cloud and your Windows network.

Planning Federation

Even if you create user accounts in the cloud for your users, these accounts will not automatically map to the user accounts your staff uses to log into Windows. As a result, they will be prompted to enter their cloud credentials when they visit. The solution is to connect your Windows Active Directory to the cloud via Active Directory Federation Services. This brings its own risks from a disaster planning perspective, so I will deal with it next.

While your new cloud may be floating high above your network, your user's Active Directory is still tied to the ground. This means you will still have to add infrastructure to your network if you want to keep your users' network accounts in sync with their cloud accounts. If you don't, users will have to keep logging in when they visit the cloud site, rather than having it just open because it picks up their credentials from Windows. If you do set up this type of identity federation, there are HA considerations. While it is beyond the scope of this book to detail all the steps in planning and deploying identity federation, I will detail it enough so you know what to do to ensure the architecture is resistant to failure.

Active Directory Federation Services 2.0 (ADFS) is a Windows (as opposed to a SharePoint) service that you install to federate your Windows users' credentials to your cloud. ADFS 2.0 is a central piece of Microsoft's identity management strategy, providing a two-way gateway for sending and receiving claims-based requests, using SAML-based tokens containing information about users and what they want in terms of information and access. Security Assertion Markup Language (SAML) is an XML-based open standard for exchanging authentication and authorization data between security domains. The key point is that it is not a Microsoft-only technology. Its role is to communicate identity data in a structured way between an identity provider (a producer of assertions) and a service provider (a consumer of assertions). Another important note is that this must be a single forest.

There are two types of forest topologies: the single forest and the multiple forest. A forest represents the outermost boundary of the directory service. All resources in a forest implicitly trust each other regardless of where in the forest they are located. Within each forest, there is a common directory schema and configuration of the directory service. A forest can be comprised of one or more domains. Single sign-on with SharePoint Online (as part of Office 365) doesn't support multiple forests. In terms of credentials and prerequisites, before you add this role to your domain, ensure you have installed .NET 3.5 SP1 and that you are logged in as a domain administrator.

A Federation Server Farm

You will install this server role on more than one server on your domain to provide redundancy. Collectively you'll refer to these as your federation farm. You'll place all these federation servers in your internal domain behind a firewall and use a NLB host to create a cluster with a dedicated cluster DNS name and cluster IP address. When you create your federation service you'll want to use the same FQDN as your NLB cluster's DNS name. This will give you redundancy at the server level. Also, from a resilience standpoint, the cluster DNS name and the federation service name must be the same, such as `fs.share1point.com`. The FQDN must also be Internet-routable through your preferred third party domain registrar.

Federation Proxy Servers

Federation proxy servers redirect client authentication requests coming from SharePoint Online in the cloud into your organization's internal domain. These servers are most commonly placed in a DMZ that is segregated from your internal network. In addition to the redundant ADFS servers in your federation server farm on your internal network, you'll need at least two more ADFS servers (proxies) for hardware and DNS redundancy as well as another dedicated NLB cluster. Having another AD domain is optional, but it is common to join the proxies to an external domain rather than your internal one.

This second NLB in the DMZ must be configured with an external IP address that the domain is registered to use. For example, you would want to register a domain similar to fs.spsfaq.com with your registrar, then point it to the NLB cluster in your DMZ. The NLB cluster FQDN also must use the same cluster domain name as the internal NLB cluster domain name. For example, both clusters as well as the federation service will use the same FQDN (fs.spsfaq.com). Also, the federation proxy servers themselves must be configured with Internet-accessible IP addresses. You'll also need to set up redundancy at the database level during installation, which I will discuss next.

Certificates

All ADFS traffic that communicates through the firewall uses HTTPS on port 443 by default, so you'll need to purchase a certificate to make the traffic encrypted and therefore secure. Otherwise, someone could intercept the packages and read your users' credentials. Most organizations use the same certificate they use in their internal network.

WID vs. SQL

In the planning phase, you need to understand which database mode you should choose during installation. ADFS is set up separately from Active Directory; it's just able to communicate with it. When you install ADFS, it creates a configuration database; this can be a Windows Internal Database (WID) or a SQL server database. From a redundancy point of view, SQL is the better option. That is because with a WID, there is only one primary copy on one server where you write changes. The others simply receive propagated copies of the changes. You can only write to the primary; the others are read-only. Therefore, if you make a change to the configuration, that change has to be propagated to the secondary servers.

With SQL Server you have more control and there is only once central database. This means that you can use any server to make configuration changes and there is no propagation delay. Because your data is in SQL Server, you now have all the benefits of scalability and high availability you have applied to your other SharePoint databases. You can use SQL Server's clustering and mirroring capabilities for HA and you can add more SQL Servers to the cluster to increase throughput.

WID also has a scale limitation that may or may not affect you: you have a maximum of five servers in the federation farm. Five servers can support up to 60,000 users. If your organization has more than 60,000 users, you'll need to use SQL Server so you can add more than five servers in your federation farm. Even though SQL has many benefits not available to WID, most ADFS installations still use WID because it's so easy to configure. Irrespective of the users you have in your organization, I would recommend you have at least two federation servers to make them redundant. Also, if those servers are virtual, make sure they are split across two physical servers to prevent the host server becoming a single point of failure.

Further Considerations

You may have thought that setting up a cloud version of SharePoint would mean no longer having to plan or implement this level of technically complex infrastructure. It is possible to use SharePoint in the cloud without having identity federation. It just means users have to explicitly log on occasionally. SharePoint Online does do a limited amount of cookie caching so the user's identity is retained between browser sessions, so this is not as inconvenient as it sounds. As well as setting up this federation farm, you can use the Microsoft Online Services Module for Windows PowerShell to establish a trust with

Office 365. The Microsoft Online Services Module for Windows PowerShell is a download that comes with Office 365. This module installs a set of cmdlets to Windows PowerShell; you run those cmdlets to set up single sign-on for Office 365. Microsoft recommend you set up single sign-on before you set up Active Directory synchronization.

Microsoft also points out that activating directory synchronization is a one-way street. You can't currently deactivate directory synchronization. Once you have activated directory synchronization, you can only edit synchronized objects using on-premises applications.

Additionally, there is the task of ensuring user client machines are ready for Office 365. This means installing the required updates for Office 365 from the Office 365 downloads page to ensure that your users are running the latest Windows updates.

In *Office 365 Community*, Microsoft also recommends all client machines install the Microsoft Online Services Sign-In Assistant (MOS SIA). "This provides the end user with sign-in capabilities to Microsoft Online Services like Microsoft Office 365. The MOS SIA installs client components that allow desktop applications like Microsoft Outlook and Microsoft Lync to authenticate to Microsoft Online Services. The MOS SIA also provides an improved sign-in experience so users can access Microsoft Online Services without re-entering their usernames or passwords." There is a lot to consider beyond just the HA consideration I have detailed here.

Summary

So how is this cloud computing? It sounds like you are just as tied to servers and client machine installs as ever before. The important thing is not to believe the marketing hype. There is still a great deal of planning involved in moving to the cloud. Microsoft can consult with you to help with this transition, and there are more and more third parties that can help, too. But it should be clear that while cloud computing has many benefits, it also still has responsibilities.

This chapter has looked at the following:

- The process by which SharePoint developed into its current form.

- How cloud architecture options come down to cost and control.

- Multi-tenancy and planning federation: key aspects of SharePoint in the cloud.

SharePoint has come a long way, but right now it feels like a transitional species, half way between dinosaur and bird. It has taken wing, it is in the clouds, but it is still being pulled to earth by its history. Maybe in another version or two it will have fully made the move.

CHAPTER 11

Best and Worst Practices

A principle is the expression of perfection, and as imperfect beings like us cannot practise perfection, we devise every moment limits of its compromise in practice.

—Mohandas Gandhi

SharePoint has not yet reached its full potential. This is partly due to the time it takes to refine and perfect an application, but it is also due to the limitations and boundaries set for it by the technologies upon which it is dependent. SharePoint is bound by .NET, Windows, Active Directory, networks, latency, bandwidth, SQL Server, and the Internet, in no particular order. But the primary limiter of the potential of SharePoint by far is the decision makers who have responsibility for its planning, deployment, and maintenance. There are many perspectives you can take on why something is what it is; there are always many interrelated causes. While we can't control the hardware, software, networking, and developmental limitations of the SharePoint platform, the actions of those who run it can make the greatest difference to its success or failure.

This chapter is an attempt to distil the best and worst practices I have seen during my years as an end-to-end implementer of SharePoint solutions. Most of what makes SharePoint successful comes down to the people involved and the decisions they make. I have fit these under the following four main headings:

- *Be prepared to work hard*: Good results take resources, consensus, and effort.

- *Avoid quagmires*: Issues such as migration, metadata, customization, workflow, and others can get thorny.

- *Change management*: This is not something tacked on after a farm is deployed.

- *Governance*: Have the right people in the right roles who know the right things.

There are many worst practices to avoid. During the course of this chapter I will explain the ones that create the most difficulty in maintaining a SharePoint farm.

Work Hard and Don't Take Shortcuts

Unfortunately, there are no shortcuts to a successful implementation of SharePoint. There has to be consensus and an appropriate expenditure of resources. There is prevalent a business philosophy that makes the assumption that any attempt to do things in a methodical way is just wasting resources and the best way is always the quickest way. This approach can perhaps lead to success in the short term. However, as time passes, the results of this management approach become evident. Forging ahead without following a plan starts a process but it can't anticipate any complexity. The reflex reaction is to throw more resources at the problem without attempting to understand it. Eventually, the process grinds to a halt, leaving a mess for someone else to clean up.

For example, you can set up SharePoint on the first pieces of hardware available on the network and give people access. You can then hire some developers or a third party company to set up a boilerplate server farm, backup plan, governance plan, and branding. This can be done quickly albeit expensively. The flaw in this approach is that no detailed planning has been done to establish if and what SharePoint is indeed needed for—and this is what shapes the actual solution. If this step is skipped, the result is a SharePoint platform doomed to fail. The reason organizations find themselves in this situation is solely because of managers who avoid proper planning; SharePoint is marketed to appeal to people who think and act that way. In many cases, SharePoint is chosen and installed without any planning or a formal Request For Proposal (RFP). Even if an RFP is done, it is based on superficial needs, which are not enough to execute a proper SharePoint implementation. SharePoint must be planned properly with ownership by the business being the goal. If setup it done carefully and with full participation of IT and the business, the results will be much better.

A Typical SharePoint RFP

SharePoint is generally chosen by a manager who read some marketing information online. Then someone lower down in the organization is told to create an RFP. RFPs are not a bad thing as a rule: a RFP is the early stage in a procurement process after an RFI (Request for Information) sets up the initial process. The first step is an invitation to suppliers, often through a bidding process, to submit a proposal on a specific commodity or service (in this case, for SharePoint). The RFP process brings structure to the procurement decision and is meant to allow the risks and benefits to be identified clearly upfront. However, here the largest risks have been ignored: is SharePoint the right choice and is the organization prepared for the amount of work it will take to transition to it?

In this scenario, third party companies are invited to submit proposals on how they would meet the organizations needs, which are only very vaguely described in the RFP because even if a detailed business analysis was done internally, it was done by someone without in-depth SharePoint experience. As a consequence, these RFPs tend to take the form of a brochure for SharePoint. Here is a typical example:

TYPICAL RFP

Company X has lots of data in many different systems and people in many places. We also have lots of different applications and these are expensive to support. We want SharePoint so we can have one application to do everything and store everything. In your response to this RFP, due in two weeks, tell us how you would use SharePoint to deliver the following:

- One place where people go to put everything.

- Centralized Search so people have one way to find everything.

- Web content management, but not to replace our intranet records management, although we have not yet defined any records.

- Document management, although we don't have any policies.

- Facebook for the Enterprise.

- To migrate all our content, and to do so without any disruption to users.

- We want to migrate our business processes into workflows, too.

Also, send us a detailed design of the SharePoint farm architecture and how you would do backups.

The vendors have trouble giving any more than a generic response to these criteria and add the proviso that "further analysis will be required." It is better to perform a proper, detailed evaluation of the business' needs as this will give the respondents more information upon which to base a solution. There will always be a requirement to add some contingency time into the proposal, but this is simply a sensible risk mitigation exercise rather than time that will certainly be used to perform a more comprehensive business analysis.

Good Practices

An ounce of practice is worth more than tons of preaching.

—Mohandas Gandhi

For a large organization, it could require hundreds of workshops with every team to establish their business processes and how SharePoint could be used to do them better. The assumption is always that SharePoint is the answer and that it is now the task of the third party company to frame the question exactly to fit that. Good consultancies guide the client through the process of setting up SharePoint in a small way initially and then hand over ownership to them as soon as possible so they can learn about and own the platform themselves. A good consultancy supports their client in establishing internal processes for the assessment of user requirements and how these can be translated into out-of-the-box (OOB) solutions with SharePoint, not ones that require custom code and thus usually can't be owned internally. Good consultancies will establish the business needs for SharePoint before they build a scalable, secure, and available architecture. They will also take into account that different content will have different RTOs and RPOs and that these can't be defined without a proper business impact analysis. This is information I have covered in previous chapters and should be familiar to you by now.

Putting the Cart Before the Horse

SharePoint is Microsoft's fastest growing product in its history. This is partly because of the need for something that provides users with better and faster information sharing, but it is also because of Microsoft's unique position in the majority of enterprises. This position creates a situation where SharePoint is installed before anyone has assessed what it can and should be used for: no business case has been prepared. This is putting the cart before the horse (see Figure 11-1). Here are the main reasons SharePoint can be leveraged into organizations by Microsoft in this way.

Figure 11-1. Slow and inefficient

Office and Windows

Office in all its versions is the dominant productivity tool used by most people in business. How many of us could function without Word, Outlook, or Excel at work? The same is true of Windows; for most businesses, it's the only PC OS available to users. SharePoint integrates better with Office and Windows than any third party product. This is a compelling driver for organizations to reduce the risk of non-user adoption. It also helps Microsoft bundle SharePoint with Office and Windows, but they only do this indirectly via licensing bundles.

Licences

SharePoint Server and user licenses are bundled in an Enterprise Agreement with Microsoft for Office and Windows. That means many companies have SharePoint licences "for free." The true cost of setting up SharePoint is in planning; a lack of a proper analysis means this is not given the attention it deserves. It is important to take into account the cost of purchasing, installing, and managing the hardware for the multiple farms. A large enterprise could need 15 or more servers. Even with SharePoint Online, synchronisation with Active Directory requires hardware. The licenses may seem free, but a functioning SharePoint platform that meets your business needs is not.

With a beginning like this, there is a risk that things will simply get worse for the SharePoint platform. Seeing SharePoint only as an IT product, rather than a business process mapping tool, means it is not perceived correctly from the start. With this misperception, the pressure is placed on IT services to make SharePoint "work." IT thinks that their role is to support the infrastructure; it's up to the business to decide what and how to use it. Even if the organization does have a services arm that supports an internal consulting role, they are unlikely to have SharePoint experts in house. If they hire someone to support the business, this person is rarely given the authority to make changes to how the business operates so that it can get the best benefit from SharePoint; as a result, they become an expensive support person. SharePoint becomes a quagmire that no one wants to get stuck in.

Sidestepping Quagmires

Worst practices don't seem that way at first. We all try to do the best we can. It is only in retrospect we realize our mistakes and try to learn from them. At first, we see what appear to be structured, pragmatic approaches to implementing SharePoint. It is only when we look back do we see that they are based on a natural misunderstanding of the nature of SharePoint. In this section I will describe the worst of these practices and the alternative best practices. I'm describing the worst practices as quagmires because there are a number of characteristics of real quagmires that are the same as the metaphorical SharePoint quagmires I describe here. They are detailed here so you can spot them and avoid them.

1. A quagmire looks like normal, flat, clear ground that is perfectly safe to enter.

2. It is usually alongside a hard, uneven path, so the quagmire looks like a great shortcut. You feel very clever for taking this seemingly better route.

3. As you enter, it seems fine—maybe a little soft under foot—but you still make progress as there are no obvious obstacles.

4. As you move further in, the footing gets softer and progress is slower, but you still move forward hoping it will get better.

5. Now you are in the middle of the quagmire. Your feet are stuck, and you can't go forward or back.

6. You start sinking and look for help. Anyone coming to help you gets stuck, too.

7. Once you've fully disappeared, the quagmire returns to looking flat and inviting for the next person coming along looking for a shortcut.

The metaphorical quagmires you can get in when planning to implement SharePoint are the same.

1. The approaches appear to be quite easy and safe.

2. There is another alternative but it is obviously harder and more uncertain.

3. Initially, you make progress with this approach.

4. You gradually notice it is taking more and more effort to make less and less progress.

5. Eventually you have gone so far in this approach that it will be just as costly to go back as forward.

6. You contract with the wrong external expert, buy an ill-suited third party tool, or write overly complex software to try to move forward again.

7. All of your wasted efforts lead nowhere and you are forced to give up. The reason you gave up is not fully explained, so someone else eventually starts making the same mistake.

Let's see how this pattern applies to the most common quagmires in SharePoint implementations, starting with migration—easily the biggest and most dangerous of them all.

Migration

History in its broadest aspect is a record of man's migrations from one environment to another.

—Huntington Ellsworth

Implementing SharePoint should be seen as a migration of business tasks and processes, but it is very often mistakenly seen as a migration of content. This is due to a mistaken understanding of the nature of SharePoint. It is not a file storage system with drives and folders like Windows. This misunderstanding of the terrain of SharePoint is the first step into the migration quagmire. The mistaken perception is that migrating content to SharePoint is surely as simple as moving files and folders from one drive to the next. If you explain that SharePoint is in fact a collaboration tool and not simply a storage tool, this point is dismissed as it leads to a harder road: an analysis of all the tasks and processes in the business and how these can be mapped to functionality in SharePoint. This path means real commitment from the content owners and lots of work: once the processes have been identified, there needs to be a new taxonomy created in SharePoint and then a slow, manual migration of content to the correct locations. The business would prefer not to go down this path, so it fixates on the idea that migrating to SharePoint is simply a copy and paste process.

There are simple ways to migrate content to SharePoint: users can drag files and folders in via Windows Explorer view of Document Libraries and Lists can be imported from Excel. An initial site structure can be created that reflects the organizational hierarchy and Active Directory groups can be used to grant access to these. At this point, progress seems fast and the idea that SharePoint is easy to set up seems vindicated. But as more content is dumped into SharePoint, the progress becomes slower. Users complain that they don't know when or how to use SharePoint, and it appears to be just another location for files to be dropped and forgotten. The site hierarchy is not helpful as the sites quickly become "cobwebs" as no-one updates them or uses them for any real business task except some meeting agendas or announcements. The question is asked as to the benefit of SharePoint to the business.

Now, however, there is a lot of real business data in SharePoint, but SharePoint is not really doing anything for the business. The solution at this point is to talk to the business and work out what is effective and what is not. Build on the parts that are effective and try to improve those that are not by giving more direction and guidance on how SharePoint can and should be used. External tools can help but should be evaluated carefully and even tested before purchase. This is because they usually require a lot of analysis and training to use effectively. By taking this approach you avoid the quagmire of choosing poor advice or mismatched tools.

Best Practice

Now the stakeholders on the company are bewildered as to why the initial promise of SharePoint was not fulfilled, so they mothball the project. SharePoint stagnates until someone else in the organization decides to revitalize it. They either avoid this quagmire or step into it again. The best way to avoid the migration quagmire is to follow these steps. These are more complex than the "easy" approach, but they do work.

1. Understand that SharePoint is a process and collaboration tool.

2. Hold workshops with key teams within your organization who will act as early adopters of the technology.

3. In advance of these workshops, give the teams a questionnaire that asks them about key sharing and collaboration processes that they want to improve.

4. Map their requirements to OOB SharePoint functionality.

5. Give the users a chance to pilot, understand, and take ownership of what you have set up for them.

6. Hand over ownership of the SharePoint processes to the teams.

7. If the users would benefit from some content being migrated into SharePoint, they can move it manually themselves. Occasionally, there is a benefit to migrating intranet content.

It can be difficult to promote this approach as it requires users to be directly involved and take ownership. It is then necessary to show them the benefits to them of doing it this way. Focus on the fact this will make their lives easier, not harder. Also explain how content migration is not a way to implement SharePoint. This is not the easiest path, but it is the best. It is also the first quagmire most organizations step into. Unfortunately, there are other quagmires that have to be avoided, too. The next is not based on the inherent problem of moving content into SharePoint, but of moving information about content.

Metadata

The metadata quagmire is based on the mistaken assumption that all properties and content types must be defined before the system can be used and that strict, centrally managed metadata has to be applied to all content. The opposite is also true: content can be added before a useful metadata structure is applied. While it is true that SharePoint can centrally manage metadata, and keep properties and content types consistent across site collections and even farms via the managed metadata service, it is not true that everything has to have detailed metadata and that this all has to be defined in advance. Some content doesn't need any metadata and some only requires user-defined tags that don't have to be consistent with a central store of properties, although any properties can be promoted to that level.

At the beginning, the complexity of options leads some at the planning stage to reduce everything to one hierarchical tree of metadata that all content will sit on. Figure 11-2 shows one such example of a complex tree.

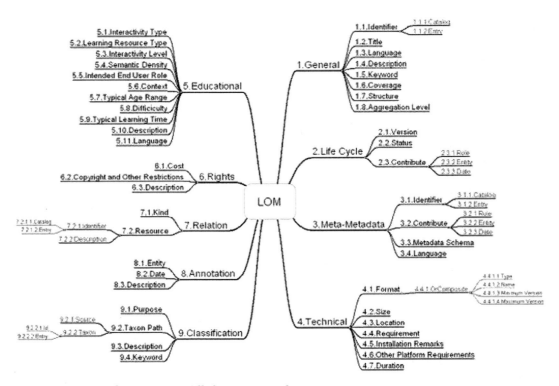

Figure 11-2. *Metadata maps rapidly become complex*

At first, this seems simpler than enabling all of the other metadata options. When SharePoint is initially installed, it is clear that there are many ways to provide users with the ability to tag content. SharePoint allows your users to create "folksonomies" of metadata for tagging their content that is only useful to them and only consistent within one list or library. Libraries can be navigated just using metadata, and groups of content can be given the same metadata using document sets. Rather than understand this complexity, the owners of SharePoint go for the one-tree approach.

This approach quickly starts to run into trouble when it turns out there are potentially hundreds of document types and that it will take a huge amount of time to identify every document type. Then each of those document types will need multiple properties, and each of those properties could have multiple predefined options in drop-downs or radio buttons.

Soon, they find themselves in the middle of the quagmire. They have hundreds or thousands of document types and properties, and they realize no user wants to have to choose which of these to use when they upload a document. They think the solution lies in a third party tool and employing external contractors to write code that will apply all this complex metadata automatically.

This seems to work for a while until the metadata becomes out of date and a complex process has to be entered into by the developers to update the metadata. They now realize it is not possible to push changes out to existing documents. It turns out that they should have used the OOB SharePoint metadata functionality that gives users more flexible ways to select and modify metadata. It also makes sense for metadata in different parts of SharePoint not to be consistent.

Following this one-tree approach to metadata gives users far too many potential content types, properties, and drop-downs to select from or fields to fill in before they can upload a document. It inevitably needs a custom solution, which is very slow to change, and so the metadata gets out of sync with users' needs.

Best Practice

The way to avoid this danger is to identify what content that will benefit from being in SharePoint with metadata and what will not. You should identify specific business benefits to assigning metadata to items. If you follow this approach, you will see that much of the benefit of SharePoint around collaboration can be achieved without needing strict metadata. Some content can use a looser folksonomy; this will give users all the benefits of tagging without restricting them to a large complex tree. This way, you avoid the quagmire.

Customization

SharePoint is a web application but there is an erroneous assumption that it is as simple to modify as a standard HTML web site. Microsoft is guilty of fostering this misperception by marketing tools like SharePoint Designer as being easy to use by users with no prior training. As a result, they try to make changes themselves to the branding or even the standard SharePoint functionality. Their first efforts are successful: they change the site logo and theme, but when they attempt to do more, they quickly realize SharePoint is more complex than it first appeared. It takes more and more time to achieve what appear to be small changes, such as changing the appearance of the Search box. SharePoint use is falling away and the company is building something much more complex to achieve the same purpose (Figure 11-3).

Figure 11-3. Custom does not always mean better.

Now they have moved so far from the standard SharePoint UI. Users demand more and insist SharePoint look and function exactly like they want it to, not as it was designed. As a result, the only way forward is to contract an external company to make the changes. They successfully make the changes, but now the system has become very complex and can only be updated by experienced developers from the third party company. This sends the cost of ownership higher than its value to the business. Once again, it stalls and is stuck until someone else in the business tries again to improve the UI.

Best Practice

The key point here is that SharePoint is a finished application and not as malleable as a web site. The more you bend it, the more likely it is to break. I would recommend as a rule of thumb that 80% of your SharePoint implementation be out of the box. About 17% could be extensions that don't require a feature or solution package. The final 3% can be custom code. The reason for these proportions is that the cost of managing customizations is high. If you don't have the skills in house to perform and maintain them, I recommend you don't do them. That may seem overly stringent, but as a principle, it's a good one to follow and a good target to have even if you don't always meet it.

Workflows

Workflow is another deceptively simple quagmire to slip into. Initially, the prospect of using a technology like SharePoint to make a work process more efficient is attractive. SharePoint offers built-in workflow templates. Other tools include SharePoint Designer, Visual Studio, and tools like Nintex which make the creation of workflows seem deceptively simple. Creating a workflow is seen as a better alternative to the more difficult path of changing and improving inefficient and time-wasting business practices.

At first, as before, the basic business processes are easily mapped to the approval workflow (for example) and the steps are defined. Then things become more complex. There is no official delegation policy if the approver is not available; in fact, there is no definitive list of approvers. It seems anyone in the department could potentially approve something. Then it becomes clear that the organization has no idea of the actual business process. The process has simply grown organically over time; while it doesn't really work and constantly breaks down, the stakeholders persist with the idea that the problem is not with the business process but with the workflow technology. Once again, expensive alternatives are explored. A detailed bespoke workflow is built with Visual Studio that it is believed to be able to capture every obscure eventuality even as the business comes up with new, contradictory rules for it to follow. As before, eventually the money and effort sinks into the quagmire and the workflow development team gives up.

Best Practice

No technology can fix a broken work process. If the business process is complex, inefficient, and ultimately doesn't work, the workflow will simply reflect that and be complex, inefficient, and ultimately not work. Using SharePoint or a very good third party workflow visualization and creation tool like the one from Nintex (Figure 11-4) should be seen as an opportunity to improve the business practice—to make it clear and efficient. Then the workflow will reflect that. The creation of a workflow is not a solution to a bad business process; trying to make it so is a quagmire of wasted time and effort.

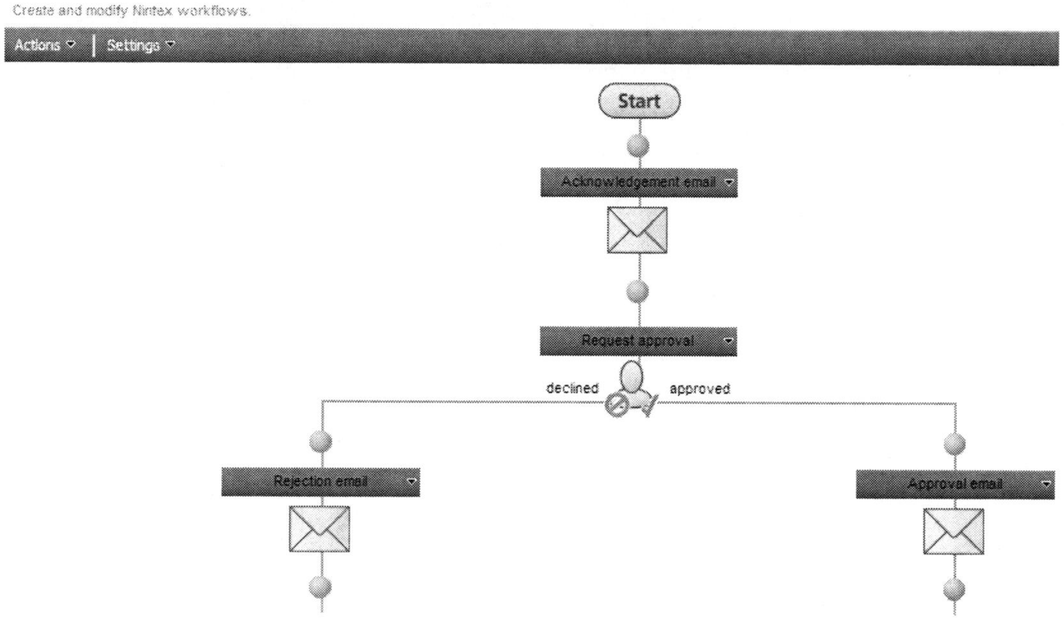

Create and modify Nintex workflows.

Actions ▽ | Settings ▽

Figure 11-4. Clear business processes make clear workflows.

Intranet Conflict

This is a definite quagmire to avoid in relation to SharePoint and that is not defining its purpose as opposed to the purpose of the existing intranet. In your organization, if anyone is asking why you need SharePoint if you already have an intranet and there's no clear answer, you know that you have a cart-before-the-horse situation: someone has decided to implement SharePoint without clearly knowing what it can be used for.

At first, setting up SharePoint alongside the intranet seems deceptively simple. Someone says that SharePoint is for "collaboration" while the intranet is for sharing news, templates, policies, and procedures with the company. After the two have existed alongside each other for a while, it becomes clear users are putting content on SharePoint in order to share it with the broader company community. This is because putting anything on the intranet takes weeks to submit, get approval, and format the pages for the custom intranet application. It also takes weeks to change the navigation to add links to the new pages. As a result, the business is putting documents in SharePoint, then e-mailing around links to them. This creates a conflict with Corporate Relations or Marketing or whatever the department owns the intranet. They want to control the message. As a result, they either insist that nothing be shared via SharePoint or that it only be linked to from their intranet. Progress grinds to a halt.

At this point third party vendors or contractors are brought in to look at how the intranet can be migrated to SharePoint. Now the organization is in the migration quagmire. Both SharePoint and the intranet are out of favor and both fall into disuse.

Best Practice

Many intranets become out of date and thus trapped in a quagmire of their own. The main reason for this is that they are overly complex to update and users can't contribute to them without passing through a slow approval process. As a result, they are either out of date or have such a narrow use they are little more than an internal brochure for the organization. The basic one-to-many sharing paradigm of intranets has had its time; users expect something more participatory like public forums on the Internet where they can instantly contribute or blogs where they can post a comment. SharePoint can work alongside an intranet as they serve different needs. The key recommendation here is to have both, but clearly define to users what content goes on which platform. It is also possible to replace the intranet completely with SharePoint publishing pages, although this is a separate and bigger task.

Records Management

SharePoint does indeed have records management functionality. As a result, people try to use it to create records management operations. At first, things go well: the company looks at the record management functionality of SharePoint, and it seems to be something the company can use. Then there is an immediate roadblock because the company doesn't actually have an information management strategy or a records management policy (Figure 11-5). SharePoint is just a tool, after all. Like with workflow, it is not a substitute for established business processes. It can't in itself improve processes either. The best approach is to begin a process of defining a strategy and a policy before you implement the policy on SharePoint. SharePoint is a great opportunity to begin records management as it will facilitate the process. Once again, don't skip the planning phase.

Strategy, Tactics and Operations

Figure 11-5. SharePoint might be the "how" but it can't give you the "why" or "what."

Best Practice

It may be that the desire to use SharePoint for records management underlines the fact that this is something the business needs and has matured to the point where it is ready for it. Like with workflow, having SharePoint can be seen as an opportunity to define why records management is needed and what the policy should be. Use this opportunity to bring the business together and analyse its needs. Then work out how SharePoint can meet those needs. Once again, there is no shortcut when it comes to records management. It represents a large upfront effort to put in place, but SharePoint can help bring the policy into practice.

Corporate Facebook

Gage: Mr. Zuckerberg, do I have your full attention?

Mark Zuckerberg: [stares out the window] No.

Gage: Do you think I deserve it?

Mark Zuckerberg: [looks at Gage] What?

Gage: Do you think I deserve your full attention?

Mark Zuckerberg: I had to swear an oath before we began this deposition, and I don't want to perjure myself, so I have a legal obligation to say no.

Gage: Okay. No, you don't think I deserve your attention.

Mark Zuckerberg: I think if your clients want to sit on my shoulders and call themselves tall, they have the right to give it a try, but there's no requirement that I enjoy sitting here listening to people lie. You have part of my attention—you have the minimum amount. The rest of my attention is back at the offices of Facebook, where my colleagues and I are doing things that no one in this room, including and especially your clients, are intellectually or creatively capable of doing.

[pauses]

Mark Zuckerberg: Did I adequately answer your condescending question?

—The Social Network (2010), Aaron Sorkin (screenplay), Ben Mezrich (book)

Many companies see their staffs as resources. A common belief is that if the staff shares information about themselves and their skills and knowledge, it will lead to better identification of resources and communication within the company. With Facebook, the site is provided for free to the users because the users are the product that is being sold to the advertisers. Everything people put in Facebook is valuable to the companies that use it to target their products to the people they perceive as their customers. The rule is simple: if you are getting something for free, it is because someone else is paying. In the case of Facebook, you are what they are paying for.

Translating this into a corporate setting is not so simple. There has to be an incentive for employees to share information about themselves. Since they are already paid to work there, it quickly becomes clear that building a sophisticated duplicate of Facebook in SharePoint is not enough. The organization becomes disillusioned because the employees don't see any reason to use this corporate networking application. It doesn't help them do their job or make their job easier. As a result, it stalls and you are back in the mud.

Best Practices

The key to the success of applications like Facebook is they offer people status and exclusivity. Popularity is the driving force of Facebook: who you are friends with is just as important as how many you have. In a corporate setting, presenting yourself well is key to advancement within the organization and perhaps out of it. There are reasons and incentives to network; getting known by the people who have the power to promote you or offer you a raise is a powerful incentive to use a corporate version of Facebook. If the corporate Facebook is presented to people from this perspective of self interest, then they may begin to invest the time and effort into it. And if they really use it, it becomes valuable to the organization. But to gain peoples' attention you have to appeal to their interests. You can't sell them something they don't want to buy just because you want them to buy it.

Change Management

As mentioned in Chapter 9, the management of change is crucial to a stable SharePoint system. But the worst practices around change management occur because initially it seems you can simply make changes to SharePoint without needing a proper process. However, that is only because the majority of SharePoint's functionality is supposed to be user-driven and can be changed through the web UI. Also, it initially contains very little production data that users depend on to do their jobs. As SharePoint becomes more adopted and integrated into the business's daily functioning, it becomes more essential to manage changes to it properly. It is likely that more customizations have crept in, and these require careful testing before they go live. More customizations mean greater risk because they may begin to have an impact on each other.

The best practice with change management is to have a clear process in place from the beginning, even before it is really necessary. This gives you a chance to perfect the process before any flaws have a significant impact on the business. This approach also gives the stakeholders and content owners time to learn and get used to the process. As an example, users are sometimes unaware that after an InfoPath form, approval workflow, and reporting dashboard go live, making a change to one will impact the others and may potentially destroy data. If there is no separate development and test/UAT environment, the changes have to be made in the live environment and the owners simply have to brace themselves for the support calls. This is not the way things should be done. Ensure the process is being used from the very start; this will make it more effective when it is really needed.

The biggest change in SharePoint to manage is the moment of going live. This is where users have full access to the system and can use it in earnest. This is frequently done too soon or not in a strategic way. The best practice is a phased release. This gives you a chance to identify problems early but minimize the impact to a few users. Think of this as being like the beta phase of Gmail or Google+. The product was live, but users could only get access if they were invited. Google was able to get feedback from real users, not just testers, before it was made available to everyone. Web applications can be released this way more easily because everything is on the server; it only has to be changed once for users to see the change, unlike when a CD had to be used to uninstall/install beta version of software. The crucial consideration here is that no changes can be made that will destroy content. Once a system is live, you are constrained by the fact that the user (and their content) is king.

Another error is not to have HA, DR, and backup plans in place from the very beginning. Many organizations only add these later when the system has grown until it is at risk. The HA and DR plans will be simple at the beginning, but they must be in place; a failure of the system early on can destroy user confidence, which is almost impossible to win back.

Governance

A house divided against itself cannot stand.

—Abraham Lincoln

The worst practice in relation to governance is to see SharePoint as either purely owned by the business or purely owned by IT. In both cases, SharePoint is missing vital input into its governance. Unless there are regular meetings between the content and the infrastructure owners, SharePoint as a platform will suffer. Without either, SharePoint can't grow and develop. The users provide the change and growth to the content and structure. IT provides the capacity and resources to support that change and growth. The two are interdependent. This must be clear to the owners of SharePoint and they must communicate.

SharePoint is a user-driven tool. Another worst practice I have seen is to over-centralize it. This means site creation, granting access, and even adding content are controlled by a small team. This is counter to the way SharePoint is designed to work and will eventually lead to frustration and non-user adoption. If your organization wanted a centralized content management tool and not a collaboration tool, SharePoint was the wrong choice. Train users who want to own sites and manage them. Give them guidance and encouragement in running SharePoint properly and you will have a healthier system in the long run. The following are just some good principles to pass on to users.

Folders Are Bad

A small bad habit of users to discourage early on is the creation of nested folders within libraries. Show users that the main way to sort content is columns and views, and the main navigation elements are sites and lists. There are some that would argue that only metadata matters as a structuring and organizing element in SharePoint, but sites and lists are still necessary for putting content into different containers that can have different audiences with different levels of access. No organization is completely flat and no SharePoint structure can be either, but folders are simply a throw-back to file servers and are rarely necessary in SharePoint.

Have Skills in House

Give a man a fish; you have fed him for today. Teach a man to fish; and you can sell him fishing equipment.

—Author Unknown

It may seem obvious but the golden rule of deciding if someone external should be asked to make a change to SharePoint is this: if no one internally understands how they did it, you need to recruit someone who does. This is true of branding as well as custom code. It is always cheaper in the long run to have skills in house than to develop a dependency on external providers. If you can't afford to take on someone new, train an existing employee. If no one can take on the ownership of changes, you will be dependent on third parties for any new changes. This is inefficient.

Permission Inheritance

I have also seen children successfully surmounting the effects of an evil inheritance.
That is due to purity being an inherent attribute of the soul.

—Mohandas Gandhi

The worst practice I find from users is a lack of understanding of the concept of permission inheritance. This is the concept that the children of an object will gain the same permission settings as the parent, so it's logical to group content that requires the same permissions. When you arrange it hierarchically, it's also logical to grant access at the highest level to avoid complex granular permission management that becomes impossible to track. Another principle in relation to permission management that it is very important to convey to content owners is the idea in SharePoint (indeed in many systems) that you group rights into permission groups, that you associate these permission groups with SharePoint groups, and then you add Active Directory user accounts and security groups to those SharePoint groups. This relationship structure is very important; as the architect of the system, you have a responsibility to convey the importance of this to the users.

Summary

Ultimately, when it comes to best and worst practices in SharePoint, there is no such thing as perfection and no implementation is all bad. But it is possible to improve and to avoid obvious pitfalls. The quote at the beginning of this chapter points out that while principles are expressions of perfection, we as imperfect beings can never fully attain them. But they do give us something to strive for and a direction and motivation for our efforts.

Primarily, you have to avoid the easy path of short term results, the quagmires of weak assumptions, a reactionary approach to change, and an irresponsible approach to governance. Those four principles will get your SharePoint platform off to a good start and keep it on course to the end of its voyage.

Final Conclusions

My basic principle is that you don't make decisions because they are easy; you don't make them because they are cheap; you don't make them because they're popular; you make them because they're right.

—Theodore Hesburgh (American Clergyman, University President)

The purpose of this chapter is to extract the key guiding principles from each from the preceding chapters. As I said in the introduction, SharePoint, like all technology, is constantly changing. I have worked on four versions of it now and have had to learn new technology and features each time. Luckily, I've been able to take the most important and hard-won lessons from version to version. This means that the lessons here will be useful to you now and in the future, no matter how the application changes.

This book doesn't attempt to proscribe one definitive path to HA and DR nirvana. There are too many different circumstances, people, and organizations in the world that make every implementation distinct, albeit similar. Like a suit, you can make one size that fits all, but it won't really look good on anyone.

The following are lessons that I apply to every new SharePoint project I embark upon. They are the most useful and valuable tools I have to create the individual SharePoint Architectures I build. The core principles of SharePoint are

- You have to understand SharePoint to manage it. Simplistic metaphors are a trap.

- Embrace change in SharePoint and manage it well.

- Make your platform as user-centric as possible.

- The business and IT must communicate and work together.

- Keep processes and procedures current.

- People and documentation are more important in a recovery than tools.

- Monitor to anticipate problems before they occur.

Key Points By Chapter

This section is in a sense a "cheat sheet" for the whole book. In it I distil the main messages of each chapter so that you can keep them clear in your mind during your own work and refer back to them quickly rather than having to read the whole thing again. If, dear reader, you have not bought this book and are perhaps flicking through it in a bookshop somewhere, you have come to the right place! If you have read the book up to now, congratulations! This section is to help refresh your memory and hopefully crystallize what has gone before.

Chapter 1: Steering Away from Disaster

A resolution to avoid an evil is seldom framed till the evil is so far advanced as to make avoidance impossible.

—Thomas Hardy

The metaphor of the Titanic disaster is a common thread through the book. The reason for referring to the ship is partly as a cautionary tale: complacency can lead to disaster. Moreover, no matter how much protection you have, disasters do happen. But I also wanted to highlight it because it is probably the most examined man-made disaster in history. As a result, there are many lessons to be learned from it that can be applied to HA and DR planning.

The disaster has a lot in common with modern IT disasters, such as the following:

- Multiple contributory factors.

- Over-reliance on resilience and redundancy.

- Profits and low cost valued more than safety.

- Poor monitoring.

- Confusion when the disaster did occur.

- A lack of means to recover.

Ultimately, the sinking had a huge effect on the fortunes of the White Star Line, the company that owned the ship. Their focus on building a cheap ship and getting to New York quickly was their ultimate downfall: they were bought out by Cunard and no longer exist.

The same thing might be true of your organization: it may rely more on SharePoint now than was initially thought. The first principle in this chapter is not to ignore how dependent materially as well as from a brand perception point of view your organization is on technology.

The next point is one of responsibility. The sinking naturally led to apportioning blame, and some people came out of the disaster looking heroic and self-sacrificing. One example is Arthur West: he left a lifeboat to get a thermos of warm milk for his daughters, then climbed down the rope as the lifeboat was lowered to give them the thermos before climbing back up to the ship. His body was never found. Some looked selfish and cowardly like J. Bruce Ismay, who pressed the captain to travel as fast as possible but was one of the few men to take a seat on a lifeboat. The principle here is that responsibility has to be taken early on when running SharePoint; you can't just take credit when things appear to be going well.

The final principle is that measuring success by the fact that there has not been a disaster yet is not enough. Reporting of near misses is an established error-reduction technique in many industries and organizations, and it should be applied to the management of SharePoint systems. There are always clues that something could go wrong. Recognizing, recording, and responding to these near misses is an essential part of owning the SharePoint platform.

Chapter 2: Planning Your Plan

Unless commitment is made, there are only promises and hopes; but no plans.

— Peter F. Drucker

This chapter focuses on the importance of preparation. Before you can even create a disaster recovery plan, you need an understanding of what it is you are trying to protect. You must have management buy-in. Getting this sometimes means refuting overly-simplistic understandings of technology. You must conduct a business impact assessment. This means bringing together key stakeholders in the business to quantify in detail the effect of an interruption of SharePoint service on the different teams and departments at different times of the year.

With sign-off from management and more insight into the business needs, you can define recovery point objectives and recovery time objectives for different parts of the system. A key point this chapter makes is that not all content requires the same high level of availability. Multiple tiers can be established so that priority can be given to recovery of the most important content over the least important. After the Titanic sank, there were accusations that priority was given to passengers in first and second class. The figures, sadly, bear this out (Table 12-1).

Table 12-1. Tally of the Titanic Disaster by Class

First Class	Second Class	Third Class (Steerage)
Total: 319	Total: 269	Total: 699
Died: 119	Died: 152	Died: 527
Survived: 200	Survived: 117	Survived: 172
Percentage Survived: 63%	Percentage Survived: 43%	Percentage Survived: 25%

Whereas the actions on the Titanic are indefensible, careful prioritization and corresponding planning with your SharePoint implementation is a sound practice. While all people should be cherished and their intrinsic equal worth defended, the opposite is true of content stored in SharePoint.

This chapter also emphasises the importance of coordination during a disaster, otherwise known as 4Ci. This means there has to be command, control, communications, computers, and intelligence. Without making sure that these resources are available in advance, no plan can be put into action. Properly training your staff is crucial in any disaster, including the Titanic (Figure 12-1).

Figure 12-1. A Titanic lifeboat and crew member immortalized in English ale.

Preparation of a plan is essential, but preparing specifically how to put the plan into action will determine if it is effective or not. An undrilled crew can't save anyone, including themselves.

Chapter 3: Activating Your Plan

Suit the action to the word, the word to the action.

—William Shakespeare (Hamlet, Act 3, Scene 2)

Disaster is by its nature unexpected. The key principle in this chapter is that you must know when and how to activate your disaster recovery plan. In the case of the Titanic, many passengers thought the sinking was only a drill. The ship sank very slowly and people took time to understand what was actually happening. After the disaster, the press also had trouble figuring out what happened, as the Oakland Tribune's early headline clearly shows (Figure 12-2).

Figure 12-2. This incorrect early headline stated all aboard were rescued.

With SharePoint, the disaster recovery plan itself is always given attention, but how do staff and users know the time has come to use it? Who makes that decision? What if that person is not available? A disaster can be a confusing time; the normal processes do not apply and the right people may be unavailable. Your SharePoint disaster will likely be part of a larger IT or network disaster or even a general disaster, such as a flood. There has to be clearly defined processes and procedures. The main principle in this chapter is that having the right people in the right place at the right time is the number one way to ensure your plan will be executed correctly. The warning here is that resources need to be focused on the sudden change in circumstances and not on tasks that no longer take priority (Figure 12-3).

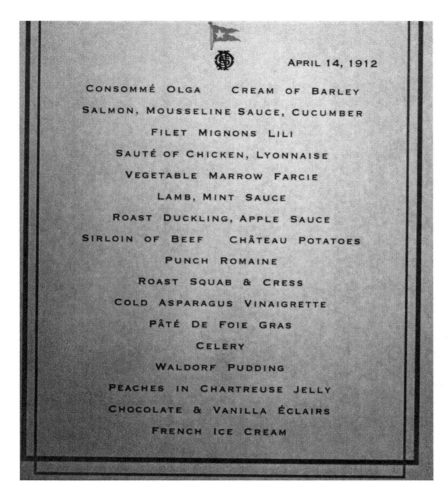

APRIL 14, 1912

CONSOMMÉ OLGA   CREAM OF BARLEY

SALMON, MOUSSELINE SAUCE, CUCUMBER

FILET MIGNONS LILI

SAUTÉ OF CHICKEN, LYONNAISE

VEGETABLE MARROW FARCIE

LAMB, MINT SAUCE

ROAST DUCKLING, APPLE SAUCE

SIRLOIN OF BEEF   CHÂTEAU POTATOES

PUNCH ROMAINE

ROAST SQUAB & CRESS

COLD ASPARAGUS VINAIGRETTE

PÂTÉ DE FOIE GRAS

CELERY

WALDORF PUDDING

PEACHES IN CHARTREUSE JELLY

CHOCOLATE & VANILLA ÉCLAIRS

FRENCH ICE CREAM

Figure 12-3. Preparing menus was no longer a priority when the ship began to sink.

Chapter 4: High Availability

Simplicity is prerequisite for reliability.

—Edsger Dijkstra

Helping you achieve high availability is one of the key goals of this book. The key principle of this chapter is that unmanaged change is the main risk to the availability of a system. While emphasis has to be put on building a technically highly available platform, technical faults are not the primary cause of failure. SharePoint fails because people fail to take into account the potential risks of the changes they are making. This is sometimes driven by a requirement being classed as urgent by someone high in the organizational hierarchy who insists the change be made without considering the consequences. They "pull rank," in other words. That is why change management processes must be in place.

Availability targets based on a simple percentage of uptime per year do provide a simple empirical goal to aim for in a calendar year, but they rarely include planned maintenance. They also don't measure the impact of the unavailability.

Resilience and redundancy are necessary; they depend on high quality hardware and constantly monitoring the system to ensure it is working correctly. It's never wise to recycle old servers into a production farm; always have the best quality your company can afford. In the case of the Titanic, space on the deck for passengers to walk about during the voyage was given priority over having enough lifeboats to save them all (Figure 12-4). Putting SharePoint users' immediate needs or a desire to save money over the long-term integrity of the content in the farm is never a good idea.

Figure 12-4. Lifeboats from RMS Titanic recovered by the SS Carpathia.

Chapter 5: Quality of Service

Quality has to be caused, not controlled.

—Philip Crosby

Quality of service is a cost-effective compromise between user satisfaction and a not overly complex architecture. Complex architecture costs more and has more points of failure. It is also less flexible to change. Latency is a physical limit that can't be removed simply by increasing the size of a metaphorical pipe. The further two places are from each other on the globe, the slower the transfer rate of data. This is because of the limitation of the speed light can travel in fiber optic cables.

The Titanic would have likely crossed the Atlantic in 5.5 days had it not struck the iceberg two thirds of the way there (Figure 12-5). This estimate is based on the fact that the Olympic made the journey in that time. Nowadays a flight to New York from London takes 7.5 hours (although the Concorde completed the flight once in under 3 hours).

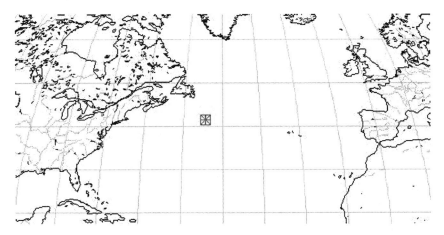

Figure 12-5. *Where the Titanic sank: haste makes a terrible waste.*

Generally, organizations are behind the curve in terms of available bandwidth. Bandwidth should be charged on the same utility model that cloud services, electricity, and water companies use. More bandwidth is not the solution to all speed issues, but it can help.

The principle with quality of service is to put the content geographically near the people who need to use it. If there is more than one group of users and they are geographically dispersed, put the content at a point between them. Remember that some content is only of use to the people who uploaded it, so it is sensible to store it near them.

Chapter 6: Back Up a Step

Backup is my computer's shepherd, My data shall not want. It lets me download software with good pleasure, knowing my data is untroubled like still waters. It restores my system. It lets me surf the paths of cyberspace for information's sake. Yea, though I walk through the Silicon Valley of the shadow of death, I will fear no evil for my backup system is on standby. My backup software and online backup, they comfort me. They prepare me a fresh backup in the presence of mine enemies, They anoint my head with peace, my cup runneth over. Surely goodness and security shall follow my data all the days of my life, and my data will continue to live on forever.

—T.E. Ronneberg

Some focus on SQL Server to back up SharePoint, some use third party tools, and some use SharePoint itself (either the Web UI or PowerShell). But the first step in understanding what to use to back up a system is to thoroughly understand the system itself. This can't be known by just one person—what if she is not available to do the restore?

Maintenance of effective backups is not primary about the tools you use. It is about documented and tested processes and procedures. The backup and restore process must be reviewed constantly to keep it relevant and reliable. Prioritize in backups not only what is most valuable to the organization but also what will take the longest time to recover manually. Hint: this will be developer-coded solutions and content that is not replicated anywhere else.

Restores should be tested regularly, if not daily. Originally, a lifeboat drill was scheduled to take place on board the Titanic on April 14, 1912—the day the Titanic hit the iceberg. However, for an unknown reason, Captain Smith cancelled the drill. Many believe that had the drill taken place, more lives could have been saved.

There are three primary things to remember when you think of what you need for backup, not just tools:

- People

- Processes

- Documentation

There are three primary things you have to be able to restore:

- Configuration

- Code

- Content

Keep these things in mind and practice your restore drill regularly. This will give you the best chance of success.

Chapter 7: Monitoring

Where observation is concerned, chance favors only the prepared mind.

—Louis Pasteur

With backup I emphasize not to be overly dependent on tools, but the opposite is true of monitoring. Monitoring tools are underutilized in the majority of SharePoint farms. Monitoring is conducted on two levels: Windows and SharePoint. Both levels are essential to a healthy SharePoint environment. SharePoint depends on the network it sits on like the mind depends on the body. As I quoted at the end of Chapter 7, *mens sana in corpore sano* (a sound mind in a sound body). Don't neglect either.

It is essential to have regular updates on key indicators of the health of your SharePoint system as well as the environment is exists in and is dependent on. Before a disaster occurs, there are usually clues that proactive monitoring can detect so that preventive measures can be taken.

Ironically, while the news that the Titanic was sinking travelled slowly throughout the passengers, the Titanic actually had its own newspaper on board. *The Atlantic Daily Bulletin* was printed every day on board the Titanic. The newspaper included news, advertisements, stock prices, horse-racing results, society gossip, and the day's menu. Information is important, but make sure you're looking at the most important pieces.

Chapter 8: DIY DR

Freedom is the greatest fruit of self-sufficiency.

—Epicurus (Greek philosopher, BC 341-270)

SharePoint backup and disaster recovery is moving from being the responsibility of the owners of the IT infrastructure and into the hands of the users themselves. The move with all technology is to make it less obscure and difficult to use, so more people can do it themselves. Beyond creating content, preserving it is the next most important step. Giving users the ability to maintain it themselves gives them freedom to be certain nothing will be lost in the event of a disaster.

Users can take advantage of several SharePoint tools to do their own recovery in the event of a disaster. Some are only for farm administrators, but some can be used by the people who create content. Obviously, the users know their content best and can back up what they know needs protection and when. The opposite is also true: content that doesn't need multiple backups won't be given them. It's as if democracy is coming to SharePoint: it's now less of a centralized autocracy and more of one where the users have more freedom and self determination.

Chapter 9: Change Management and DR

To improve is to change; to be perfect is to change often.

—Winston Churchill

Change is essential to keep SharePoint viable to the organization. No organization is perfect, so it needs to refine and improve all the time. Users generally don't know what they want from SharePoint until they see it; when they do see it and understand it, they want more. This should not be seen as a bad thing; it's a sign that the system is full of potential to make the organization more productive and meet user needs.

Once a system is in production, however, change must be managed properly to avoid the risk of the system being compromised. SharePoint is not like compiled applications like Word; it has much more scope to be extended and changed, not just through code but through configuration and structure directly by the users. Without change management, there is a risk of system failure; without change, it is certain.

Change should be primarily out of the box because the risks to the overall system are much lower and can be made without a slow change management process. There must be a policy in the business and IT to keep custom code and change to a minimum.

Chapter 10: DR and the Cloud

A cloud is made of billows upon billows upon billows that look like clouds. As you come closer to a cloud you don't get something smooth, but irregularities at a smaller scale.

—Benoit Mandelbrot

The cloud changes how SharePoint is architected and managed in many ways because the hardware and software are more under the control of a third party. But rather than making SharePoint more restricted, the cloud platform allows for more freedom because there are fewer resource restrictions. Capacity and processing power can be allocated when needed and are not underutilized. Cost of setup is much lower as the infrastructure is already there.

Moving to the cloud as the platform for SharePoint doesn't mean there is no longer a need to understand and maintain a disaster recovery plan, however. To integrate with your existing Windows user accounts, you still have to plan for and deploy additional servers and software. They now become the focus of your on-premises disaster recovery planning. But it's a great leap forward for platform computing and one what will have long-term repercussions on how we perceive computing.

Chapter 11: Best and Worst Practices

Wise men profit more from fools than fools from wise men; for the wise men shun the mistakes of fools, but fools do not imitate the successes of the wise.

—Cato the Elder

There are four main principles in this chapter.

- Focus on the long-term results of decisions, not just the short term ones.

- Avoid the quagmires of weak assumptions.

- Avoid a reactionary approach to change.

- Take a responsible approach to governance.

People make SharePoint succeed or fail. They make the technology decisions. It's too simple to blame the application. More can be achieved with a constructive and positive approach. Learn your lessons and apply what you've learned next time. If you don't, you will just keep making the same mistakes again.

Summary

High achievers spot rich opportunities swiftly, make big decisions quickly, and move into action immediately. Follow these principles and you can make your dreams come true.

—Robert H. Schuller (American Reformed Church Minister, Entrepreneur, and Author)

Networks, specifically the Internet, have made the communication of information faster and easier for millions of people around the word. SharePoint is the main tool that enables this in organizations and businesses. SharePoint has come a long way in 10 years, and it's now at a significant turning point where it may become more of a cloud solution rather than an on-premises one. Time will tell. Safeguarding your SharePoint environment means swiftly putting into action the principles I have conveyed in this book. Actions speak louder than words, so this seems the most appropriate point for me to end this book and stop speaking myself. Good luck to you in all your endeavors.

Index

■ Numbers and Symbols

D

▨ S

CPSIA information can be obtained at www.ICGtesting.com
Printed in the USA
LVOW110339231211

260829LV00012B/20/P